GROWING UP GARDENING: GATEWAYS TO GARDENING WITH CHILDREN

GROWING UP GARDENING: GATEWAYS TO GARDENING WITH CHILDREN

ARLENE MARTURANO

© 2025 ARLENE MARTURANO. ALL RIGHTS RESERVED.

The book is dedicated to my daughter Paris, who grew up gardening.

Acknowledgements

The birthing of a book takes much longer than nine months but the delivery process was made much less painful with a dedicated team of publishing professionals.

I am grateful for the email exchanges with indie author and GardenComm member Carol Michel and her verbal nudge, "If you are serious about self-publishing a book, DO IT!"

Plantsman, garden designer and author, Jenks Farmer, shared his self-publishing experiences, referrals, and suggestions, which provided momentum and support.

Tom Alewine is an interior designer of books with the technical skill of bringing together text and photographs to lay out a reader-friendly document.

Graphic designer Rob Barge skillfully and magically meshed thoughts and words into images for the exterior cover design and chapter titles of the book.

Shelley Quattrocchi, president of the American Society for Indexing, was enthusiastic, perseverant, and thorough in preparing the index.

Special thanks to Margaret O'Shea, content editor, copy editor, and proofreader extraordinaire for her insightful and inspirational suggestions and disciplined patience.

I appreciate the calm computer wizard Stephen Maluck for answering my many questions on computer conundrums.

Thanks to journalist and content designer Paris Ward for sharing a colorful sticky-note strategy to assist me in organizing articles into chapters.

My sincere appreciation to the many students, teachers, and gardeners who welcomed me into their garden space to share their stories.

I'm indebted to *The State* newspaper for publishing my monthly Kids Gardening column for thirteen years. Cheers to *The Columbia Star* for allowing me to continue to grow gardens in print for twenty-five years.

Tussie mussies to all!

Introduction

Collecting the spicy seeds from my chaste tree, *Vitex agnus-castus*, takes me back to childhood in my grandmother's Midwestern garden, where together we enjoyed watching butterflies and bumblebees collect nectar and pollen at the fragrant vivid blue spires.

I gardened beside a quiet, patient earth mother who used biointensive organic methods before the Rodale Institute, Center for Ecoliteracy, or Mother Earth News existed. Welcoming wildlife came naturally to her. Spiders, birds, toads, and frogs consumed garden pests. Tools like the hoe, weeder, and hand controlled weeds.

Flowering trees and shrubs -- crabapple, peach, mulberry, mock orange, snowberry, viburnum, althea, vitex, and currant -- framed the explosions of color, scent, and taste she created. I was introduced to gender in plants and saw what happened to birds eating fermented fruit.

The kitchen garden was a 36-by-36-foot victory garden with rows of corn, tomatoes, green beans, peas, spinach, lettuces, cucumber, radishes, beets, carrots, green onions, asparagus, parsley, and dill. Rhubarb was prominent and prolific for strawberry-rhubarb pie and rhubarb sauce. I learned vegetative propagation in the strawberry patch. Arbors of grapes fenced the back of the food plot.

Bushel baskets of fresh produce were served and shared all summer. In fall the kitchen became a cannery for peach, grape, strawberry and currant jellies and jams, dill pickles, tomato juice, and whole tomatoes. Preserving the flavors of summer coaxed anticipation for next year's garden.

Every inch of soil not producing food was yielding fragrance and colorful motion -- old roses like Mademoiselle Cécille Brünner, tiger lilies, peonies, hollyhocks, larkspur, and sweet peas bordered the white picket fence, which I painted for a penny a picket. Zinnias, marigold, bachelor button, calendula, cosmos, snapdragon, petunia, and portulaca were tended in foundation beds around the Colonial brick house. Sweet alyssum, lobelia, and baby's breath laced flagstone stepping stones. Under the stones we would find friendly earthworms and garter snakes. At night, fireflies danced fireworks. We would catch them in a canning jar to make a lantern.

In spring, iris, daffodil, crocus, tulips, hyacinths, and violets announced a new gardening season following the long, harsh dormancy of a 42° North latitude winter.

Grandma introduced me to annual mail-order seed catalogs – Burpee, Ferry-Morse, Gurney's, Henry Fields, Landruth, Park Seed, R.H.Shumway's, and Stark Brothers. The pictures of coach pumpkins, giant sunflowers, yard-long beans, potato-tomato plants, and fruit cocktail trees captivated my imagination. I longed to create the first white marigold for Burpee and began reading about George Washington Carver, Luther Burbank, and Linnaeus.

When my father built a cedar playhouse for my sister and me, I planted the perimeter with zinnias, cosmos, bachelor buttons, and an experimental plot of marigolds. Flower boxes under each window were seeded with alyssum, petunia, and portulaca.

The rich, deep, black prairie topsoil amended with Grandma's compost recipe assured my success. I made bouquets for our dining table and then started a cottage industry so everyone would have fresh flowers. Before hearing of Eliza Doolittle or the flower ladies of Charleston, I set out on foot selling bouquets door to door for a dime. Earnings would be invested in more mail-order seeds. When my parents discovered their daughter was vending flowers, they stopped me.

But I found another venue for my plants. My elementary school encouraged family gardening. Each fall the school had a contest for fruit, flowers, and vegetables grown at home. My blue ribbons pleased Grandma.

The childhood teaching garden internship with Grandma was both a prelude to my career of teaching children and pre-service and in-service teachers and a template for continuing a dialog with the natural environment.

As you reminisce about your gardening roots when reading this book, extend a green thumb to a new crop of seedling gardeners by volunteering at a nearby school garden, botanical garden, or community garden.

Table of Contents

Section One – Kinship Across Species

Chapter 1 - Amazing Animals

The Dance of the Squirrels 1

Keep the Firefly Light Shining 2

Hummingbirds at Home 3

A Munchie Tree for Birds 5

Growing a Birdhouse 6

Dogs and Gardens Really Can Coexist 7

Planning a Garden with My Feline Friend 8

Welcome Toads into Your Garden 10

Spider Watching in the Fall Garden 11

A Wildlife Safari at Home 12

Ms. Slither Goes to School and Summer Camp 14

Chapter 2 – Flying Farmers – the Pollinators

An Insectary to Bring Back the Bees 17

Pollinator Populations 18

Pollinator-Friendly Family 19

Barbara's Bees 20

Bees and Blooms 22

A Pollinator Picnic 23

Plant Trees to Attract Larvae 24

A Perennial Vine with a Passion for Butterflies 25

Section Two – The Occupation of Gardening

Chapter 1 – School Gardens

How Parents Can Help Grow a School Garden 27

Special-needs Students Grow Plants and Life Skills 28

A Classroom Without Walls 29
Heathwood Hall's Teaching Gardens... 31
Cabbage Dreams 32
Cultivate Ingenuity in an Organic School Garden 34
Maintaining a Wildlife Habitat at School 36
The Making of a Milkweed Meadow... 37
Scientific Method Rules in the Garden.. 39
Stimulus Packages for School Gardens 40

Chapter 2 – Garden Systems – Sow Many Ways to Grow

The Magic Box 43
Restoring Habitat with Seed Balls 44
Build a Doghouse with a Green Roof.. 46
Square-Foot Gardening for Calculating Minds... 47
A Grow-Bucket Greenhouse 48
Build a Teepee Trellis and Beans will Grow... 49
Instant Fall Gardens for Children 50
Picket Fences Make Good Childhoods 52
Unlocking Literacy with Keyhole Gardens and Cameras.. 52
Growing Food and Flowers in Buckets 54

Chapter 3 – Growing Healthy

Planting Winter Greens.. 57
Grow A Family Pizza Pie 58
Launching Lunch 59
Growing a Healthy Family... 60
Nutrition and Fitness Nuggets in a School Garden.. 61
Visit a Strawberry Patch or Grow Your Own.. 62
Fall is the Season for Planting 64

Toss a Salad in the Garden 65
Serve a Wild Dessert for Thanksgiving 66
Fresh, Fast, Fun Food Gardens to Go 68
Nutrition Gardens: Growing Healthy through Gardening 70
MyPlate Inspires MyGarden 71

Chapter 4 – Recycling

Turning Trash into Treasures 75
Possibilities with Pumpkins 76
Black and White and Read All Over 78
Turn the Christmas Tree into a Bird Bar 79
Returning Your Christmas Tree to the Wild 80
The Days of Wine and Rabbits 81
Composting with a Wiggle 83
Snip Seeds and Store for Planting Later 84
Can't Wait? Start Early from Seeds 85
Nature's Free Fall Podcast 87
Seed Saving in the Library? Check It Out! 88
The Poinsettia Project 89

Section Three – Nature Play

Chapter 1 – Playful Plants

Props for Child's Play Abound in Nature's Toyland 91
Plants to Play With - and Maybe to Eat 92
Play Potential Can Hide in Gardens Unless You Seek It Out 94
We're 'All Ears' in the Garden 95
Vines Like Children Thrive with Support and Training 96
Planting Secrets 98
Have Bushels of Fun Growing and Harvesting Potatoes 99

Making Moveable Gardens and Landscapes for Children 100

Growing Stones Instead of Throwing Them 101

Hollyhock Days 102

Party Favors in One Perennial Plant 103

Walking with Wildfllowers 104

Growing Sunshine and Smiles 106

Chapter 2- Indoor Gardens

Houseplants Sprout Lessons for Healthy Living in Every Pot 109

Call Plant 911 110

The Plant Hospital 111

A Lesson in Beauty in Wake of Tsunami 113

A Terrarium is a World unto Itself 114

Budding Botanists Trick Winter by Forcing Blooms 115

An Avocado Plantation 116

Chapter 3 – Holiday Gifts from the Garden

Gifts Grow in Every Garden 119

A Flamboyant Flower for the New Year 120

Picking and Preserving Poinsettias 121

The Best Flowers for Giving Their Hearts 122

Fireworks from Flowers 124

Celebrating Christmas with Cats 125

Ms. Slither Trims a Holiday Tree 126

Section Four – Recreation in the Garden

Chapter 1 – Games

Circling Around the Yard in a Maze 129

Explore Nature with Garden Games 130

Challenge Your Family with a Puzzle Garden 131

Spelling and Vocabulary Grow with Scrabble® Gardening 132

Weather Detectives 134

Chapter 2 – Crafts

Branching Out with Trees 137

While Away an Afternoon with 'Miss Hickory' 138

Write this Lesson on a Leaf 139

Painting with Colors from Earth's Palette 141

Peeking Inside Nature's Closet 142

Tie-Dye from the Garden 143

Keeping Fresh Colors Through the Fall 144

Grow a Garland, Braid a Chain 146

Joining Hands for Wreath Making 147

Eggshell Garden Crafts for All Ages 149

Section Five – Ethnobotany

Chapter 1 – Intergenerational Gardening

Reconnect Nature and Your Child 151

Gardening Binds Generations 152

Jozefine's Catering Garden 153

Grow A Family Floral Clock 154

Hope Grows in Your Back Yard 156

Bolster Your Garden with Family Reading 158

Chapter 2 – Horticulture and Human Culture

Garden like a Native with the Three Sisters 159

Trailblazing a Garden with Lewis and Clark 160

Poinsettia's South Carolina Roots 162

Around the World with Aromatic Herbs 163

Hands-On Hmong Farmers 165

Three Students Script a Teacher's Vision for Education..................................166

Section Six – Community Collaboration

Chapter 1 – Natural History Programs

Riverbanks Nature Preschool: Where Learning Comes Naturally 169
Feast Your Family's Eyes on Nature's Wonders 169
Recharge with a Walk at Belser Arboretum 170
The Plant Circus in Charlotte..172
The Outdoors Were In at the Conservation Station 174
Your Neighborhood Urban Forest..175
A Schoolyard Herbarium 177
Healing Through Giving and Gardening 178
A Walk on the Wild Side..179

Chapter 2 – Data Dialogs via Citizen Science

Winter is for the Birds... in Your Back Yard and Schoolyard 183
Budburst – Citizen Science with Plants 185
Data Dialogs with Natural Phenomena...186
Lure a Luminous Landscape..189
Grow Some Shade..191

Chapter 3 – Carolina Children's Garden

Planting Future Generations of Gardeners...193
Spotlight on Youth Gardening Across the Nation...196
Selecting Plants Helps Kids Grow to Love Their New Home..................................200
The Autumn Garden ABCs 205
Peek a Boo...Imagine Pooh and Friends Waiting for You.......................................206
The World at Your Feet 207
Experience is the Best Teacher 208
The Children's Garden Was For the Birds 210

Mesozoic Memories: A Dinosaur Garden 213
Trees: From Our Garden to Yours 214
Signs of Spring Hopped Out of the Children's Garden 216
It's a Pleasure To Find Peter Rabbit 217
Butterflies Flutter Amid Nectar-Rich Flowers 218
Food Chains in the Garden 219
Blueberries for Annika and You 220
Index 223
About the author 239
Reviews 240

SECTION ONE

KINSHIP ACROSS SPECIES

"Biophilia is our innate tendency to focus upon life and life-like forms and, in some instances, to affiliate with them emotionally."
E.O. Wilson

Chapter 1
Amazing Animals

"Cultivating relationships with animals, real and imagined, is one of the best ways to foster empathy during early childhood. Children want to run like deer, to slither along the ground like snakes, to be clever as a fox and quick like a bunny." David Sobel

The Dance of the Squirrels

Whether we are planting bulbs, mulching with pine straw, raking leaves, harvesting fall greens, drying seed heads, or stocking bird feeders, the agile and ambitious gray squirrels watch our every move. They like to watch us, and we enjoy watching them too.

When we move from one task to another, the inspectors descend from their treetop villas to review and rearrange our work. They dig up bulbs and replant them in the lawn or, alas, in the neighbor's yard. Perhaps they have seen current bulb catalogs encouraging gardeners to tuck bulbs under the turf for an early spring splash of color against the dormant lawn. Or is this a squirrel experiment with naturalizing?

Using front paws like hands, they stuff their mouths with leaves before climbing up a tree with cleated claws to furnish a high-rise den. If garden gloves are nearby, they disappear, carried upward to insulate a nest. They uproot salad greens and nibble them on site. They find seed heads drying on the deck and disperse them. Any nuts they find get concealed in random fashion across the property.

And we've all seen what happens when squirrels visit bird feeders!

Watching squirrels change your garden to accommodate their lifestyle and habits can be ongoing family entertainment with the bonus of learning about animal behavior. Since fall is one of the busiest times for squirrels, it is one of the best times to commence squirrel watching.

Their bodies are programmed to scatter hoard nuts like acorns, walnuts, hickories, and pecans. The cache of nuts is the primary food for the winter pantry. Although squirrels do not remember where the nuts are buried, their keen sense of smell enables them to unearth nuts on demand. Nuts not retrieved become our forests. As he "squirrels away" food, the squirrel facilitates the start of the tree-planting season. Each squirrel can bury a thousand nuts per season. How many trees will you plant this fall?

Hoarding behavior isn't limited to nuts. Mushrooms are gathered and dried on twigs like marshmallows awaiting roasting. Pine cones may be piled at the base of squirrels' favorite treetop feeding stations. The foraging list also includes buds, flowers, berries, fruits, seeds, insects, vegetables, twigs, bark, and tree sap.

As rodents, squirrels have two upper and two lower chisel-shaped incisors which continue to grow throughout their lives. Gnawing on hard surfaces wears down the incisors to keep them from growing too long and prohibiting eating. This is why we see squirrels gnawing on nuts, tree bark, and even decks, fence posts, wooden siding, swing sets, outdoor furniture, and wires.

While autumn marks the flu season for us, squirrels show evidence of health issues, too. Two of the most visible problems are caused by parasites. To reduce parasite problems squirrels abandon infected nests and build anew as many as ten times a year.

Squirrels communicate with us, their kin, and other animals with both voice and body language. Squirrel vocalizations warn of enemies, invasion of territory, or predators, such as owls, hawks, coyotes, foxes, raccoons, and hunters. Squirrels have sounds for calling a mate, scolding their young, and screaming when attacked or injured. Their flexible tail can signal fear, curiosity, playfulness, friendliness, and anger.

A squirrel's tail is a multipurpose tool. It serves as a blanket in cold weather, a flotation device when swimming, a surface to break falls, a rudder to control direction when leaping, a balance pole when walking on wires, a rain umbrella, and a sunshade.

Take delight in the antics of the gray squirrel. The garden acrobat entertains while educating us to an array of behaviors needed for survival. The observant squirrel also heightens our awareness of the plants in our surroundings.

Grey squirrel consuming camellia blossom.

Keep the Firefly Light Shining

Most adults remember the childhood delight of observing and chasing fireflies in summer. The fireflies came out like stars - first one, then another - until their blinking filled your back yard or the nearby woods. Today the lightning bug of our childhood seems to have disappeared from some landscapes. For me, only on a recent owl prowl in the Congaree National Park did appreciable numbers light up the night.

The decline of fireflies has been attributed to several factors. Municipal mosquito spraying controls more than targeted pests with fireflies and bees among the victims. The destruction of habitat that has reduced butterfly and bird populations also affects fireflies. Fireflies need darkness to find light mates, and humans have polluted their dating scene with vehicle, street, and security lights.

These nocturnal insects are members of the *Lampyridae* family in the order of beetles with 2,000 species worldwide; 125 are found in the United States.

As insects, fireflies have three body parts: head, thorax and abdomen. The light organs are on the underside of the lower abdomen. Light is produced when oxygen breathed in through abdominal trachea combines with luciferin in the presence of the enzyme luciferase. Fireflies regulate airflow, to create the pulsating pattern.

The flickering adult beetles we observe have a life span of three to four weeks. Their predecessors live underfoot as larvae or glowworms. Adult females lay eggs (which also may glow) on or just beneath the soil surface. In the larval state, fireflies overwinter burrowed in the soil.

Carnivorous larvae hatch in four weeks and survive by consuming snails, slugs, earthworms, and other soft-bodied invertebrates. Adults feed on pollen, nectar, and juice of fruits like mulberries. But the adult's main mission is to mate. Males attract females with a luminous Morse code to which females respond with a flash.

From 2016 to 2024 the Museum of Science in Boston hosted a program called Firefly Watch to gather data on fireflies. In 2024 they turned the program over to the Xerces Society's Firefly Atlas program, a collaborative effort to better understand and conserve the distribution of fireflies in North America. Families may register to provide data. Find information at https://www.fireflyatlas.org/.

Here are a few ways to entice fireflies into your garden: Knowing the life cycle of fireflies and their preferences helps. Generally fireflies like the same moist conditions as mosquitoes. They frequent undisturbed wild spaces and unkempt overgrown areas of a garden. Leave unmowed grass and weeds along the edges of your land. Preserve a parcel of unsuppressed wilderness in your yard. Allow leaf litter to remain on the ground. Rake and cultivate carefully to avoid injuring overwintering pupae. Go cold turkey on the use of pesticides, herbicides and fungicides. Fireflies will reward you by dropping by the friendly space you've made for them.

Hummingbirds at Home

Create a hummingbird habitat with your children this summer. A family's backyard hummingbird habitat can provide learning adventures for a lifetime. Our home property is really a time-share with wildlife. Once hummingbirds discover the habitat created for them, they will remember to return to it year after year.

The ruby-throated hummingbird, the most common hummer to the Southeast, returns to its breeding grounds in the Midlands by April after wintering in Central America. Following courtship and mating, males and females go their separate ways. Females establish a nesting territory, where they weave a tiny cup-shaped nest of spider silk and plant parts disguised with lichen. There they lay and incubate two 8mm-13mm white eggs, and remain to raise their young solo in neighborhood oaks, sycamores, sweet gums, maples, red cedars, and pines.

To build a hummingbird habitat at home you will need to create an ecosystem which includes flowers, feeders, perches, abundant insects and spiders for food, and trees for nesting. Hummingbirds also need dense cover to hide from predators as diverse as cats, snakes, frogs, hawks, and robber flies.

The diet needed to keep these high-energy birds healthy and active comes from insects, spiders, and floral nectar. Refrain from using lawn and garden chemicals in the habitat. Since 60 percent of the bird's diet consists of protein from arthropods, the hummers provide natural pest control. Females feed nestlings a slurry of regurgitated pollen, nectar, and insects, a good reason to keep the baby food organic.

Many of the nectar plants that hummingbirds rely on have coevolved with them and have specific characteristics to allow hummingbird access but exclude other pollinators. The flowers are tubular with protruding stamens covered in pollen, scentless, bright red or orange, and easy to hover in front of.

Each flower species deposits pollen in a particular place on the bird's head to increase the chances for cross-pollination. Fuchsias leave pollen on the throat; pinks dust pollen on the bill; lobelia deposit on the crown and jewelweed on the forehead. Catch sight of pollination elation as hummingbird tongues probe your flowers.

The ruby-throated hummingbird's black bill and tongue are long and tubular like the flower form. The tongue laps up nectar via capillary action.

Plan the plant palette to offer a menu of nectar sources to span the entire length of the hummingbirds' temporary annual residency. Perennial vines like honeysuckle and the crossvine welcome the spring migrant. Trumpet creeper vine, annual salvia, and perennials like lobelia, monarda, and weigela, will take them through to fall.

Adding a hummingbird feeder will bring hours of delightful aerial antics and iridescent traffic flow in the habitat. Select a feeder that comes apart for easy cleaning with a bottlebrush and hot soapy water. Regular visitors may even drink from hand-held floral feeding tubes. Mix four parts boiling water to one part plain white sugar. White granulated sugar is sucrose and mimics the chemistry of flower nectar. Never use honey or corn syrup because they promote harmful fungus growth. Molasses and other sugars contain iron concentrations lethal to tiny hummingbirds. Nectar is naturally clear so there is no need to add red dye, which also may be harmful to the birds.

Water is another habitat requirement for hummingbirds. They enjoy flitting through a mister and will bathe in shallow birdbaths.

National Audubon Society scientists have been interested in finding out what nectar sources hummingbirds are using nationwide. They detected a mismatch between the blooming times of flowers and migration arrival times of hummingbirds. To monitor nectar sources Audubon conducted a citizen science project, Hummingbirds at Home, from the spring of 2013 to December 2021. Families participated by gathering data on hummingbird feeding preferences in their home hummingbird habitat or any patch of property selected for observation. The program yielded good data and made families aware of native plant options and how climate influences migration and food sources for hummingbirds. https://www.audubon.org/hummingbirds-home-wind-down

Journey North, a citizen science program, has a hummingbird migration component. Volunteers track spring and fall migration of rufous and ruby-throated hummingbirds across North America. Sightings are recorded on maps. Participants are encouraged to contribute photos and commentary and to make predictions based on the data collected. https://journeynorth.org/hummingbirds/

12 Top Hummingbird Plants

Trumpet creeper, *Campsis radicans*

Crossvine, *Bignonia capreolata*

Trumpet honeysuckle, *Lonicera sempervirens*

Hollyhock, *Alcea rosea*

Scarlet sage, *Salvia splendens*

Bee balm, *Monarda didyma*

Red buckeye, *Aesculus pavia*

Cigar plant, *Cuphia ignea*

Pineapple sage, *Salvia elegans*

Cypress vine, *Ipomoea quamoclit*

Cardinal flower, *Lobelia cardinalis*

Indian pink, *Spigelia marilandica*

A Munchie Tree for Birds

Birds decorate our gardens with color, plumage, flight, song, courtship, and nesting throughout spring and summer. Winter is the season to decorate your garden for their benefit.

Start by taking the family on a walk across your property to inventory the natural foods available. Look for berries, seeds, nuts, pods, and cones. Then have a family tree-trimming party or host one for friends of all ages.

Select an evergreen on your property such as an eastern red cedar or magnolia, a container-planted Alberta spruce, or a shapely, sturdy deciduous to become the birds' holiday treat. Or if you've waited until after Christmas, recycle the indoor evergreen to an outdoor buffet of edible ornaments for wildlife.

Organize the tree-trimming party around workstations. Stock one station with a variety of natural trimmings such as evergreen boughs from eucalyptus, loquat, pine, cedar, juniper, holly, boxwood, podocarpus, and deciduous grapevines. These can be shaped into wreaths, garlands, nosegays, swags, and other ornaments. Send the finished products to the next station.

At station two, participants attach to the ornaments berries from wax myrtle, beautyberry, dogwood, pyracantha, and holly, and pods from crape myrtle, wisteria, mimosa, magnolia, okra, and chili peppers.

A third station has popcorn, cranberries, raisins or grapes, peanuts in the shell, cheese cubes, and dehydrated apples, pears, and oranges. Use needles threaded with dental floss to make chains of food to drape around the tree.

A fourth station contains pinecones, sweet gum balls, peanut butter, and sunflower seeds. The cones and balls are flocked in peanut butter, then rolled in sunflower seeds. Attach a hook or loop of dental floss before placing on the tree.

The fifth station is where guests make a log feeder to take home to their back yard. Have three-inch-diameter logs cut into 12-inch lengths. Drill holes two inches deep around the log to fill with a high-fat snack.

One holiday-spread recipe for birds is one cup each of peanut butter, Crisco, and white flour mixed with four cups of cornmeal. The spread can be refrigerated to refill the logs. Attach a screw eye to the top of each log for ease in hanging. Chickadees, titmice, wrens, nuthatches, and woodpeckers will parade and probe up and down the Yule log.

After the tree is trimmed, scatter acorns, walnuts, hickory nuts, pecans, peanuts, and dry corn around the base for ground feeding birds and squirrels. Refresh and replenish the edible ornaments throughout the winter.

In February reunite with your tree-trimming guests to take part in the Great Backyard Bird Count sponsored online by the Lab of Ornithology at Cornell University. Households across America report birds visiting their feeders. For more information, see https://www.birds.cornell.edu/k12/gbbc/.

Growing a Birthday

If you are looking for a long-term project to enthuse, enchant, and educate children from summer into fall, purchase a packet of birdhouse gourd seeds. For centuries gourds have captured the imagination and creativity of humans. It takes only one seed of the birdhouse gourd, *Lagenaria siceraria*, planted in June to produce a twenty-five-foot vine covered in flowers first and by fall a wheelbarrow full of large pear-shaped gourds. Cured gourds can be crafted into birdhouses for next spring's nesting season.

Gourds need a hot, sunny, spacious spot to grow. Sow the seeds in mounds like squash and pumpkins, their next of kin, or directly in flat ground. Use a vertical structure like a fence, trellis, teepee, or tree for vines to climb upward and keep fruits off the ground where they are susceptible to rot.

Children of all ages become entranced with growing gourds.

The Amish are bountiful gourd growers. They recommend preparing the soil well by digging a full wheelbarrow of composted manure into the ground under wherever gourd seeds are planted. This method self-fertilizes throughout the growing season. Otherwise, you will need to use an aromatic organic blend of fish emulsion and kelp fertilizer weekly.

Gourd seeds have a hard seed coat. Soaking seed twenty-four hours in warm water hastens germination. Plant seeds one inch deep, four to a hill, or pairs of seeds six inches apart along a fence. Seeds sprout in fourteen days, and within a few weeks the vines take off rapidly with tendrils grabbing onto supports.

Water well at planting and continue to water thirsty gourds throughout the summer. Test soil moisture daily by poking finger into the earth near each plant. Reduce watering when fall comes to harden off gourds.

When the vine reaches six feet tall, pinch the growing tip to shock the plant into growing lateral branches. The main vine produces only male flowers and pruning encourages the growth of females. If your goal is birdhouses, you must have female and male flowers on the vine.

Provide a hand lens so children can be on the lookout for the two kinds of flowers. Male flowers form first. The structure of the flowers provides clues to gender. The female flower comes with a miniature embryonic gourdlet below the base of the petals. Gourds are insect-pollinated, but young gardeners may help the process along by transferring pollen from the male stamens to the stigmas of the female flowers with an artist's fine soft-hair paintbrush.

Have children use a ballpoint or permanent marker pen to write their names on the skin of a young gourd. As the gourd grows so will the name.

Harvest time for gourds usually comes after the first frost but gourds may be ready to harvest before then. When gourd stems turn brown, they can be removed by a clean cut leaving two inches of stem on the gourd. The stem acts like a chimney releasing moisture from inside the fruit as it cures.

Cure gourds atop a screen or palette or string them up to dry in the sun or in a dry well-ventilated shed. Gourds can take six months to dry. Dry gourds feel lightweight and when you shake them you hear the seeds inside.

The final step is to make the birdhouses. Soak gourds in soapy dishwater for fifteen minutes and scrub with a copper scrubbing ball to remove mold and skin. Rinse and dry thoroughly.

Gourds attract cavity-nesting birds, and the entrance hole size will determine whether nesters are wrens, titmice, chickadees, nuthatches, bluebirds, woodpeckers, or purple martins. For example, Carolina wrens need a hole size of 1.5 inches in diameter. Drill one entrance hole on the outermost face of the gourd. Remove and save the seeds from the inside for next year's garden. Then drill two quarter-inch drainage holes in the bottom of the gourd. Drill a quarter-inch hole in the neck of the gourd to thread a wire for hanging.

Birdhouse Gourd Seeds
www.parkseeds.com
www.rareseeds.com
www.sowtrueseed.com

As the gourd grows from seed to a vine with fruit, and fruit is transformed to a birdhouse with residents, children will have fledged in their capacity to sequence a series of changes to cultivate life in the garden.

Dogs and Gardens Really Can Coexist

Pets are members of the family. Being pack animals, dogs especially want and need to be with the family indoors and out. Just as we make outdoor space safe and enjoyable for our children, we can design gardens to promote a good life with our dogs.

One of the first features to consider is a fence to keep Fido in and strays out. The fence could become part of a dog run or the backdrop for a new flowerbed.

Dogs make pathways where they want to go. Incorporate their pathways into the garden by installing brick pavers or stepping stones. Dogs can be trained to stay on the paths. Edging around flowerbeds gives dogs a visual reminder of off-limits. You add the verbal command "No" or "Off."

When introducing new plants in the garden, consider the age and size of the dog. Puppies often view plants as chew toys and require tough plants. Add woody plants (trees, vines, shrubs) before tender herbaceous ones. Cluster shrubs or ornamental grasses to keep the dog from invading private areas, and make sure trees provide essential shade. Sturdy-stemmed bulbs like narcissus, iris, and gladiolas planted en masse will discourage doggie detours.

Bare soil is an invitation to dig -- for both gardeners and dogs. Use groundcovers like thyme, creeping juniper, prostrate rosemary, verbena, periwinkle, or mondo grass between beds or woody shrubs. Create a shady and dry pit and teach Fido to use it as his digging nirvana.

Dogs require turf for training, exercising, playing, and lounging. Keep their outdoor toys nearby.

Training a puppy to use one designated area of the yard will prevent "dog spots" in the lawn. A potty surface of wood chips or pea gravel will be absorbent. Screen the zone with a trellis and evergreen vines. Male dogs benefit from a vertical structure like a post or stump. Getting the dog to use the potty zone will require at least a week of consistent leash training, but is well worth the time. If you don't train for a potty zone, hose down urination areas promptly and remove solid waste regularly to reduce loss of lawn.

Humans and dogs perceive the garden differently. We know our garden best by sight; dogs know it best by scent. Any garden is a perfumery to the canine nose, so expect paw prints to the most fragrant flora.

Dogs are colorblind to green and red. They see yellow, blue-violet, and shades of gray. Their rod-dominated retinas enable them to see better at night and to see moving objects better than stationary ones. Let the dog lead you on a night walk in the garden.

Lawn and garden fertilizers, chemical and organic, are unsafe for dogs. Chemicals burn their paws and irritate the skin. Organic fertilizers like fish emulsion, blood meal, and bone meal appeal to pets but should not be used either. Baits for slugs, snails, voles, and moles are as lethal to children and pets as to the pests.

Pesticides, herbicides, and fungicides have no place in a family garden. By eliminating them, you allow beneficial insects, birds, bats, snakes, lizards, toads, and frogs to work for you. Handpicking and squishing solve many pest problems, as does conscientious surveillance and maintenance. Homemade compost and compost tea enhance soil fertility and healthy plants. An enclosed compost bin fits neatly into any garden.

Dogs like to survey their territory from a raised deck, table, doghouse roof, or berm. Celebrate the presence of your garden companion by planting a dogwood tree.

Planning a Garden with My Feline Friend

When Ferdinand and I first met, he was reluctant and shy. Our friendship grew over shared interests. We discovered a mutual love of birdwatching. We enjoy the outdoors, but while I take pleasure in walking, he prefers to climb trees, jump over fences, or lounge in my lap. We enjoy the same foods: salmon, sea bass, liver pate, turkey, and chicken. We both exercise daily.

In other ways we are less alike. I tend to be work oriented, and Ferdi reminds me to take time to play. Something as simple as a leaf blowing in the wind or a ball of aluminum foil catches his eye.

I am definitely a daytime person, and he is a night owl. We travel together, each with our own special luggage. My carry-on Skyway goes in the overhead bin. His Samsonite carrier goes under the seat. As a "preferred" flyer his tickets are always less than mine.

Now after ten months of friendship, we are planning a garden together. Both of us gravitate to plants and gardens. While my eyes guide me through, his nose and whiskers lead him.

Ferdinand's favorite plant is catnip, *Nepeta cataria*. The scented leaves send him into playful fits and frenzies. The easy-to-grow hardy perennial germinates in seven to ten days and in sun to partial shade reaches three feet tall. Only after plants are well established will Ferdi enter the bed to bite the foliage, shred the stems, and roll in rapture.

Like its popular mint relatives -- peppermint, spearmint, apple mint and chocolate mint -- catnip spreads rapidly by root and self-seeding. To control spread gardeners often cultivate mints in containers. We plan to cut plants back in midsummer, tie the stems in bundles, and hang them upside down to dry. Then we strip the dry leaves off the stems and store them crumbled in a glass airtight container. Ferdi will use pinches of catnip at play, and I will brew hot minty tea.

Catmint, *Nepeta mussinii*, has the same appeal to Ferdinand as catnip but grows to a height of only fifteen inches with bluish-purple blossoms instead of the white with lavender of catnip. Ferdinand rolling in nepetas is comparable to me applying an insect repellant. Scientists with the U.S. Department of Agriculture are testing the insect repelling properties of nepetalactone, the essential oil of nepetas, to derive safer insect repellents for humans and their pets and for commercial pesticides for treating termites and cockroaches.

Another insect-repellant plant Ferdinand chose for the garden is chamomile. After drying the apple-scented leaves and yellow and white blossoms on a screen and crushing the dried plant parts, we place the herbal bouquet inside a small soft fabric dream pillow to deter fleas.

Ferdi's grain garden will contain rye, wheat, oats, barley, and rice grown from organic seed purchased at the health food store. We will start the seeds in pots on the windowsill where he watches birds. He can taste the tender sprouts as they mature.

Ferdi grooms himself daily but doesn't like bubble baths or shampooing. When he does get his hair washed, he prefers a natural rinse conditioner from rosemary. Both upright and spreading rosemary are available from local nurseries. To make a rinse pour two cups of boiling water over two or three five-inch sprigs of rosemary and allow it to cool to room temperature. In addition to sharing my cat's rosemary rinse, I'll use the plant in cooking.

As the final touch to our garden we will add a pot of aloe as a gesture for long life and good health. This useful plant is a natural first aid kit to treat cuts, scratches, and insect bites. Just pick off a leaf from the base of the plant, split it to expose the inner gel, and apply to the sore. The gel dries quickly and soothes the wound.

Ferdi doesn't care about the details. He just enjoys our time together and what we do with the plants we grow. We sense our friendship will

Ferdi's grain garden

continue to grow along with our garden.

Welcome Toads into Your Garden

When exploring the outdoors in summer, children find many treasures to share with family members and camp counselors. One treasure which fits comfortably into the palm of the hand is a toad.

The enchanting adventures of toads, which have captivated children in Kenneth Graham's *Wind in the Willows* and Arnold Lobel's "Frog and Toad" series, can't match the first-hand fun of welcoming and living with toads on your home turf.

Four species of toad are commonly found in South Carolina gardens: American, Southern, Fowler's and Oak. While toads have been erroneously reported to cause warts and to be a witch's familiar, their virtues as an insect vacuum have been obscured. The toad's long, sticky tongue flicks, nabs, and swallows prey faster than you can blink an eye. Cutworms, caterpillars, mosquitoes, slugs, spiders, moths, crickets, and beetles vanish. Scientists estimate one toad consumes between one and two hundred insects and other invertebrates per night. They are most certainly a gardener's animal, one of a cadre of natural pest patrols and controls.

Toads are not fearful of human contact and can become quite tame if given conditions conducive to their nature. To encourage toads to live on your property ask, "If I were a toad, what would I need?" Basic starters are camouflaged surroundings that are cool and moist with shallow water, plant cover, and plenty of insects. Since toads are sensitive to chemicals, absorbing toxins readily through their skin, a toad-friendly garden must eliminate insecticides and lawn chemicals.

Here are a few family projects to retrofit your yard for toads:

Toad Abode. Recycle cracked terra cotta or ceramic flowerpots into cool shelters. Along the pot's rim chip away a doorway large enough to accommodate a toad. Set the pot upside down in a shady bed surrounded by plants visited by insects.

Toad Spa. Being amphibians, toads require moisture to live. Instead of drinking water through their mouth, toads absorb it through skin patches when sitting in water. Nestle ceramic saucers, aluminum pie pans, or birdbaths without pedestals into a shady plot of soil and fill with fresh water.

Rock Pile. Toads like to hide in cool dark places during the day. Arrange flat rocks in a damp area near an outdoor spigot, downspout, air conditioning drain, or low spot that collects rainwater.

Toad Tunnel. Place a hollow log, ceramic pipe, or recycled coffee can on its side partially buried in soil so toads may meditate inside.

Ground Cover Cabana. Shade-loving plants harbor toads by day and attract appetizers at night. A few of the many ground cover options include pussytoes, foamflower, wild ginger, Japanese holly fern, marginal fern, Virginia creeper, common periwinkle, hosta, and pachysandra. Include a clump of your amphibian's namesake plant, the toad lily.

Brush Pile. In a corner of the yard build a mound of limbs, twigs, broadleaf evergreen trimmings, and woody plant parts to shelter toads. The debris will attract insect tidbits for the toads.

Once your yard is retrofitted for toads, throw a habitat warming party. Celebrate the enchantment of toads in your garden with neighbors and friends by raising glasses of lemonade in a toast to toads.

Spider Watching in the Fall Garden

Parents and teachers are bound to encounter bugs when gardening with children. All types of arthropods seem to show up in fall. Many insects and spiders are laying eggs, which will overwinter and yield hatchlings to reside in the garden come spring.

One of the most conspicuous, attractive, and interesting spiders for children and adults to watch is the large black and yellow garden spider, *Argiope aurantia*. The colorful patterns on *Arigope's* body and legs help with identification. Her head (cephalothorax) is covered in silver hairs. The abdomen is black and yellow. The eight legs are black with orange or yellow bands near the body. The female garden spider's body is an inch or more long compared to the rarely observed male, who is only about one-fourth of an inch long.

She constructs an orb web as wide as two feet among flowers and vegetables or anchored to outdoor structures in sunny locations. The web is an extension of a spider's sensory system and a snare for prey. An extraordinary sense of touch alerts garden spiders to prey in the web.

Males and females communicate via the web. When courting, the male plucks strands of the outer web to signal interest. If his signal is misread, he becomes prey. If his signal is accepted, the male builds a separate small modest web beside his mate's spacious one.

The round flat webs of orb weaver spiders are made of many types of silk. One can observe the anatomy of a web from the outer frame to the inner hub. The spider attaches a frame to vegetation or structures. From the frame she extends radial dry spokes supporting sticky spiral threads of silk. The hub is an open free zone where the spider stays in waiting, head side down, atop a white zigzag nonadhesive silk called the stabilimentum.

This monogram gives the spider the nickname "writing spider." Scientists conjecture the monogram carries silent messages of protection for the spider by startling predators, camouflaging the spider, and warning birds to steer clear of the web. The stabilimentum could alert predators to the web and cost the spider a meal. Hungry spiders don't seem to stitch the zigzag.

Another theory on the function of stabilimentum posits that the thickened zigzag threads are highly reflective of ultraviolet light and serve as a lure to insects. Children will come up with theories too.

The female eats her web each night and spins a new one in the same place. Eating the web is a way to recycle protein and conserve energy before spinning a new one. Females can handle prey much larger than themselves, including cicadas, katydids, grasshoppers, beetles, and wasps.

The garden spider is a beneficial inhabitant of the garden because of its role as a biological control of insect pests. The female puts on quite a show of horror and suspense when an insect hits the web. She sprints to the entangled victim, wrapping a silk strait jacket around it and anesthetizing the mummy with a poison bite. Later she will dine on bug juice. She goes about her spider chores adeptly without getting herself entangled in the web.

In fall the female lays eggs in a brown silken sac about the size of a large grape. The sac, which can contain three hundred to fourteen hundred eggs, stays next to her in the web until she dies, usually by the first frost. When eggs hatch, hatchlings overwinter inside the sac and in spring spiderlings emerge.

Although observation of garden spider behavior is best done outdoors, teachers can bring spider observation indoors with a spider picture frame. Students construct a fifteen-inches-square wooden picture frame with one-by-three-inch untreated lumber. Set the frame inside a large empty rectangular glass aquarium. Place the garden spider on top of the frame. After she builds a web, students can release live prey (crickets, grasshoppers) onto the web.

Following indoor observations, release her back to nature. Since spiders are an integral part of a healthy food web in the garden, there are specific things humans can do to integrate spiders into the home or school landscape. Plant a wide variety of flowers to attract flying insects so spiders will have a rich food supply. Leave the tall, sturdy stems of grasses and decorative seed heads standing as scaffolding for webs. Don't use pesticides so there will be insects for spiders to eat. Seek out these garden allies and their dazzling dew-spangled webs on early morning walks in your garden.

Teachers build a spider frame for indoor observations.

Wildlife Watch
Gearing Up
butterfly net
hand lens
journal
sketch pad
pencils
camera
binoculars
Field guides to:
birds, insects, butterflies and moths, reptiles and amphibians

A Wildlife Safari at Home

A family can find the wonder and adventure of exotic places in their own back yard. With a tad of imagination, ecotours -- natural history excursions exploring the life systems in an area -- exist within the confines and contours of your property line. Like a long-distance excursion, tours will require planning, team effort, attending to scheduling time and duration, gathering and packing gear, and designating a theme. May is a perfect planning month so when school is out, tours can begin. Just be sure to pick a time that works for you.

Here are some preparation and programming suggestions for a holiday at home:

Wildlife Watch

Part of taking a wildlife watch includes installing features to attract wildlife around your home. Bird-nesting boxes along with bird baths are a start. Plant natural feeders like crab apples, hollies, blueberries, figs, wax myrtles, pyracantha, grape vines, and mulberries. Advertise your yard to hummingbirds with scarlet sage, bee balm, agastache, and trumpet creeper.

The summer air show provided by avian residents and itinerants can be complemented by butterflies' levitators lighting on sun-filled airstrips specially designed for their metamorphic life cycle. The nectar brewery might include cosmos, butterfly bush, Joe Pye weed, purple coneflower, lantana, verbena, and butterfly weed. Host plants used by butterflies to lay their eggs and caterpillars to feed include parsley, dill, fennel, maypop, senna, and milkweed.

Once the stage is set, the ecotour begins. Plan close observation of wildlife using binoculars or hand lens. Look into the compound eye of insects. Feel the barbed legs of butterflies and watch the long proboscis of butterflies uncoil to sip nectar. Use the Golden Guide series of field guides to identify the birds, insects, and wildflowers on location. After identification of species, keep a list of observed specimens.

As part of your wildlife watch, plan side-trips to local sites that have lured wildlife to the area: Congaree National Park, the trails at Sandhill Research and Education Center, and Sesquicentennial State Park.

Interstellar Safari

Explore nocturnal flora and fauna under a canopy of stars and planets while camping in your yard. In background research for the trip, investigate the layers of the atmosphere that sight will travel through to see beyond the atmosphere of Earth and into space. Clouds, airplanes, satellites, and meteorites reveal evidence of atmospheric layers.

Evenings of stargazing with star maps to locate and identify constellations and tinker toys to model them can be accompanied by voices from mythology, stories of how

Interstellar Safari
Gearing Up
camouflage clothes
night net
flashlight
red cellophane
tinker toys
capture jars
firefly lantern
binoculars
telescope
star maps
journal
sketch pad
pencils
camera
Field guides to:
stars and constellations,
clouds,
mammals,
moths

the constellations were named. Track one star or constellation's position on an hourly basis until starset. On successive nights draw or photograph the phases of the moon. Track the moon's path in one night.

Since we humans are diurnal and visual creatures, darkness evokes our other senses for survival. Listen to the insect and amphibian orchestra and identify the individual musicians. Identify the scents of night. Draw the shadows and silhouettes of plants and of each other. Play a game of shadow tag in the moonlight.

Make a temporary firefly lantern for use first as you hike the perimeter of the property and then venture into the interior rooms of the landscape. Coleman® makes a lightweight plastic firefly lantern for kids with a screen mesh cylinder.

Make an inventory of the creatures of the night. Nocturnal creatures are very light sensitive. From a hammock, a deck, or a tree house and wearing camouflage clothes and a head net, watch for night mammals using a flashlight or head light covered in red cellophane. This will enable you to see an animal without it seeing you. Flying squirrels will entertain throughout the night.

If you have planted a moonlight garden in anticipation of the summer sojourn, walk among the moonflower, four o'clock, nicotiana, night phlox, and evening-scented primrose. Hold a primrose party at dusk to see the petals open and then be alert throughout the night for the large moth that pollinates primroses.

By planning ahead, a family can experience the wonder of no place like home and stay on a shoestring budget.

Ms. Slither Goes to School and Summer Camp

When I was a child, our family garden had garter snakes-- garden snakes as neighbors called them. The harmless yellow-striped reptiles hid under our flagstone stepping-stones. We were told not to lift rocks to disturb them. We learned these carnivorous reptiles ate earthworms, snails, slugs, frogs, toads, salamanders, fish, and tadpoles, not people, pets, or plants.

Nowadays, I travel with Ms. Slither, a twelve-year-old, five-foot-long corn snake, also known as a red rat snake or garden snake native to the southeastern United States. Ms. Slither is a captive-bred 'designer' snake with markings and color of a corn snake but with noticeable variations. She has orange and reddish brown striations along her back instead of the typical orange blotches outlined in black of wild relatives. Instead of a belly looking like Indian corn, hers is solid tan. In the wild corn snakes are often found in corncribs and cornfields where rodents feed on the grain.

Corn snakes are rodent-eating constrictors, an important service they provide to the ecosystem we share. They also feed on young mammals, birds, lizards and small snakes. Ms. Slither eats locally grown feeder mice kept in the freezer. Fresh locally grown food is good for reptiles as well as humans.

Since she is a wild animal and feeds as such, I don't want her to associate my hand with food. At feeding time I place her in a large plastic tub in which a thawed mouse has been placed first. By instinct she may constrict the limp mouse but usually she uses her two-pronged flickering tongue to sniff around the body and then clamps down on the head first with open jaws. She swallows prey whole. As the rodent disappears, the snake's skin bulges and undulates as muscles in neck and body contract and push the mouse into the stomach.

As snakes eat and grow, they shed their skin. A week or two prior to the molt, her entire body looks cloudy, even the eyes. After shedding, Ms. Slither's new skin is bright and shiny. Ms. Slither brings a set of shed skins to school so children can calculate growth between molts.

Ms. Slither was the education snake at the Carolina Children's Garden. Corn snakes are model reptile representatives. They are elegant, graceful, and a comfortable size to handle. Their docile nature allows children to feel the musculature and touch the scales. Their calm, cool and curious disposition is not prone to biting or attack. Ms. Slither elicits numerous questions, one of which is "Teacher, can we have a snake in our classroom?"

During the school year Ms. Slither visits classrooms spreading messages on snake safety and reptilian lifestyle in the wild and in captivity. In summer she is invited to summer camps where children (and adults) inquire about her name, internal anatomy, sense organs, shed skin, habitat, and diet. Why is she called a corn snake? Does she have a heart and lungs? Why is her tongue flicking in and out? Does she have teeth? Where does she live? What does she eat? Is she slimy to touch? Do corn snakes lay eggs? How do they hear without ears? Can they see in color?

Thirty-eight species of snakes reside in South Carolina. Only six are venomous. Learning to identify the venomous is a good family summer activity. Many species use camouflage to protect themselves and to catch prey. Attempting to catch a snake, poking a stick at it, or stepping on one is likely to provoke a snake's natural defense mechanism to strike at danger.

Follow these snake safety tips from Ms. Slither (and the South Carolina Department of Natural Resources):

- Never put hands, arms, feet, or legs into places where you cannot see them.
- Wear long pants, socks, and closed-toed shoes when walking in the woods or high grass.
- Walk around fallen logs instead of stepping over them.
- Use a flashlight if walking at night.
- If you encounter a snake in your path, step back and let it pass.
- If a snake is on your property, let it alone.
- Learning to identify snakes reduces fear of them.

The Savannah River Ecology Lab has an online snake ID page at https://srelherp.uga.edu

Chapter 2
Flying Farmers – the Pollinators

"The hum of bees is the voice of the garden."
Elizabeth Lawrence

An Insectary to Bring Back the Bees

Seventy-five percent of flowering plants on earth require pollinators to set seed or fruit. Humans consume one-third of these plants and a much larger percentage is eaten by wildlife. But declining bee populations are threatening world food supply for humans and wildlife.

Pollinators like bees, butterflies, moths, bats, birds, beetles, and other insects visit flowers when foraging for food in the form of nectar and pollen. When visiting a flower, the pollinator touches the reproductive parts depositing pollen along the route. Bees are considered the most important group of pollinators because the females deliberately collect pollen as food for offspring and transfer large amounts as they travel to hundreds of flowers on each foraging foray.

Fragmented habitat, habitat loss, fungal diseases, parasites, and environmental contaminants like pesticides are variables implicated in declining bee populations. It's an ominous problem, but the simple practice of creating an insectary on your property can help to bring native bees back. An insectary is a pollinator planting of wildflowers and wild grasses, which provide food, shelter, and nesting area for the life cycle needs of pollinators.

How to attract and protect native bee pollinators was the subject of a daylong pollinator short course conducted in 2014 by the Xerces Society for Invertebrate Conservation at the Clemson University Sandhill Research and Education Center in northeast Columbia, South Carolina. The Xerces Society is a non-profit organization headquartered in Portland, Oregon, with the mission of protecting biological diversity through the conservation of invertebrates and their habitat. Workshop participants came from a broad spectrum of interest groups including homeowners, farmers, extension agents, entomologists, educators, gardeners, naturalists, park managers, beekeepers, biologists, natural resource specialists, and U.S. Department of Agriculture crop consultants.

Instructors were Nancy Lee Adamson of the Xerces Society and Sudie Thomas of the USDA's Natural Resources Conservation Service. They guided class participants outdoors into the field to plant a pollination demonstration plot on a quarter-acre strip of land, which had been cleared of all weeds and grass. Roundstone Native Seed of Kentucky supplied the pollinator mix with over thirty native wildflowers and grasses including beardtongue, goldenrod, coreopsis, baptisia, bergamot, purple and grey coneflowers, Indian grass, and yarrow. Roundstone provides Ecotype seed, meaning the seed comes from parent stock that has evolved over time and adapted to southern eco-region soils, geology, temperature, rainfall, elevation, insects, and disease pests.

Wildflower and grass seed is mixed with a carrier prior to sowing. A carrier is an inert material that will dilute the seed mix for even distribution. Carrier agents include sawdust, kitty litter, rice hulls, soy hulls, sand, pelletized lime, or cracked corn. Seed and carriers are mixed in plastic tubs and transferred to five-gallon buckets for hand scattering. Broadcasting seed by hand is an old-fashioned, low-tech, low-cost option and very effective on a quarter-acre plot.

When broadcasting over a large area, it is recommended that seed be sown in two directions to enhance even coverage. First, seed lengthwise down the field. Then seed perpendicular to the first seeding.

Regular watering is important for newly installed insectaries but tapers off once plants mature. Hand weeding is the best practice for weed control.

The insectary plot provides the forage and shelter. What about nesting sites? Wooden nest blocks, bundles of hollow stems from bamboo or reeds, and dense brush piles can be added to support the life cycle of native bees.

For additional information on insectary gardens, visit www.xerces.org/

Pollinator Populations

Who are the two hundred thousand different species of pollinators among us? Invertebrates like bees, wasps, flies, beetles, mosquitoes, butterflies, and moths, and vertebrates like birds, bats, and rodents are the primary pollinators conducting ecological services for humans and wildlife nonstop year round.

Worldwide animals pollinate three-fourths of the staple crop plants humans eat, thereby assisting and improving food production and, concomitantly, contributing to food security and nutrition. Scientists estimate that one in every three bites we eat is made possible by an effective animal-plant pollination partnership. Pollinators also contribute to crops that provide biofuels, fibers, medicines, livestock forage, and building materials.

Ninety percent of flowering plants depend on animal pollinators for fertilization. Pollination as an ecosystem process involves transferring pollen grains from the male anther of a flower to the female stigma by wind or animals, resulting in the production of fruit and fertile seeds for reproduction of the plant. When animals forage at flowers, they do so for the reward of food for themselves and offspring in the form of pollen (protein) and nectar (carbohydrate). Pollination is the unintended ecological service of their visit.

Where have all the pollinators gone? There was a time not so long ago when a drive on a country road or interstate demanded frequent stops to wash the bugs from the windshield and grill. Entomologists call it the windshield phenomenon. Millennials have had little splat experience to report. What's on your windshield?

While splattered insects may not seem scientific evidence, whether bugs are on or missing from windshields raises questions about diversity and density of insect species. German scientists studying insect abundance in over one hundred nature preserves from 1989 to 2013 found an eighty percent percent decline in biomass, an alarming decrease. Similar results were recorded across the globe. The decline is likely to have far-reaching effects on plants and other animals, such as insect-eating birds. Ninety-six percent of songbirds feed their nestlings insects even if the birds do not eat insects as adults.

Pollinator population decline is attributed to multiple factors. One is habitat loss to aggressive agricultural practices that plant crops on every accessible acre, eliminating wildflower patches and cover crops that provide pollinator food. Another is increased pesticide use by farmers, the seed and horticulture industry, commercial applicators, lawn and garden services, homeowners, and gardeners. Pathogens and parasites also affect insects, and so does changing climate. Warmer earth temperatures alter the territories of plants and animals, leading to the speculation "Will pollinators be available when the flowers need them?"

What can the home gardener do to provide a healthy habitat for pollinators to thrive and survive? As animals they require four basic ingredients: food, water, shelter, and nesting material.

Pollinator Resources

www.fao.org/pollination/en/
http://pollinator.org
https://xerces.org
https://www.fs.fed.us/wildflowers/pollinators/pollinator-of-the-month/index.shtml

Conservation Campaigns

The global decline in pollinator populations since the 1980s has sparked numerous conservation campaigns. Each spotlights how humans can act locally to protect and enhance pollinator life cycles, lifestyles and habitat. They include:

- Bring Back the Pollinators sponsored by the Xerces Society
- National Pollinator Week (last full week in June) managed by Pollinator Partnership
- The USDA Forest Service Pollinator of the Month Program
- World Bee Day each May 20, declared by the Farm and Agricultural Organization (FAO) of the United Nations

Pollinator Friendly Family

When an old diseased oak tree was removed by the city, their front yard right of way was suddenly sunny. Columbia, South Carolina, homeowners Carla and Dylan Goff decided to take advantage of the new sunlit spot to create a low maintenance pollinator plot.

Using their natural instincts, indigenous knowledge of plants, and experimental serendipity, the pair planted a palette of perennial native plants and self-seeding annuals, providing many happy returns for birds, bees, and butterflies.

The Goffs' plant inventory reads like a checklist developed by pollination ecologists. Yarrow, *Achillea millefolium*, sunflower, *Helianthus annuus*, purple coneflower, *Echinacea purpura*, blanket flower, *Gaillardia pulchella*, and false indigo, *Baptisia australis* attract large numbers of native bees. Rosemary, *Rosmarinus officinalis*, is an aromatic drought tolerant perennial evergreen herb with blue flowers grown to attract bees, hawk moths, butterflies, and hummingbirds. Plants were chosen to deliver a succession of bloom across three seasons: spring, summer, and autumn. The spring barrage of bees and bloom starts when the redbud, *Cercis canadensis*, replacement tree from the city, invites bumblebees.

Butterflies nectar at tickseed, *Coreopsis* spp., beeblossom, *Gaura lindheimer*, red hot poker, *Kniphofias* spp., lavender, *Lavendula* spp., and the fiery red globe amaranth, *Gomphrena haageana* 'Strawberry Fields'. The carmine red *Spiraea japonica* 'Anthony Waterer' forms flat wreathlike flower clusters from spring to midsummer. The individual tubular florets of *Lantana camara* give a feast of nectar until frost.

Hummingbirds are fond of beardtongues, *Penstemon* spp., succulent Texas Red Yucca, *Hesperaloe parvifolia* and a trio of sages: *Salvia microphylla* 'Hot Lips', *Salvia coccinea* 'Jewel Red', and purple salvia.

When Dylan experimented with sowing safflower seed, he discovered the thistle-like annual composite was easy to grow and matures to three feet high with pretty yellow blossoms favored by bees.

He amends the loamy sand soil with homemade compost, "a lot." He said, "I don't use sprays or fertilizer." By using a diversity of native plants the garden ecosystem lures pollinators and beneficial insect predators.

The pollinator plot doubles as a cutting garden for gift bouquets and indoor flower arrangements. The Goff garden displays one family's motivation and model for restoring natural neighborhoods to the city.

Dylan Goff working in his pollinator plot.

Barbara's Bees

As a food and flower farm gardener in rural Richland County, South Carolina, Barbara McCoy has invited a diverse population of native bees to forage and nest on her homestead. How does she get the garden buzzing?

She knows the names and predilections of each plant as well as she knew the idiosyncrasies of the kindergarten students she taught. Scouting in the garden, she points out that lacecap hydrangeas are a magnet for bumblebees. Since bumblebees are generalists when it comes to foraging, they feed from her garden's diverse menu including columbine, foxglove, liatris, and tomatoes. By offering native and non-native self-seeding annuals and perennials in seasonal succession, pollinators receive nectar and pollen over the entire southern growing season.

Humans and bees rely on the sense of vision for the work they do. But bees and humans don't have the same color vision. Human vision views a rainbow spectrum from red through violet. Bees see from orange to blues to ultraviolet (UV). A red flower to us is a black flower to a bee. Good flower colors for a bee are blue, purple, violet, white, and yellow. Some red flowers like blanket flower, gloriosa daisy, and poppies have a UV color component visible to bees. Native bees are readily attracted to McCoy's blue Lily of the Nile, *Agapanthus*, and *Veronica*, blue hydrangeas, mauve elephant garlic blooms, and clouds of blue or white *Stokesia laevis*. *Liatris spicata* aka blazing star, a striking vertical wildflower with purple, tufted flower heads arranged in a tall, dense spike blooming from top to bottom, becomes a pollinator popsicle. Bumblebees and diminutive native sweat bees "make a beeline" to masses of *Monarda didyma* aka bee balm.

McCoy's variety of flower shapes supports more bee species too. The range of flowers from which bees gather nectar depends upon the length of their tongue. Bee tongue length correlates with body size. Short-tongued bees drink from open flowers like daisies, stokesia, sunflower, allium, and liatris; long-tongued bees secure nectar from tubular and complex flowers like foxglove, columbine, snapdragon, and honeysuckle. Flowers have nectar guides in ultraviolet color patterns that bees see to guide their foraging but humans cannot see.

The size of a bee determines how far it travels from its nest for food. Large bees fly farther than small ones. Bumblebees can forage distances of a mile or more, whereas small sweat bees may forage only two hundred yards from the nest. Barbara's bee-friendly property has long corridors of flowers lining driveways and the vegetable garden. Wide ribbons (four feet in diameter) of flowers clustered in clumps of one species encircle the perimeter of the farm. McCoy's summer food crops, tomatoes, green beans, peppers, squashes, melons, and cucumbers, are lined in bee-attracting herbs including rosemary, sages, thyme, oregano, and mints.

Bumble bee with pollen baskets

All yard waste, leaf litter, and grass clippings are composted and returned to the soil as nature's fertilizer. No landscape fabric or bark mulch covers the soil. This permits underground nesting bees such as bumblebees, digger bees, and sweat bees to nest on the property.

Hand weeding and picking off pests are preferred practices over use of herbicides or pesticides for bees and humans.

Barbara's bees work side by side with the food and flower farm gardener to protect and conserve biodiversity in rural landscapes.

Farming for Bees

https://xerces.org/guidelines-farming-for-bees/
www.nrcs.usda.gov/wps/portal/nrcs/main/national/plantsanimals/pollinate/farmers/

Bees and Blooms

The National Wildlife Federation has designated June as National Pollinator Month to raise awareness of pollinators as a key component of global biodiversity, providing vital ecosystem services to home gardens, commercial agricultural crops, and wild flowering plants. The global decline in pollinator populations threatens a catastrophic collapse of the proper functioning of all ecosystems. Bees are the most efficient and effective pollinator. There are 20,000 species of bees worldwide, 4,000 species in North America and between 400-450 native species in South Carolina.

Local education initiatives are available on pollinator conservation. Columbia Southeast Park rangers conducted Bees and Blooms, a two-hour workshop on social and solitary bee pollinators and native plants to attract them.

Ranger Alfred Burns, resident expert on pollinators and trained by the SC Mid-State Beekeepers Association, presented a talk on European honey bees, which are social bees and the most familiar and popular crop pollinators for South Carolina peaches, blueberries, and watermelon. Since commercial agriculture depends on managed pollination, beekeepers transport honey bees to flowering fields around the country. The IRS considers beekeeping a form of farming and the U.S. government classifies honey bees as livestock.

Burns described several fascinating forms of honey bee communication – touching antennae, pheromones, and the waggle dance. His display of posters "What is Pollination?" "Bee Biology," ''Inside the Hive," and "How Honey is Made" are useful for teachers and homeschool educators. After his talk, participants donned protective beekeeping veils, suits, jackets, and gloves and walked to the hive to view busy bees at work.

Ranger Walsh with a mason bee cavity nest

Honey bees as social insects live in colonies. Each colony consists of one queen, 3,000 drones, and up to 60,000 worker bees. The queen is responsible for laying eggs. Drones mate with the queen. Worker bees are responsible for collecting nectar and pollen, building and maintaining the hive, caring for the young, and making honey.

Bird netting surrounds the new park pollinator garden to deter resident deer from munching. Lori Watson, owner of Millcreek Greenhouse, recommended and sourced native species of aster, bee balm, blanket flower, boneset, coneflower, coreopsis, hydrangea, and milkweed for the garden.

https://crownbees.com/mason-bee-life-cycle/
https://www.weekshoneyfarm.com/
https://www.facebook.com/scmidstatebeekeepers/

Think of a flower garden as a pollen source for bees.

Ranger Karla Brown presented a program on native solitary bees focusing on the diminutive but powerful pollinator mason bee life cycle. Of the 4,000 species of bees in North America, ninety percent live solitary rather than social lives. Females construct and provision a nest without any help from kin. Seventy percent of solitary bees are ground nesters; thirty percent are cavity nesters. Mason bees nest in hollow reeds or plant stems, wood boring beetle cavities, or man-made bundles of bamboo. Female mason bees build cement walls in their nesting chambers with mud and clay, "masonry products" giving each developing bee its own private room in the nesting chamber.

A culminating activity for participants was to make a mason bee bamboo cavity nest to take home to place in their garden.

A Pollinator Picnic

National Pollinator Week is an annual celebration designed to raise awareness of the importance of pollinators and what we can do to protect them. Linda Suber has been celebrating bees, butterflies, flies, wasps, and hummingbirds in her Shandon neighborhood garden for fifteen years by planning and planting pollinator picnics. Menus vary by season and by pollinator preference.

The caterpillar café menu grows dill, fennel and parsley to host black swallowtail caterpillars, snapdragons for buckeyes, violets and pansies for variegated fritillary, and native milkweeds for monarch caterpillars.

The nectar café menu is composed of annuals, biennials, and perennials including balloon flower, beardtongue, canna, clover, coneflowers, coreopsis, cosmos, cuphea, daylilies, hibiscus, hydrangeas, Joe Pye weed, lantana, marigold, pentas, phlox, spiderwort, vitex, and zinnia. Hummingbirds imbibe at bee balm, red bottlebrush, cleome, columbine, Mexican petunias, salvias, and red shrimp plant. Most plants are purchased from Gardener's Outpost in Columbia and Joyful Butterfly in Blackstock, South Carolina.

How is urban soil amended? Linda and husband Von compost underground in holes using a Dig and Drop method. Von digs a hole fifteen inches deep to bury kitchen food scraps. He replaces the soil and is done. The organic matter decomposes underground and the resulting compost enriches the soil and offers nutrients to plants. Grass clippings and dry deciduous leaves are used as mulch year round to control soil temperature and moisture, smother weeds, add nutrients, invite earthworms, and prevent erosion.

Container plant pots are filled with potting soil and top-dressed with Stout Ollie compost. Linda uses Fox Farm Tiger Bloom fertilizer with earthworm castings for containers.

Rain barrels, hoses, drip line, and underground sprinkler system are used to get water to all areas of the sun-filled garden.

Since pesticides poison pollinators and can cause subtle changes in reproduction, navigation, and memory of bees and other beneficial insects, and herbicides destroy pollinator food sources, Suber uses no pesticides or herbicides and advises others to do the same.

The garden is a bird sanctuary for thirty-five species to fly, feed, sing, and nest. The bird buffet includes millet and sunflower seed, suet, and mealworms. From an ecological perspective moth and butterfly caterpillars are an important protein and fat food source for birds, reptiles, amphibians, and small mammals. Fountains and birdbaths bring feathered friends to drink, bathe, and preen.

When Suber's grandson attended Rosewood Elementary, she invited his second-grade class to the garden to observe monarchs in various stages of metamorphosis. Since the life cycle of butterflies is part of the second-grade science curriculum, Rosewood second graders continue spring visitation observing the monarch life cycle in a screen cage and rotating among four stations: Pollinator Word Search, Sidewalk Chalk of Life Cycle, Scavenger Hunt, and Pollinator Bee Sticks.

Linda Suber at the entrance to Kaleidoscope

Suber's garden named Kaleidoscope is registered with the Rosalynn Carter Butterfly Trail based in Plains, Georgia, with Monarch Watch as a Monarch Waystation and with the South Carolina Wildlife Federation as a Wildlife Habitat.

Plant Trees to Attract Larvae

On a nature walk at Congaree National Park my third-grade companions spotted several green caterpillars crawling along the boardwalk railings. The youngsters knew caterpillars chew leaves and they started looking for the food source. It happened to be right overhead. The red maple trees, *Acer rubrum*, were in autumn color but caterpillar cutwork had created intriguing "see through" leaf designs.

These vegetarians had round red-orange heads and green bodies with small black spines. The markings, measurements, and menu helped us identify the caterpillar as the green-striped mapleworm, the larva of the rosy maple moth, *Dryocampa rubicunda* -- a stunning yellow and pink winged moth with a furry yellow body. It is native to the eastern United States.

Further along the boardwalk, among a stand of beech trees, we encountered an inchworm looping along the handrail. Inchworms, also known as cankerworms, loopers, measuring worms, and span-worms represent over a thousand species of geometer moth. The size of the caterpillar is no clue to the amount of foliage these miniature mouths can consume in a forest. Beech, oak, elm, and maple trees are but a few hosts of these forest surveyors.

Observing creatures dependent on a host tree leaf brings awareness to the importance of including trees when planting butterfly and moth gardens.

The Congaree National Park trees host a varied population of caterpillar species. Your home landscape and child's school grounds can do the same.

Consider shade trees that can be planted as food sources for the larval stage of the adult butterflies and moths.

Tulip poplar, *Liriodendron tulipifera*, tops my list. Years ago I planted a tulip poplar twig from the Arbor Day Foundation and today the towering tree is visited by Ms. Eastern Tiger Swallowtails at egg laying time to deposit glistening green beads on leaves. My river birch cools the house in summer while the leaves play host to tiger swallowtail and mourning cloak larvae. On sassafras tree leaves one can find the Imperial moth's larva and the spicebush swallowtail butterfly's green caterpillar, with its snakelike head and large black eyespot.

The fast growing hackberry, *Celtis occidentalis*, and its cousin the sugarberry, *Celtis laevigata*, are hosts to a handful of butterfly larvae, including hackberry emperor, question mark, mourning cloak, snout butterfly, and tawny emperor. Royal walnut moth larvae, called the hickory horned devil, feed on hickory, walnut, pecan, sumac, and sweet gum. The lovely and large sea-foam green luna moth deposits eggs on beeches, cherries, hickories, pecan, persimmon, sweet gum, and willows.

Tour the forested areas of the metropolitan area to view host plant Lepidopteran gardens. The trees of W. Gordon Belser Arboretum offer ten acres of upscale dining for caterpillars. The tree-lined trails at Sesquicentennial State Park are a butterfly larvae buffet. Visitors to the University of South Carolina's historic Horseshoe can take a self-guided tour of the trees using a leaflet from the visitor's center at McKissick Museum. The downtown campus trees matriculate and graduate more moths and butterflies than students each year.

Trees, canopy and understory, are the backbone of a well-designed landscape for humans and larvae.

A Perennial Vine with a Passion for Butterflies

Capture children's enthusiasm for butterflies with a vine that matches their energy while rearing gulf fritillary butterflies on *Passiflora incarnata*, passion vine.

The native herbaceous perennial vine grows across the southeastern United States. While found in wilderness areas, it is also common in subdivisions and along roadsides.

The extraordinary beauty of the passion flower is dreamlike. Three-inch wide purple flowers have five sepals and five petals. The crown or corona is covered in wavy hair-like fringe. In the center of each flower are five stamens and a tripart pistil. The ephemeral flowers last only one day.

An egg shaped green edible fruit filled with seeds follows faded flowers. The popping sound made when the ripe fruit is stepped on accounts for the common name maypop.

Starting a community of passion flower vines is not difficult; containing it is. The vine spreads by underground rhizomes popping up on property like prairie dog mounds. Mow the plant down and it soon returns running for a mature length of twenty-five feet across the ground or twining its tendrils on nearby plants or structures.

By cultivating passionflower in raised beds or containers you witness plant-insect relationships, butterfly behavior, and life cycle on a daily basis. The vine hosts the eggs and larvae of the gulf fritillary butterflies. The plant is frequently passed along by gardeners or obtained at native plant nurseries. If propagating from seed, sow in early spring. Germination is slow, from days to months.

While getting passion vines established, attract fritillaries with lantana as a lure. This nectar plant brings a pageant of butterflies with its mass of colorful nosegay shaped flowerheads, each offering twenty to forty florets for tapping nectar.

Gulf fritillary butterflies have a wingspan of two and a half to three and a half inches. Upper wings are a burnt orange color with black edgings and markings. The underside of wings is brown and orange with iridescent silver spots. The body is streaked in white and orange with black specks on the orange. Head is pointed and a black-coiled proboscis extends from the front.

Females deposit single yellow eggs on the underside of the tri-lobed palmate leaves of passion vine. The plant leaves have tiny yellow bumps mimicking eggs. The plant has devised a protection device to fool butterflies into thinking eggs have already been deposited. After all, eggs lead to caterpillars and the decimation of the leaves. In four to six days miniscule caterpillars chew their way out of the eggshell, which serves as an appetizer for the leafy green entrées ahead. Larvae are reddish brown caterpillars covered with rows of ominous looking but harmless, black bristles. Caterpillars chew leaves and stem with chitinous mandibles.

As caterpillars grow, their exoskeletons become too small and they molt. After a series of molts, caterpillars pupate by finding a firm support on which to attach and form a chrysalis. Within five to ten days the dry brown chrysalis shell splits, the adult butterfly emerges hanging upside down until its wings dry and harden. The lifespan of the adult is two to four weeks.

The gulf fritillary's life depends upon the passion vine. By growing passion vine and rearing caterpillars to butterflies, children and adults come to realize their role in conserving natural systems.

Passionvine flower

SECTION TWO

THE OCCUPATION OF GARDENING

"Gardening...need not be taught either for the sake of preparing future gardeners, or as an agreeable way of passing time. It affords an avenue of approach to knowledge of the place farming and horticulture have had in the history of the race and which they occupy in present social organization. Carried on in an environment educationally controlled, they (gardens) are a means for making a study of the facts of growth, the chemistry of soil, the role of light, air and moisture, injurious and helpful animal life, etc. There is nothing in the elementary study of botany which cannot be introduced in a vital way in connection with caring for the growth of seeds. Instead of the subject belonging to a peculiar study called botany, it will then belong to life, and will find, moreover, its natural correlations with the facts of soil, animal life, and human relations."
John Dewey

Chapter 1
School Gardens

"Great was my pride and delight when I was given a garden of my own, to do just what I like with." Gertrude Jekyll

How Parents Can Help Grow a School Garden

Staying involved in your child's education is a means to ensure sustained interest and success in school. One way to become active is to volunteer with the initiation, continuation, or revitalization of the school garden program. Most school gardens function best through a partnership of parents, teachers, students, staff, and community volunteers working together with clearly defined roles.

What roles might parents take? Here are several ways to be involved:

Garden programs need publicity. The spokesperson makes the garden's goals, needs, and accomplishments visible to the PTA, school improvement council, local garden clubs, nursery and garden centers, and the press.

Prepare a publicity packet to include a letter of endorsement from the principal, a one-page description of the program, a list of supporters, drawings or photographs of the garden, and website address.

Visibility may come through direct contact, invitations to events, flyers, announcements in the school newsletter, and press releases. The computer-savvy parent could develop an ongoing virtual tour of garden activities on the school website. A parent with artistic flair could encourage students to design a garden logo, make posters and signs, and design garden theme note cards.

At Brockman Elementary School in Richland One in Columbia, South Carolina, the school garden committee was a perennial committee of the PTA. Each classroom had a garden, plus there was one large vegetable plot used by the entire school. Each classroom also had a "garden parent" who worked with the teacher to determine the objectives and activities for the garden. At least once a week that parent taught a lesson in the garden. Teachers followed up with a journaling, storytelling, graphing, or drawing activity. At the start of the school year, recovery efforts of weeding, hoeing, deadheading, watering, and harvesting were under way.

Few school budgets allocate funds for a school garden. However, a garden costs from $1,500 to $2,500 per year to maintain. Joyce Shealy, chair of the Brockman garden committee, reported that the PTA allocated a hundred dollars to each classroom garden and additional funds for bulk garden items and greenhouse supplies. Parents assisted with fund-raising too.

Grassroots fund-raising included car or pet washes, plant or seed sales, benefit concerts or dances, pancake or spaghetti suppers, roller-skating parties, and yard sales. Donations from local businesses added to the garden: wood chips from the utility company, split fertilizer and lime bags at the garden center, gravel from a paving contractor, horse manure from a stable, scrap wood from a lumber company.

Specialists in the community offer invaluable instruction to classroom programs. A parent can recruit county extension agents, master gardeners, tree farmers, soil scientists, water conservationists, horticulturists, organic growers, beekeepers, farmers, plant breeders, herbarium curators, nature photographers, chefs, even garden writers.

Barbara Collins oversees student preparing for plant sale

Parents, grandparents, and neighbors have helped the gardening program at Satchel Ford Elementary School in Richland County, South Carolina, by donating perennials, trees, time, and muscle. Families attending nearby Grace Baptist Church have installed two learning gardens.

Grants are a way to secure funds and materials. Erin Fisher, former art teacher at Satchel Ford in Richland One, had received grants from the S.C. Forestry Commission and from Clemson University's Landscapes for Learning initiative for a variety of learning gardens on campus.

Parents can assist with the grant process by finding appropriate grants and ordering guidelines. Local garden clubs, master gardener associations and state agencies offer grants to education programs.

Special-needs Students Grow Plants and Life Skills

Gardening is an exciting endeavor for all students. But the exploration, discovery, experimentation, and nurturing that gardening provides can be particularly valuable to special-needs students.

Plants are their reciprocal companions in the growth process. The greenhouse or the garden gives first-hand encounters in the real world of practical experience. Growing plants results in offshoots one can be proud to share with others in exchange for appreciation, praise, and recognition.

A longstanding program for special-needs students in central South Carolina also uses gardening to prepare for the workplace young people who otherwise might have been considered unemployable. But like the plants they tend, these students thrive and blossom in the Lawn, Garden and Gifts Enterprise course at Heyward Career and Technology Center in Richland District One.

The year-long program is one component of Richland One Works (ROW), school-based enterprises and community-based training that also includes experiential learning in welding and automotive skills, construction, jewelry-making and stitch work, and media services. Students are transitioned from high school into the workforce.

When I first observed the class in operation, veteran instructor Susan Collins, who has since retired, was teaching basic horticulture concepts using a large domed greenhouse as the laboratory for labeling the parts of plants and parts of the greenhouse; propagating plants from seed, bulb, cuttings, and division; transplanting plants as growth required, irrigating, and fertilizing. Then students were taught how to safely use power tools among plants and on lawns.

The class was run like a business. Students clocked into class as they would a business. Plant propagation throughout the year transformed the greenhouse into a jungle. Each spring students conducted a one-week plant sale open to the public. The sale gave students experience in using the business savvy, etiquette, and math and communication skills honed in class.

In 2021 Jamie Tyler began teaching three horticulture classes at Heyward - Introduction to Horticulture, Horticulture for the Workplace, and Nursery, Greenhouse and Garden Center Technology. A new Jaderloon Freestanding Greenhouse provides a lab with proper light, temperature, and ventilation for propagation and watering of plants. The irrigation system can be set to do drip, overhead, and basket automatic watering.

Students learn propagation techniques from seed starting to vegetative propagation by cuttings, division, layering, runners, bulbs, and tubers. They are introduced to basic plant care including soil types and pH, nutrients, temperature, humidity, lighting, watering, and scouting for pests in the greenhouse and in the landscape.

In addition to the science of growing plants, they learn about careers and business ventures available in horticulture. The spring plant sale gives students an opportunity to practice customer service and soft skills developed in class.

By April -- just in time for an annual week-long plant sale -- the greenhouse is a chlorophyll zoo with hanging baskets and cell packs and pots of flowering annuals, perennials, herbs, and vegetables lining greenhouse shelves.

You name it, they have it! Herb lovers will find oregano, thyme, rosemary, basil, and banana mint. Heat-tolerant varieties of gourds, tomatoes, peppers, and cucumbers will be ready for transplanting. To attract pollinators there are coneflowers, pentas, and salvias.

Proceeds from the plant sale directly support supplies, student incentives, classroom activities, and travel to local green industry businesses.

When students grew and submitted indoor plants to the S.C. State Fair Competition, several Heyward students won first and second place.

Supporting these enterprising young people will enrich your garden and their self-confidence. While growing plants might be your hobby, it is likely to become their livelihood after graduation.

When teachers like Tyler seed the future of students with inspirational educational experiences, it is easy to understand why colleagues selected her as the 2021-22 Heyward Teacher of the Year.

A Classroom Without Walls

Courtyard gardens, meadow, woodland, and bog have been an integral part of the daily instructional life of some students at Sandhills School – those lucky enough to discover that classrooms don't have to have walls. The twenty-two acre campus in southeast Columbia, South Carolina, is a wildlife campus amid a residential neighborhood. Students enter Sandhills for a second chance to learn to read, write, or calculate. The private school's mission is "to provide a successful environment for students who learn differently." Over the years some teachers have used the natural world with its multi-sensory experiences as one context and compass to unleash and develop individual student potential.

The atmosphere for natural classroom teaching and learning still exists at Sandhills. I like to share what I wrote about it several years ago because it epitomizes what the right people in the right place can do at the right time. When I wrote these words in a "Gardening with Kids" column a dozen years ago, two remarkable teachers were on the faculty, awakening students to the world around them.

This is what I wrote in 2010: "Around the bog students find deer and raccoon tracks, fox scat, green frogs, toads, dragonflies, snakes, and turtles. In the meadow, a killdeer pair returns annually to nest on the ground, unruffled by student activity. There are no bells between classes but there are birdsongs from mockingbirds, robins and Carolina wrens inhabiting the woodland. Red-winged blackbirds have been heard and sighted around the bog plants - cattail, water lilies, spider lilies, and pickerel weed.

"Jewel, a five-year-young tortoise, has an outdoor pen but accompanies classes on excursions across the schoolyard.

"Elementary students working with teacher Becky Woldt stake out study plots in the bog, woodland and meadow to compare soils and plants of each ecosystem. The abundance of flora and fauna on campus gives students a close view of natural life cycles. Students present their observations, for example of the life cycle of green frogs, in artistic representations including drawings, paintings, diagrams, or three-dimensional models.

"Jennifer Mancke teaches middle and high school science as natural history. An inveterate collector, her classroom suite is a museum of natural curiosities. She stops for road kills and is permitted to collect wild specimens for education. Among the living things indoors are a tarantula and cockatiel.

"Students look forward to going barefoot in the bog muck, a special event reserved for the last day of school each year. Usually they don boots when gathering water samples to test for dissolved oxygen in summer and winter, to observe the gambusia minnows, or to add new water plants like the spider lilies relocated from the Columbia Canal.

"The outdoors stirs student imagination, and their aesthetic sensibilities are awakened through experiences and encounters with nature and art. Mancke says, "Art is big in all classes." While closely inspecting plant specimens, students draw portraits from root to shoot. Student plant portraits won first, second, and third place in the University of South Carolina's Herbarium Picturing Plants Art Contest. Seven sculptures with outdoor themes adorn the campus and a hallway mural brings the outdoors in.

The tortoise Jewel goes for a walk on campus

"At recess students snatch wild blackberries from the scarlet vines they tracked in winter all the way through to spring buds, blooms and pollinators.

"Picture a classroom in the treetops with solar lighting and air-conditioned by the wind. The treehouse constructed around two old hackberry trees is a gathering place for instruction and camaraderie events including ice cream socials and picnics. Up in the tree Mancke's students witness the 'Battle of the Bugs at Sugarberry' while observing the farming and gardening practices of ants, aphids, and ladybugs. The eye of the naturalist is one of the lenses through which students at Sandhills come to view the world and find intrigue and success en route."

Heathwood Hall's Teaching Gardens

Heathwood Hall Episcopal School in Columbia, South Carolina, has a long tradition of environmental stewardship and sustainable use of resources. The campus was built to harmonize with the natural world. When I visited in 2009 a dozen landscape projects were underway and a new garden was on the horizon every year. Students were learning land stewardship and ecological literacy through gardening. The school environmental education or S.E.ED team involved administrators, faculty, staff, parents and students. The team oversaw all garden creation and maintenance, fund-raising, curriculum, professional development, communication, and outdoor classrooms.

A lean-to hothouse housing tools, equipment, potting table, bags of Fafard mix, hoses, and rain barrels served as command central for projects across the 133-acre campus. Plants propagated by students in the hothouse move to an outdoor garden where they were watered and nursed in preparation for sale.

In a locally grown garden certified by the state Department of Agriculture, students grew organic produce in raised beds for Harvest Hope Food Bank and for sampling in the dining hall. With an abundance of radishes, cooks prepared a radish aioli to top baked potatoes -- just one of the educational experiences students have gained from gardening.

A series of compost bins next to the food garden recycled waste from cafeteria food preparation as well as yard waste and clippings. Early childhood students fed garbage to worms in vermicomposting bins.

The xeric garden was created in a full sun area next to a parking lot with thermal updrafts. A riparian green zone bordered a water source. This waterfront garden slowed erosion and absorbed overflow as well as attracting animals.

Two butterfly gardens, one at the early childhood learning center and one at the lower school, enhanced math and science instruction and introduced ecosystem concepts like consumer, producer, predator, and prey.

The rain garden was a sixth-grade project to reduce water pollution from parking lot runoff, eliminate lawn upkeep, and restore wildlife habitat. Water quality and wetland issues were studied in this outdoor lab.

The Carolina Fence Garden used native plants as food, cover, and nesting material for wildlife.

A Medicine Wheel Garden filled with the useful native plants of Southeastern Native Americans spans 4,200 square feet. The wheel was divided into four quadrants representing the points on a compass and the four seasons. It featured the four tribal colors of red, purple, white, and yellow and four stages of human life from birth to youth to adult to elder. Plants in each quadrant mirrored one of the tribal colors in flower, fruit, or foliage.

A nature trail linked all gardens along a serpentine path marked with tree identification signage and learning stations. Heathwood Hall budgeted $2,000 to the gardens per year. The bulk of financial support came from spring and fall plant sales and from writing a dozen grants per year.

For many years teachers Todd Beasley and Jim Morris were coordinators of the S.E.ED (School Environmental Education) team and developed the garden program to a level well beyond most school gardening efforts. All too often ambitious gardening projects become abandoned when the people who worked so hard to create and use them depart, but that thankfully had not happened as of 2024 at Heathwood Hall.

In 2021 Jamie Browder, early childhood and lower school science resource teacher, took charge of the outdoor classroom and greenhouse and expanded the edible forest with native trees and shrubs. His garden-based work with students earned him the 2022 Conservation Teacher of the Year from the Richland County Soil and Water Conservation District.

In 2023 Jason Giovannone, early childhood and lower school science and STEM teacher, continued the tradition of using the beautiful 133-acre campus as an outdoor classroom for his 2K - fourth-grade students.

Giovannone is working to address student emotions about phenomena in the outdoors and to offer a safe and supportive space for outdoor learning. He believes children need to care about phenomena before they will conserve nature. In fall he uses *Leaf Man* by Lois Ehlert to introduce the colorful changing tree leaves on campus but also the autumn wind. In spring the young learners will venture outside to explore one of the five habitats on campus: pond, field, wetlands, forest, river. Each class decides on one area of interest to focus on for six to eight weeks. Through research and hands-on activities, students present their findings in a performance to parents and peers on Habitat Day in May.

While faculty and student body changes over time, the landscape's history can be read in tree rings, habitats, wildlife, and gardens.

Cabbage Dreams

When Katie Stagliano of Summerville, South Carolina, was nine years old, her class participated in Bonnie Plants 3rd Grade Cabbage Program. Each school year Bonnie Plants contributes millions of cabbage plants to schools to encourage home and school gardening. In Katie's class each student received a cabbage seedling to grow at home and see who could harvest the largest cabbage. Katie planted her seedling in the family garden and tended the plant by watering, fertilizing, and pulling weeds. With the help of her grandfather, they built a wire cage around the cabbage to protect it from deer. By season's end she had a forty-pound cabbage.

What do you do with a colossal cabbage too heavy for the grower to lift? Katie believed her special cabbage needed a unique purpose. Her mother contacted a local soup kitchen, Tri County Family Ministries, to see if they would accept a "large" donation. When Katie watched her cabbage feed 275 appreciative homeless, a dream sprouted. What if she could start a school vegetable garden to donate produce to the soup kitchen on a year-round basis and reduce hunger in her hometown?

With the help of teachers, classmates, and parents at Pinewood Prep, and a local master gardener, a school vegetable garden the length of a football field was developed to serve local soup kitchens.

Having achieved the goal of a local soup kitchen garden, Katie dreamed an even bigger dream. Could she inspire schools across the country to grow food for the homeless and hungry?

Katie's Krops was formed. The 501(c) 3 raises funds to initiate school soup kitchen gardens in all fifty states. When I first wrote about Katie, she was fourteen and five years into her mission. She had already inspired the creation of sixty gardens in twenty-six states. By 2022, at twenty-three, she had become founder and chief executive officer of the non-profit company with one hundred gardens across the United States and numerous programs to get children and families involved in fighting hunger in their own communities.

She said, "Katie's Krops is thriving and empowering kids to grow a healthy end to hunger, one vegetable garden at a time."

Along the way Katie's Krops has garnered support and contributions from organizations like WP Rawl Farm in Lexington, Safer Brand products, Disney Friends for Change, Opal Apples, Fall Creek Farm and Nursery, and, of course, Bonnie Plants.

When Katie's Krops posted a greenhouse on its wish list, Dutch Heritage Gardens in Colorado shipped a forty-eight-foot greenhouse to Summerville and the company owner flew in to help set it up. With the help of the Director of Food Service at Pinewood Prep, Katie's Krops student chefs prepare and serve monthly fresh from the garden dinners for the hungry.

WP Rawl Farm in Lexington County, South Carolina, hosted the first Katie's Krops Camp in Pelion in 2013. These camps bring together youth who have initiated Katie's Krops vegetable gardens in other states to learn new gardening practices, budgeting, garden photography, and skills to improve their community project. Campers also cook and serve a meal for the hungry.

Also in 2013 at age fourteen, Katie had a book-publishing

KATIE STAGLIANO
Founder & Chief Executive Gardener- Katie's Krops
Katie@KatiesKrops.com
843-754-0857 I www.KatiesKrops.com

contract. Young Palmetto Books, a division of the University of South Carolina Press, has since then published *Katie's Cabbage,* the story of how a cabbage plant grew into a national non-profit tackling hunger at home.

It can take only a cabbage seedling to grow a dream for a lifetime and make a colossal difference in the local community.

For more details, contact: https://bonniecabbageprogram.com

Cultivate Ingenuity in an Organic School Garden

When students are eager to spruce up the school garden for fall, the paramount consideration must be the health and safety of the gardeners, consumers, ecosystem inhabitants, and environment. That's true whether they maintain a pond for fish and amphibians or grow food to eat, flowers for pollinators and their progeny, or seed plots for birds and mammals.

Over sixty years ago Rachel Carson made the public aware of the dangers of chemicals to ecosystems through her research and book, *Silent Spring*. She warned of the use of fungicides, herbicides, and pesticides -- the "biocides" still commonly in use today in commercial agriculture and home gardens. Children are particularly vulnerable to chemicals due to their still developing nervous systems, immune system, and detoxifying enzymes.

In 2012 the American Academy of Pediatrics issued a policy statement on the harmful effects of pesticides on children and recommended ways to minimize exposure. Pediatricians will be asking parents about the use of pesticides around the home and yard during well visits and will work with schools to advocate for the least toxic methods of pest control.

The U.S. Department of Agriculture paper Food Safety Tips for School Gardens states, "Do not use any pesticides or herbicides due to potential health hazards to children."

Organic gardening offers the best practices for chemical-free gardening with children while engaging students in problem solving. Help children view the garden as an ecosystem where all components are interconnected, including them. Organic gardeners see themselves as part of nature as opposed to conquering it. Weeds and pests are part of the plan along with natural checks and balances. How does "organic" look in the school garden?

Nature is the model recycler. Emulate by composting schoolyard leaves and garden waste and then returning it to replenish beds. Include indoor pencil sharpener shavings, shredded school paper, and cafeteria food preparation waste in the composting process. Collect, dry, and store seeds from garden fruits, vegetables and flowers to replant next year.

If the garden was untended over summer, weeds would be thriving. Weeds shelter insects and compete for water and nutrients. Schedule a 'weed weigh-in' to pull weeds up by the root with hand tools and hoe. Teams compete for the heaviest harvest of weeds. Or smother the weed patch with multilayers of mulch or opaque black plastic, old carpet, or cardboard. Solarization lets the sun's heat kill weed seeds. Cover the weeded plot with clear plastic and seal the edges with soil for at least six weeks. Dead-plant mulches made from cover crops such as wheat, oats, or rye suppress weeds while adding nutrients to the soil. Mow down the cover crop and tuck in new seasonal seedlings.

Invite a weed ID expert or ethnobotanist to class and use weed field guides to identify the invaders. Find out about beneficial weeds.

Insects are a necessary part of any garden. Since ninety-seven percent of insects are either helpful or harmless, get to know the enemies and allies before waging warfare on them. Allies or beneficials work with you to protect plants and can be remembered as the three P's - pollinators, predators, and parasites. Pollinators like honeybees and bumblebees fertilize our crops. The predators like praying mantids, ladybugs, and lacewings feed on insects. The parasites like braconid wasps use insects as nurseries for raising their young. Biodiversity of plantings brings this trio to your garden.

Conduct pest patrols where student sleuths scout for insects and evidence of insects, such as chewed leaves or cocoons. Mount a garden insect collection while learning the identity. Mapping which insects gravitate to what plants and when assists in planning for the future. Merely adjusting the timing of planting can reduce insect problems.

Organic gardeners devise a variety of methods for controlling insect enemies. Larger pests like tomato hornworms are handpicked off and doused in soapy water. A strong spray of water from the garden hose targets smaller trespassers like aphids and whiteflies.

Students can compete to make and test homemade herbal recipes for battling bugs. Blast the Bugs spray combines six cloves of minced garlic, one small finely chopped onion, one tablespoon of dish soap and one quart of water. Blend all together and steep overnight before spray misting plants.

Challenge children to design and set physical pest barriers with recycled materials. Floating fabric row covers allow light, water and air into newly seeded beds but barricade pests. Cutworm collars made from milk cartons or yogurt

Organic Gardening Resources
Four Seasons Farm https://www.fourseasonfarm.com/
The Rachel Carson Council https://rachelcarsoncouncil.org/
Mother Earth News https://www.motherearthnews.com
Rodale Institute https://rodaleinstitute.org

containers cut to fit into the soil and around the plant thwart chewing and boring insects from reaching plant stems. Maggot mats -- five-inch-square carpet pieces slit to the center to surround a plant stem -- deter cabbage maggot flies from laying eggs in soil near seedlings.

Making and hanging insect traps is sticky fun. Paint bookmark-size strips of cardboard or plastic a bright yellow before coating with horticulture glue like Tanglefoot. Students scrape off insects and recoat as needed.

Growing 'trap crops' like amaranth, buckwheat, nasturtium, or sunflowers around the perimeter of the garden attracts pests to them rather than to your food crops. When pests enter the 'trap,' hand pick off or snare with an insect vacuum.

Design scarecrows to deter birds from harvesting your crops.

Organic gardening cultivates inventive thinking and problem solving while maintaining the integrity and safety of the ecosystem.

Maintaining a Wildlife Habitat at School

Newly constructed schools where population is not dense provide teachers and students countless opportunities to create outdoor classrooms that support curriculum and bolster teaching and learning as well as native wildlife. Catawba Trail Elementary in South Carolina's Richland School District Two set a good example for this concept in 2011, starting with its building, constructed under criteria of the Leadership in Energy and Environmental Design, the most widely used green building rating system in the world.

The new LEED school decided to go green on the surrounding grounds as well.

The rural campus in Elgin is a marine terrace landscape. The native vegetation on site is well adapted to sandy soil. It includes catawba (catalpa) trees, sparkleberry, live oaks, Carolina cherry laurel, sassafras, hawthorn, longleaf and loblolly pines, muscadine, and smilax. Students observed winter residents like yellow-bellied sapsuckers consuming the berries and drilling rows of holes in the bark of a hackberry. Keeping wildlife and bringing wildlife on campus was one goal of Victoria Pasco's conservation-minded science lab students since the school opened in 2011 because of what already thrived on campus.

During the first year a nature trail was built through the woods with the help of an Eagle Scout. A pair of bluebirds took up residence in a new nesting box mounted on the fence.

Pasco's students planned and installed a wildlife garden in 2013.. The project required lots of learning on the job and generated more questions than answers at first. What do organisms need to stay alive? What plants grow in sand? Which plants and animals are native to the area? How can we build a garden to support the life and life cycles of many different plants and animals? What plants bring butterflies and hummingbirds?

As students discovered the wildlife garden needed the same basic requirements of the "Ark" of animals in their classroom - food, shelter, water, and a place to raise offspring. (They called their classroom "The Ark" because that's where the class housed and cared for cockatiels, parakeets, brook trout, bearded dragons, guinea pigs, gerbils, and a tarantula.)

The centerpiece of the wildlife garden was the twenty-eight-inch-deep pond, which was excavated, lined, edged, and stocked with goldfish (comets) by students. Bullfrogs provided predator-prey observations instantly.

While most animals use water for drinking and bathing, fish, amphibians, reptiles, and some insects need water for breeding. Birds and amphibians catch insects around ponds. Layers of flat rocks edging the pond offered shelter from heat, cold, wind, rain, and predators, and became basking zones for butterflies.

Vegetation surrounding the pond included not only water plants like corkscrew and horseshoe rushes and pickerel weed but also fruit trees, blueberry shrubs, and strawberries for frugivorous birds and small mammals. Sunflowers were chosen to attract seed-eating birds. Red tubular nectar-rich cuphea, salvia, and penstemon were chosen to bring hummingbirds. Butterflies were welcomed with columbine, fleabane, gaillardia, speedwell, scabiosa, and yarrow.

Sandy soil as the substrate for a garden requires an abundant and continuous supply of organic matter for plant nutrition and to slow the drainage of water. Students composted cafeteria food preparation waste like fruit and vegetable peels, wilted lettuce leaves, and vegetation in several compost bins to make compost, a soil amendment. They found that mixing and shaking the food waste hastened decomposition.

Since they needed compost quickly, they 'hired' red wiggler worms to eat food waste within a Worm Factory® unit, a tiered worm bin that separates food waste, castings, and liquid leachate. They harvested worm castings to add to planting holes and to topdress around plants.

In 2014 students added a vegetable garden adjacent to the wildlife garden. It was an exciting expansion for them. They began by removing sod, adding their homemade compost, and selecting crops for the late winter, early spring, and summer sequence of plantings. They were excited to find out what additional wildlife this new garden would bring.

The outdoor classroom program developed by Pasco was one of the Columbia-area sites visited in 2016 by participants in the American Horticultural Society's National Children and Youth Garden Symposium.

Pasco was a sixth-grade science teacher at Blythewood Middle School where she continued an outdoor learning program.

The Making of a Milkweed Meadow

While it may take a village to raise a child, it takes teachers and a yearly crop of students to restore habitat for monarchs. For the past nine years as of 2023 Team Migration Nation (TMN) at Irmo Middle School in South Carolina under the wings of seventh-grade science teacher Will Green has been on a learning expedition of habitat restoration on their school campus in the Irmo community.

Through field and published research students discovered that North American populations of monarchs and milkweed have declined precipitously over the last twenty years. A cluster of factors implicated in the decline include mowing of wild areas; herbicide and pesticide use to kill weeds and eradicate pests like caterpillars; the introduction of non-native milkweed; deforestation and ice storms in the monarch's overwintering sites in Mexico; and habitat conversion to agriculture and development of highways, housing, and malls.

Aware also of the symbiotic relationship between monarchs and milkweed, that means you can't have one without the other, TMN focused on one factor: restoring habitat. With district permission classes removed a field of turf and seeded the area with native milkweed, the only plant monarch females lay their eggs on and the sole food plant for monarch larvae. They added lantana, butterfly bush, weigela, and verbenas as nectar plants to attract adult butterflies and to fuel the monarch's fall migration to Mexico.

When tilling turf brought up weed seeds to compete with milkweed seedlings, they persevered. Horticulturists at Ernst conservation seed advised, "It takes time, at least three years, to establish a meadow." When seed did not germinate, they practiced cold stratification to break dormancy. After seeds started in the classroom grew tall and spindly, they moved milkweed propagation to the greenhouse under proper light, temperature and humidity. Now they grow hundreds of *Asclepias tuberosa* and *Asclepias syriaca* for their garden and to sell in the community to support the ongoing work of the expedition.

Students took steps to affect and direct public awareness of the monarch and milkweed connection through civic engagement. They provided native milkweed to Irmo's Public Service Department for the children's garden at the community park. This spring students planted milkweed in Saluda Shoals Park. Students authored, illustrated, and published a children's book, *The Monarch Story*, for dissemination to all Lexington-Richland Five elementary school libraries. TMN partners with Wingard's Market, SC Wildlife Federation and the SC Garden-based Learning Network.

Everything students did brought them in touch with interconnections in nature and with concepts related to all school subjects. They mapped migration in social studies, graphed migration data in math, contributed monarch tagging data to the real scientific community, wrote ad content on milkweed species in English Language Arts, and modeled monarchs overwintering in oyamel trees in art.

At an end of the year Celebration of Learning students conducted garden and greenhouse tours, read *The Monarch Story* aloud, sold milkweed, and displayed their interdisciplinary projects around the Milkweed Meadow. An elegant metal monarch sculpture created by high school student, Connor Hollis was unveiled in the center of the meadow.

Imagine what might happen if each North American school campus converted a portion of turf to a milkweed meadow!

Milkweed Meadow at Irmo Middle School

Question or Problem:
The daylilies were stunted. What is causing the lack of growth?

Hypothesis:
From prior experience with plants and reading, I knew daylilies require more sunlight than shade to flourish. So I hypothesized, "If I move the plants from a shady location to a sunny one, then their leaves will grow and they will flower again."

Experimental Procedure:
My procedure was to transplant the daylilies from a shady location to a sunlit one.

Observations and Findings:
Throughout the spring I will observe and measure the growth and record my findings in a journal.

Conclusions:
By reviewing and interpreting the data collected, I will be able to find out if my hypothesis is confirmed. My data might suggest that other factors might be affecting daylily growth such as soil pH, soil moisture retention, or nutrient levels.

Scientific Method Rules in the Garden

Recently when moving a bed of daylilies to a new location in my garden, I was reminded of how gardeners use the scientific method instinctively.

For several years the daylilies had been puny and failed to bloom. The once flamboyant flowers seemed stunted. Nearby fast-growing shrubs had shaded the bed. I surmised a lack of sunlight, the elixir for daylilies, might be the problem. Hence, the daylilies have been transplanted to a sunlit area.

Only the upcoming months of observation will reveal if sunlight is the factor or just one of the factors needed to revive my plants. Any conclusion must await the observable evidence.

In the classroom children learn and recite steps or phases of the scientific method. Science fairs are held to display the results of learning and instruction.

The garden at home or at school has always been a context for practicing scientific thinking. Let's fit the above scenario to the ingredients of the scientific method.

Our gardens do not flash signs bearing the steps of the scientific method, and our minds don't use the steps as a ladder in lock-step order. The nature of the experience of gardening summons the method in our psyche. Our natural reaction to a problem is to think it through and solve it.

Parents have many opportunities to assist children in practicing scientific thinking in the home garden. First of all, work as a team. Your child is your apprentice in practice and thought.

Parents can model cues in our language, which signal scientific thinking. Some of those cues include questions like "What happens when... ?" Or, "What happens if...?" And "What happens then?"

By verbalizing the reasons for actions in the garden, parents articulate the hypotheses embedded in their actions. "If we mulch the vegetable garden, then . . ." or "We stake the tomatoes because . . ."

We want children to voice the hypotheses of their actions as well.

Parents can guide children's actions into experiments. Children love to plant seeds. Observe your child's planting method. He might poke holes into the soil and bury the seeds deeply or he might mound soil on top of the seed making a little hill. Allow him to use his method, but add another trial in which the seeds are planted at the depth recommended on the seed package. Mark the sowing date on the calendar and observe for germination of each trial plot. This experiment can introduce the concept of seed depth as one factor or variable affecting germination.

Another concept important to plant growth and development is spacing of plants. Thinning seedlings is done to promote maximum growth. Develop an experiment to demonstrate the importance of thinning. Plant two rows of carrot seeds following package instructions. When seedlings emerge, thin only one row. Observe leaf and root development on each row. What happens when carrots are not thinned?

Experiments give first-hand observable information to the child. Our world becomes predictable from the results of experimentation. Confidence comes from being able to say, "I saw it for myself."

Evidence is the stuff of science. Evidence hunts can instigate interest and inquiry. Evidence is everywhere in the garden -- a chewed or curled leaf, footprints, cocoon, exoskeletons.

Objects and events are clues to an expanding understanding of the garden ecosystem.

As you enjoy the flavors and fragrances of another garden season, use the garden as a center for growing inquisitive, experimental minds as well.

Stimulus Packages for School Gardens

As communities across the country sprout school gardens, one situation hasn't changed. School gardens are rarely included in the school budget. Sometimes parent-teacher organizations contribute funding but more often than not teachers must turn to external funding sources to initiate and sustain school gardens. In a 2008 South Carolina Department of Agriculture school garden survey teachers reported needing $500 up to $1,000 to initiate a school garden. The same respondents indicated that the annual ongoing budget for gardens was from $300 up to $500.

Fortunately there is a growing pool of resources available to teachers to support planning and maintaining teaching gardens. The grant stimulus packages described below are just the tip of the turnip. Once grant fever sets in, you can dig deeper into foundation directories.

Some popular grants enable you and your students to go shopping for garden supplies. **Kids Gardening**, a national nonprofit with the mission "to create opportunities for kids to play, learn, and grow through gardening," offers a variety of youth garden grants annually.

Seeds and plants are one part of the school garden budget. Third graders can grow to the head of the class through Bonnie Plants Cabbage Program. Teachers register their classes at **Bonnie Plants**. Each student receives a cabbage plant to nurture and compete for the biggest head across the state.

Add an edible orchard to campus for teaching environmental education and nutrition with the Fruit Tree 101 program from **The Fruit Tree Planting Foundation**. Fruit trees, design, professional installation and curriculum are included in the school package.

Teachers already trained in Project Learning Tree may apply for **GreenWorks**! a grant integrating service-learning projects with real world environmental problems. Students develop and design an action project to green their school or to improve their community.

The Herb Society of America Samull Classroom Herb Garden Grants reward innovative herbal education projects beyond the growing of herbs.

Primatologist and anthropologist Jane Goodall's **Roots and Shoots** offers mini-grants for educators to start, support, or celebrate community action projects positively affecting humans, other animals, and/or the environment.

Monarch Watch, a non-profit education outreach program based at the University of Kansas with a focus on research, education, and conservation of monarch butterflies offers free milkweed plugs to schools for monarch waystations through an online application.

The **National Farm to School Network** augments the relationship communities have with fresh, healthy food, and local farmers by changing food purchasing and education practices at schools, day cares, and other education venues. Each state's department of agriculture and/or Farm to School Nutrition coordinator puts teachers in contact with farm to school grants and mini-grants.

National Garden Clubs, Inc. provides grants to local garden clubs who work with youth to plan and plant Pollinator Gardens.

Scott's Miracle-Gro has made a commitment to connect children to the benefits of gardens and greenspaces. Their **Gro More Good grants** for the National Head Start Association teach kids, families, schools and communities how to grow fresh healthy food for life.

Wild One's **Lorrie Otto Seeds for Education Program** provides funds for native plant pollinator, rain, tall grass prairie, monarch waystation, and natural play gardens across the United States.

Schools are surrounded by corporate good will, companies that support the people, and communities where their employees work and live. **International Paper** (IP) supports literacy, health and wellness, and environmental causes in communities where employees live, work, and can participate. Grant requests must be submitted to the nearest IP facility via the online grant application available at www.ipgiving.com.

Georgia-Pacific funds projects in more than thirty states where it has facilities. If a project meets the online eligibility survey, schools may apply for funding.

CSX Community Service Grants support programs protecting natural resources and teaching environmental stewardship. Online applications are accepted from January 1 through December 15 annually.

The good neighbor **State Farm** makes grants available to K-12 schools for service learning projects integrating curriculum with community service. Apply for grants via your state grant contact.

Tractor Supply Company partners with 4-H Paper Clover spring and fall events and Future Farmer's of America (FFA) middle and high school agriculture programs with grants for growing.

WalMart local community grants fund public and private K-12 schools in after-school enrichment and tutoring for low-income students, environmental sustainability practices, and hunger relief and healthy eating. Application is sent to your neighborhood store.

Whole Foods Foundation Garden Grant program funds K-12 public and private schools that convert outdoor spaces into hands-on-learning edible food gardens.

Contact your state environmental education association, state department of health and environmental control, and county soil and water conservation district regarding grants for school gardens.

Realizing that grants are highly competitive, your application must be written to stand out from all the rest. Recruit parent volunteers or colleagues with editing experience to proof the application before pressing Submit. When the harvest of grants begins to rain down pennies from heaven, be sure to thank and recognize your donors with student handwritten thank you notes, social media posts showing what has been accomplished, signage, and galas in the garden inviting students, their families, and donors.

Chapter 2
Garden Systems – Sow Many Ways to Grow

"One 3 × 3 Square Foot Garden box (9 square feet) will supply enough produce to make a salad for one child every day of the growing season. Adding a second 3 × 3 box will supply supper vegetables for that child every day. Just one more 3 × 3 box will supply the child with extra of everything for show-and-tell or science projects at school, special crops, showing off, or giving away." Mel Bartholomew

The Magic Box

Whether building castles in sand, towers with blocks, or labyrinths with LEGOs, a child must use his hands to develop his mind. Building a cold frame is a project the family can join hands to accomplish.

To an adult, a cold frame is a miniature greenhouse at ground level; a raised bed with a transparent, movable lid; or a bottomless crate with a lid admitting light. To a child, a cold frame is a magic box.

Cold frames extend the gardening season by trapping the sun's heat, thereby encouraging plant growth. In spring, cold frames are used to start seeds or to "harden off" seedlings started indoors. Cool-weather salad greens, root crops, and cruciferous vegetables can be grown throughout fall and winter. Cuttings of perennials and shrubs also will propagate within the protected enclosure.

Locate the cold frame in a sunny, southeastern exposure protected from the wind. The site should have good drainage.

Cold frames can be made from hay bales, concrete blocks, bricks, wood, or recycled plastic lumber. If wood is used, select untreated timber like yellow pine or spruce. Treated lumber and wood preservatives should not be in contact with food crops. Decay-resistant wood like cedar, redwood, and cypress is excellent but expensive.

There is no standard size for a cold frame, but often they are three to four feet wide and six to eight feet long. The front and back may be eight inches high, or you may create a slanted frame with a twelve-inch-high backboard. The slant is not necessary but catches more sun than a flat surface during winter and permits rain to drain from the lid. Some gardeners slope the soil instead of the box.

The lid or "light" is made of a used window sash or a new frame with glass, Plexiglas or three-mil plastic. Since glass lids pose a safety hazard for children, opt for the plastic or Plexiglas. The lid should be at least an inch or two larger than the frame to keep water from dripping into the box.

The microclimate formed inside the box must be monitored for temperature and moisture to achieve success with plants. The lid will need to be slid off or propped up to control temperature and moisture. Lids are propped up during the day and lowered at night. Include an outdoor thermometer to keep track of the heat buildup and to know when to adjust the venting. Aim for a daytime temperature of seventy in spring and sixty-five in fall and winter. Water plants gently by hand or fine hose spray in the morning.

Once the frame is ready to be occupied, decide if plants will be housed in pots, flats, or directly in the ground. If transplants or seeds will go directly in the ground, prepare the bed with a mixture of potting soil, compost and fertilizer. To reduce the opportunity for weeds to emerge, cover the ground with layers of newspaper before adding potting soil.

Throughout the winter and until May you can enjoy salad greens like arugula, chard, lettuce, mizuna, mache, rapini, sorrel, spinach, or tendergreen; herbs such as coriander, parsley, and chives; and root crops like beets, carrots, celeriac, and parsnips. The magic box will flower your winter with pansies, aconites, miniature narcissus, sweet violets, and snowdrops.

Cold Frame

Insulate the frame on the outside by piling leaves, straw, or hay around the perimeter in cold weather. On nights of extreme or extended freezing, blankets, feed sacks, or pine needles might be needed over the lid.

The hands creating the magic box and the harvest from it will be preparing to build a future of resourceful living.

Restoring Habitat with Seed Balls

It just takes seed to get the ball rolling. Throughout the world adults and children are using marble-size seed balls to plant gardens, create meadows, rejuvenate vacant lots, revegetate deserts, and establish or restore habitats.

Seed balls are handmade compressed globes of seed, compost, clay, and water. Legend has it that Native Americans protected their seed from elements, predators, and transport by hiding them inside clay balls. In the 1940s a Japanese soil scientist, Masanobu Fukuoka, reintroduced the seed ball concept to rebuild habitats in arid regions. He viewed the seed ball as a portable habitat awaiting only the opportune rain to stimulate growth. Rain melts the clay and the seeds sprout in the nutrients of the compost and clay.

Fukuoka's method of broadcasting seed balls on barren land without weeding, tilling, or fertilizing is widely used today in rehabilitation projects. Students in San Diego provided two million seed balls to replace a 200-acre coastal sagebrush habitat destroyed by wildfire. Likewise, fourth-, fifth-, and sixth-grade students in Los Alamos, New Mexico, made seed balls of native grass and wildflower seeds to restore fifty-eight acres of burned forestland.

Children, with the encouragement and guidance of adults, can take an active part in restoring a community eyesore, greening a compacted schoolyard, or creating a wildflower bed at home simply by making and scattering seed balls.

The recipe for seed balls is simple and just what kids like -- messy. Plan to make seed balls outdoors, if possible, or cover the indoor work area with a plastic tarp.

Supply large bowls or plastic bins for mixing ingredients.

Seed ball recipes are written in proportions or parts. "Parts" are imprecise measurements. "1 part" means any equal part of the total volume. When making a recipe using "parts", begin by determining your basic unit of measurement. In the recipe below "1 part" could mean one cup. Then divide or multiply the ingredients to maintain the ratio "2 parts" would mean "2 cups."

Here's the seed ball recipe:
1. Pour 1 part seed mix into bowl.
2. Add 3 parts compost or humus.
3. Mix with fingers to coat seeds in compost.
4. Add 5 parts powdered red clay (terra cotta clay).
5. Mix thoroughly into the compost/seed mixture.
6. Add 2 parts water gradually (may not need all).
7. Knead to a cookie dough consistency.
8. Mixture needs to hold together without sticking to hands.
9. Pinch off pieces and roll into 1-2 inch diameter balls.
10. Dry seed balls in the sun 24 to 48 hours.
11. Since seeds are already planted, toss on the surface at a density of 10 balls per square meter.
12. Watch what happens after a penetrating rainfall!

The seed mix selected will depend on the project goals. Native plants have the greatest success in large scale habitat development projects. The Lady Bird Johnson Wildflower Center at www.wildflower.org is an excellent resource for selecting natives for your area.

Where I live, the South Carolina Native Plant Society at www.scnps.org features articles and profiles on native plants. Red clay is everywhere in the Piedmont of South Carolina. However, one can purchase red clay dirt cheap at Bethune Pottery in Kershaw County. Owners get it from a natural clay deposit in the Lynches River. Seed-Balls.com sells powdered red clay in various weights for making seed balls.

With Mother's Day on the horizon, a nonfattening box of seed balls containing her favorite herb or perennial seeds would make a unique and surprising gift. Let the good times roll.

Making Seed Balls for Butterflies

Build a Doghouse with a Green Roof

Dogs are eager and interested participants in the garden. While their versions of transplanting, burying, pruning, path making, and vermin control may not coincide with our design plans, dogs dig gardening from a perspective rooted in wolf ancestry. Today when most households have at least one dog and many schools have added dogs to their staff, we have the opportunity to learn from and with our canine coaches.

One way to successfully pair a dog's pack behaviors with the human desire to grow plants comes by building a den among natural vegetation, specifically a doghouse or doggie veranda for Fido with a roof garden. A green roof atop the doghouse is a veneer of plants on a traditional roof.

Green roof technology has been active in European countries like Austria, France, Germany, and Switzerland for a century. Major U.S. cities such as Chicago and Washington, D.C., have encouraged green roofs on residential, commercial, and government buildings. You can find green roofs on the University of South Carolina's Green Quad and at the administration building at Clemson University's Sandhill campus.

Advocates for green roofs point to a number of environmental benefits, including reducing heating and cooling bills, doubling the life of a roof, filtering rainwater, lessening stormwater runoff, improving air quality, buffering noise, adding growing space, and reintroducing flora and fauna in a new habitat.

Designing and building a green roof doghouse at your home or school provides a miniature model of how green roof technology works and opens the world of green architecture and engineering to our children. Instruction integrates STEM concepts and skills in a project for man's best friend.

Children can research blueprints for green roofs, durable products, and local resources, while adults and children can talk about the contrasts of traditional roofs with green ones.

The components of a green roof: To be viable over time a green roof must provide the ability to shed excess water, to filter water so soil remains intact and drainage isn't clogged with sediment, and to store water for plants to use. Green roofs are constructed in layers similar to making lasagna.

The basic layers from roof deck upwards are:
- Waterproof membrane – usually a thermoplastic material
- Root barrier – a membrane that defies root penetration
- Drainage system – permeable lightweight material to carry away excess water
- Filter cloth – material to repel soil particles from entering drainage layer
- Growing medium – lightweight soilless potting mix
- Plants – vegetation to cover soil

In a classroom the project is a natural way to form groups to research, present to fellow students, and build. Since each layer is dependent on the others, students must work with other groups as engineering design teams would do.

While your dog gets a climate-controlled environment, warmer in winter and cooler in summer, the home or school has a protected garden space to grow anything from pollinator pads for butterflies and bees to seasonable edible herbs and salad greens to sedum and moss quilts or a simple sod pod. Fido's rooftop garden must be maintained just like any garden. Inspect the layers yearly to look for signs of leakage.

What are you waiting for? Get out and garden on your woof's roof.

Square Foot Gardening for Calculating Minds

The square-foot garden (SFG) is one of the easiest, most affordable, low-maintenance, highly productive, and fun growing systems for families and classrooms.

Civil engineer Mel Bartholomew introduced the basic design and principles for the intensive organic gardening method over forty years ago. The SFG, a space-saving alternative to growing food in long parallel rows, requires a good measure of math. The basic square-foot garden is a bottomless box measuring four feet on each side. The box contains sixteen squares. You can anticipate quite a variety of produce within arms reach.

The number of plants per square foot is determined by the recommended spacing for the particular plants. For example, larger plants like tomato, pepper, corn, okra, cantaloupe, okra, eggplant, and sunflower each require one square foot. Help children read the seed packages to find optimal plant spacing after thinning. Then they must calculate how many seeds or transplants for each square. For example, if radishes are to be spaced three inches apart, then sixteen seeds will fit in one square foot. If lettuce is to be spaced six inches apart, one square foot holds four transplants. How many carrot, beet, parsley, onion, pea, or marigold plants can be grown in each square foot?

Most boxes are constructed of untreated rot-resistant lumber such as cedar, black locust, or redwood. Bartholomew recommends using two two-by-six-by-eight-inch boards cut in half to create each four-by-four-foot box. Brick, concrete blocks, and plastic lumber are also appropriate materials for box construction. Or one can purchase raised bed kits. Having children draw a scale diagram of the box brings the concept of ratio to the garden.

The box is constructed and placed directly on top of the ground in a well-drained location receiving six to eight hours of sun per day and away from natural or man-made structures that might shade the plants.

Rather than tilling, double digging, and amending the soil Bartholomew advises mixing a new potting medium just like one would do for container plants. His "soil of thirds" recipe – peat moss, vermiculite, and compost – challenges the gardener to calculate the total volume needed within the box before ordering the ingredients and mixing them.

After soil is added to the box, a grid is created to mark off the square foot sections. The grid gives an excellent opportunity to practice multiplication tables and to visualize square root. String or twine makes a temporary grid but a rigid permanent wood or plastic grid is necessary. Bartholomew would not consider the box a SFG without the framework of parallel strips designating each planting square. Without the grid the temptation is to revert to rows, which would be wasteful of resources such as space, seed, soil, water, tools, time, and labor.

Will one box produce enough vegetables and herbs for a family of four? Probably not. A family might consider constructing one box (bed) for each member. For classrooms basic boxes may be placed together to form beds that measure four by eight or four by twelve feet. Maintaining the four-foot width of boxes removes the need to enter beds and compact the soil. Most children can reach halfway across the bed and then walk to the other side to reach the remaining half. Allow pathways three to four feet wide between raised beds.

Weeding, watering, and pest control are easy to accomplish in the compact SFG.

Mel Bartholomew conducts workshop at Riverbanks Botanic Garden.

Bartholomew handpicks weeds and pests one square at a time. With a family or class these chores are swiftly completed weekly. His watering equipment fits any school budget. It's no more than a strong bucket and cup or dipper gourd. Hand dipping from the water pail is a method consistent with a child's way of gardening.

The SFG can be as versatile as your imagination. The basic box structure can become a Food Pyramid by constructing concentric boxes -- three-by-three feet, two-by-two feet, and one-by-one -- and anchoring them upward to one corner atop the basic four-by-four-foot box. The pyramid has a fountain effect too.

Some gardeners add vertical structures to one side of the basic box to support vines like squash and pumpkins. During winter the box may be converted to a cold frame or mini-greenhouse with plastic or glass windows over the top.

The square-foot garden maximizes the yield at harvest time and the acuity of the calculating mind.

A Grow Bucket Greenhouse

A grow bucket is a portable indoor greenhouse made by recycling five-gallon plastic food service buckets and lids. Inside the greenhouse a sprouting gardener can germinate seed, propagate plants from cuttings, and conduct experiments with plants. The portable greenhouse can be used to harden off transplants too.

The staff of the Bottle Biology Project in the Department of Plant Pathology at the University of Wisconsin-Madison initially developed the grow bucket for classroom use. Depending upon the project a classroom might need one bucket, one bucket per growing team, or one bucket per student.

Grow Bucket Greenhouse

Assembly takes less than an hour at a cost of under $40. Working with parents and grandparents will make the work faster and safer. Construction class students at technical high schools or community colleges may be able to help drill ventilation holes. Once assembled the greenhouse is ready to grow.

Use a Grow Bucket for sowing a strawberry patch, wildflower seeds for Earth Day, marigolds for May Day, tea herbs for Mother's Day, organic grass for feline friends, forget-me-nots for Teacher Appreciation Day, cut-and-come-again salads, and, of course, summer vegetable six-packs.

Here's how to make a Grow Bucket Greenhouse:

Materials
- One recycled 5-gallon plastic bucket with lid
- One screw-in circular white fluorescent light bulb (22 or 27 watts)
- One screw-in light bulb socket (lamp) with cord
- Electric drill with hole cutter

Instructions:
- Cut one hole just large enough for the lamp socket to fit in the center of the lid without falling through and four other ventilation holes each two inches in diameter spaced equidistantly around the top of the lid.
- Drill a series of ventilation holes (½-1 inch diameter) about two to three inches from the bottom all around the base of the bucket for more air circulation.
- Insert the lamp socket screw-in end down into the center hole of the lid.
- Screw the circular fluorescent bulb into the socket. If done correctly, the lid will be sandwiched between the socket and the bulb.
- Place the lid atop the bucket and turn on the light switch. The lighted bucket greenhouse is ready to nurture young green thumbs all year long.
- Position plants inside the bucket greenhouse with their tops two to four inches from the light bulb. Use recycled butter tubs turned upside down as plant container risers or elevated platforms.

Build a Teepee Trellis and Beans will Grow

Children are drawn to enclosed hiding places like tunnels, caves, and teepees. By building a teepee trellis in the garden, you can provide nutritious flavorful food for the family and a secluded cool spot for children to run for cover.

Trellis teepees are popular vertical systems for pole beans, garden peas, cucumbers, summer squash, melons, grapes, and gourds.

Since legumes such as beans and peas are one of the largest plant families prepared in the home kitchen, plant a legume teepee along with menu items for the school/work lunch bag and picnic fare.

Here's how to do it:
Prepare the soil in a sunny location. Use flour to mark a circle with a four-foot diameter. Divide the circle into eight wedge shapes like pieces of pie. Arrange and insert eight eight-foot bamboo poles six to twelve inches deep into the soil. Tie the poles together tightly with twine four to six inches from the top. Stabilize the frame and support the crop by wrapping twine around the bamboo frame every 12 inches from the ground upward and leaving one open segment for the entranceway.

Plant seeds according to package directions around the base of the teepee. Water after planting. When seedlings appear, steer them in the direction of the trellis to set them on their way skyward. Beans are super easy to grow, assuring success for the young gardener. Select climbing beans rather than bush varieties. Pole beans like "Kentucky Wonder" and "Kentucky Blue" are excellent starters. "Kwintus" are ready to eat in forty-three days.

Beans are big for teaching history and geography lessons. Native Americans forced to relocate in the nineteenth century carried with them the "Cherokee Trail of Tears" bean. "Mountaineer" white half runner is a German heirloom growing five to eight feet. "Green Anellino" is a crisp Italian crescent-shaped bean tasting prized by European chefs for its Romano cheese flavor.

Beans don't have to be green. *Trionfo violetto* pole bean is an Italian heirloom with a dark violet bean. "Marvel of Venice" is a yellow Italian heirloom climbing bean. "Rattlesnake" is a pole bean with purple streaked green pods that curl like a snake.

Two ornamental beans are also edible. Scarlet runner beans have showy red flowers and multicolored seeds. Hyacinth beans produce lovely purple flowers, pods and beans and the young pods are edible. Don't be surprised to find hummingbirds coming to the vibrant flowers of these beans.

For variety, consider inserting limas into the bean pot trellis.

"Florida speckled" butter beans take hot and humid weather producing prolific small lima beans. "Christmas" and "Snow on the Mountain" are heavy-producing heirloom limas with curious names.

Mix and match beans and peas since they share the same growing requirements. "Calico Crowder" is an heirloom climbing crowder pea.

David Bradshaw, horticulturist and professor emeritus at Clemson University, has been saving heirloom vegetable seed and offers beans and pea varieties through the South Carolina Seed Foundation, 1162 Cherry Road, Clemson, SC 29634 and online at http://www.clemson.edu/public/seed/heirloom.html.

The Southern Exposure Seed Exchange at www.southernexposure.com carries heirloom pole beans and southern peas.

Instant Fall Gardens for Children

Take the toil and tedium out of gardening by adopting a child's perspective when planting the fall garden. Children not only have preferences about what to plant but also have ideas on growing systems. Simplify starting fall planting with these child-tested instant gardens to satisfy children's tendency for instant gratification.

Pillow Pack Gardens are plastic bags filled with potting mix. Pillow packs can be made from polyethylene bags, freezer bags, or garbage bags. A plastic bag of potting soil from the garden center is a ready-made pillow pack. Punch drainage holes in the underside before placing the bag in a sunny location. Space seed or transplants in holes punctured on the bag's top surface.

Use a liquid plant fertilizer according to package instructions. Most fall flowers, herbs, and vegetables will flourish in the pillow pack as long as they do not get overwatered. Inserting fingers inside the bag can test the soil moisture.

Bucket Planters are plastic buckets obtained from restaurants and bakeries in one- to five-gallon sizes. Buckets with handles are easily positioned to a plant's light requirements. The circular growing surfaces resemble bowls, making them suited to salad greens, cereal grains, and edible flowers. Cut a drainage hole in the bottom with a utility knife and place coffee filters or newspaper strips over the hole to keep soil inside. Add moistened soilless potting mix to the bucket.

Straw Bale Gardens are made of wheat, oats, rye, or barley bales. Straw bales are more than just attractive autumn outdoor decorations. Planting in bales is a great alternative if you have poor soil, rocky ground, or excessive weeds, or if you need a raised planting platform.

Bales can last for several seasons if they are tied with synthetic twine. Fresh bales need cooling down prior to planting seeds or transplants. For best root development set bales with twine running horizontally and straw set vertically in desired location. Then soak bales with water and give them a week or two to cool down before adding a top dressing of commercial potting mix or a three-inch layer of homemade compost. A compost thermometer can be used to measure interior temperature of the bale.

Cool season broccoli, cabbage, collards, chard, kale, and spinach will thrive in bales. Annual herbs, salad greens, mesclun mixes, marigold, calendula, and nasturtium prosper too. Root crops do not grow well in bales nor do top-heavy crops like corn.

Straw Bale Garden

Square-Foot Gardens are raised box beds divided into one-foot squares, each square featuring a particular number of plants depending on their size. Mel Bartholomew, originator of the square foot garden model, recommends that a child's square foot plot be three by three feet due to short height and arm length while a basic adult square foot plot is four by four feet. Since the gardener is not to walk on the soil in the box and compact the soil, planting, weeding, and harvesting are done at arm's length.

Once the box frame is built atop your yard's regular soil, fill it with a soil mix. Bartholomew's suggested mix is one-third each of vermiculite, compost, and peat moss. You may opt to obtain bags of a commercial potting mix instead. Once soil is leveled, add a wooden grid separating the square foot planting sections. In fall in South Carolina and other states with mild autumns and winters the squares could be seeded with cool-season Chinese greens like bok choy, tat soi, napa cabbage, mustards, and radishes.

Picket Fences Make Good Childhoods

Once toddlers master walking, youngsters know no boundaries. A picket fence establishes safe boundaries on one's home territory. The space between pickets provides fun too.

Ever peek through a keyhole or cracked doorway? Picket fences are designed for peeking, a wonderful way to eavesdrop or play peek-a-boo with the surroundings.

Picket fences form the background for a child's first cutting garden or spread of spring bulbs. Add twine to the pickets to support sweet peas, morning glories, or other glorious vines such as gourds, bitter melon and garden peas.

Fences promote sharing garden plants, produce, and problems with the neighbors. The latest news and gossip fly fast over the pickets. Cool glasses of lemonade and freshly baked cookies pass easily over the pickets too.

Even though gates allow easy entrance and exit, fences must be climbed to test one's balance and bravado. Being poked by a picket is a childhood rite of passage. Home runs of many kinds depend on fences to scale.

Gates are not just meant to open and close; they are to swing upon. Swinging upon a garden gate gives a feeling of freedom for a child coming to terms with boundaries.

What child doesn't beg for a puppy? Picket fences assure a secure haven for the family pooch which also must learn boundaries. Fences bring wildlife to closer range. And wildlife can give children more ideas on how to use the fence.

As an artistic and aesthetic element, the fence frames the garden similar to a frame bringing a painting into focus. Picket fences are favorite models for landscape drawing and painting classes because they exemplify line, foreground, background, shadow and perspective.

Picket fences are even fun to paint especially as a family project. Children contribute to a fun endeavor and see immediate results from their effort. Whether they work pro bono or for a penny a picket, the experience will be memorable.

Picket fences make good childhoods and even better adulthoods.

Unlocking Literacy with Keyhole Gardens and Cameras

What happens when a keyhole, cameras, and kids come together in the out-of-doors?

One answer came the summer of 2013 when Beth Costello, faculty member in the College of Education at the University of South Carolina, and Seth Guest, staff member from USC's Sustainable Carolina garden, teamed up to offer a two-week gardening camp for children, -- Camp GLEA, Gardening and Literacy Education through the Arts.

At that time Costello was an advocate of Literacy Through Photography (LTP), an approach to learning which encourages children to explore their world by capturing scenes from their lives in photographic images. The images then become catalysts for verbal and written expression.

Guest was fluent in gardening and farming practices and manages the large organic garden at USC's Green Quad. He chose to introduce children to keyhole gardens, a small family size no-dig garden easy to replicate with children. By merging their interests in literacy, photography and gardening, Costello and Guest developed the day camp for children ages seven to twelve from families below the poverty line. Camp sessions took place at the Sustainable Carolina Garden off Main Street on campus.

Camp GLEA curriculum combined the science and math of gardening along with the arts of photography and writing. Children learned how to plant and nurture seeds and seedlings, the parts of a plant, and how to prepare fresh food from the garden for themselves and family members. They practiced composting and conducted soil experiments. As growers they found out how farm and garden food is distributed to consumers and they compared conventional and alternative food systems like local, organic and cooperative.

Measurement math was required to layout the dimensions of the concentric circular keyhole garden plot and space seeds and plants. Students used compasses and rulers to draw scale models in planning the six-foot-diameter plot. They planted basil, parsley, sage, and tomatoes in the outer circle of the garden. The center twelve-inch-diameter circle was a compost basket which distributed nutrients to the roots of outer circle plants.

Seven Steps to a Keyhole Garden

- Measure a six-foot diameter circle in a sunny spot.
- Outline the perimeter wall with bricks or stones to support weight of soil.
- Cut out a wedge for walking to the center of the circle for composting.
- Use wire mesh to create a one-foot-diameter central chimney three to four feet high for composting.
- Fill the outer circle with assorted compostable materials finishing with a four-inch layer of topsoil.
- Fill the central mesh tube with alternating layers of green and brown organic materials to feed the outer circle plants. Water the compost during drought.
- Plant your crops within the outer circle and celebrate your accomplishments.

Students explored and documented their gardening experiences through digital photographs and writing. At the start of each new day children used the previous day's photos to review yesterday. At the end of camp each child took home a photo book.

The 2013 program received grants and support from the City of Columbia Community Gardens Project, Eau Claire Promise Zone, City Roots, Earthfare, Sustainable Carolina, City of Columbia Parks and Recreation and USC's College of Education. The 2013 camp was a pilot for future Camp GLEA programs. How did the children feel about camp? One student summed up his feelings this way, "I didn't have a good day today...I had a great day today."

Growing Food and Flowers in Buckets

Buckets, barrels, and pails are cost-effective, convenient containers for introducing children to gardening. Pickle and ingredient buckets from fast food franchises, ice cream parlors and frosting buckets from donut shops and bakeries provide child-sized portable planting systems. Use only food-grade buckets-- not plastic buckets -- made or used for paint or other chemicals.

The advantages of buckets for home or school gardening are numerous. Most buckets have handles making them easily movable to change the shape of the garden, insert newcomer or delete old buckets instantly, adjust location for sun or shade, rearrange the color effect of a rainbow, isolate plants to control pests and diseases, and add in companion plants. Buckets discourage dogs from digging or trampling tender seedlings.

Buckets are manageable for the multiple tasks of young gardeners. Bucket gardens rarely need weeding since crop coverage is intense. While container plants dry out faster than in-ground gardens, children enjoy messing with watering. Scouting and pinching off insects gets them up close and personal with plants. Teachers can more easily keep tabs on a class of children tending to their buckets.

To assure success with bucket gardening, an adult must assist with several basic preparations. Drainage is important for all plants but especially those grown in containers. Drill or cut holes in the bottom of containers to allow adequate drainage. Children can place coffee filters or layers of newspaper over the holes to prevent soil loss.

Buckets are lightweight and should remain so even when soil is added. Home or schoolyard soil should not be used. Potting soil should drain well, hold moisture like a sponge, and offer support and nutrients to plants. Assist children in measuring and mixing one of the following recipes for potting medium:

- Equal parts of potting soil, peat moss, perlite
- Equal parts of potting soil, compost, builder's sand
- Equal parts of peat moss, vermiculite, compost

Alternatively, purchase a premium premade soilless potting mix by Soil3, Daddy Pete's or Stout Ollie.

After filling buckets to three inches from the top rim, small hands are ready to fill containers with herbs, flowers, or vegetables as seeds or transplants.

Planning the garden themes should precede or run corollary to the above preparations. Children's gardening should foster imagination and experimentation. School container garden themes should support curriculum objectives and will often integrate subject areas like health, physical fitness, and science or social studies, art, and math.

In spring and fall the buckets can become individual Snip-and-Serve Salads since greens, mesclun, lettuces, spinach, peas, carrots, beets, and radishes prefer cooler temperatures. In March each student could contribute a different vegetable to a "classroom community garden." When school ends in May, students tote buckets home to nurture their crops over the summer. In September they bring back some of the harvest for a fall food festival and grower's contest. Starting a Snack Garden at home or school is simple with seeds of strawberry popcorn, cherry tomatoes, and Tom Thumb carrots.

Flowers and herbs flirt with a child's senses and are fodder for fantasy. Some children may experiment with buckets of bouquet flowers such as bachelor buttons, marigolds, zinnias, or cosmos. Others might plan a mint medley garden of apple, orange, pineapple, peppermint, and spearmint for tea or a storybook tea party with chamomile plants for Peter Rabbit. Or consider growing a bucket of Herbs For Drying as used by Mr. Badger in *Wind in the Willows*.

A Flavoring Garden with herbs like basil, chives, cilantro, dill, garlic chives, oregano, parsley, and thyme will give student chefs practice in seasoning food without salt.

Native American Three Sister Gardens of beans, corn, and squash can be started in buckets at school in spring before moving to the child's home to mature over the summer.

Bucket gardens move with our children and keep our children moving more.

Chapter 3
Growing Healthy

"After 25 years of Edible Schoolyard, I know one truth: if kids grow it and cook it, they all eat it." Alice Waters

Planting Winter Greens

While home gardeners are harvesting the last summer tomatoes, eggplant, peppers, and okra, in a turn of the trowel it's time to prepare and plant the winter garden. Get the whole family involved in planting a healthy garden that will yield food for the table and taste buds twelve months of the year.

Fall and winter gardens have the advantages of fewer pests, lower humidity, and cooler temperatures.

Rejuvenate the soil by adding homemade compost, aged manure, and slow-release organic fertilizer. Vegetables grow best in a slightly acidic soil with a pH of 6.0 to 7.0. A south-facing site with full sunlight is ideal.

Plan the garden to include the imagination, interest, and effort of all family members. And don't forget to include the young ones. Arrange fast-growing cool-season greens such as mustard, cress and radishes to spell out toddlers' names in the garden. They will enjoy seeing their names sprout out of the soil. And teens enjoy experimenting with herbal flavors to make drinks, desserts, dressings, and dips.

Create a winter rainbow with a circular salad-bowl garden with rows of cool-season mache, tendergreen mustard, red giant mustard, mizuna, komatsuna, tatsoi, joi choi, pak choi, spinach, winter purslane, arugula, chicory, red and green oakleaf lettuces, kale, and Bright Lights Swiss chard. Create a tossed effect by placing a garden fork and shovel on each side of the "bowl" to simulate tools used to toss the salad.

If the garden is seeded in early October, your family can have a cornucopia of mesclun for Thanksgiving dinner. The cut-and-come-again greens will linger until the heat of May. Check your local garden nurseries for a wide selection of cool-season greens. Local garden centers are likely to offer broccoli, Brussels sprouts, cabbage, cauliflower, and kale in cell packs for quick transfer to the garden.

For suspense from beneath the surface, plant root vegetables--beets, celeriac, carrots, leeks, onions, parsnips, radish, and turnips. Protect from freezes with a six-inch layer of mulch.

Containers make personal plots for individual family members who want to experiment or compete for the first or fastest bounty. Five-gallon buckets, gallon milk jugs, waxed milk and juice cartons, and two-liter soda bottles are useful containers.

Grow A Family Pizza Pie

Children's favorite foods can stimulate interest and effort in gardening. Spaghetti and pizza are popular entrees that make nutritious meals when they include homegrown ingredients.

A round plot in the shape of a pizza pan, and at least six feet diameter, will accommodate the basic vegetable and herb ingredients--tomatoes, peppers, onions, basil, Greek oregano, parsley, and garlic. By adding vertical-growing systems, young gardeners can make room for zucchini and spaghetti squash. Or select squash varieties bred for limited-space gardens.

A plan or model is important to success in any garden. Use a large circular piece of paper or a cardboard pizza tray. Mark off slices - perhaps six, seven, or eight - making sure one wedge is larger for tomato plants. Tomatoes are the ingredient you're likely to use the most.

Children can cut out pictures from garden catalogs and glue them onto the plan. The tallest plants should be placed at the north side of the plot. If they use bedding plants, children can draw the plants' pictures onto the cardboard at planting time.

Other data to record on the plan include planting dates, maturity dates, and liquid-fertilizer schedule. Keep the pizza plan on the refrigerator or a bulletin board to build anticipation. Take it to the garden center when selecting seeds or plants.

When you have the plan in hand, you're ready to build your garden.

Choose a sunny location. Use a garden hose or clothesline rope to outline the circular bed. Use a garden fork or spade to dig and loosen the soil. Remove organic debris to the compost bin. Break up clumps of earth. Spread a one-to-two-inch layer of aged, bagged manure onto the area. Mix into the surface soil with a rake and then level the soil. Sprinkle flour along the circular outline and use flour to mark off the "slices."

When selecting plants, consider their use and space requirements. For example, the best tomatoes for sauce are plum or Roma, but children love cherry tomatoes as a topping. Peppers come in a rainbow of colors and flavors, so each member of the family can pick a favorite.

To add "cheese" to the garden, border the circle with bright golden marigolds or sprinkle them between vegetables. The tasty blossoms can garnish the pizza, too. Marigolds and the herbs are your best pest controls as well.

As the plot thickens with foliage, remember to tend to these tasks:
- Pinch off basil flowers to keep the plant producing leaves until frost.
- Weed weekly.
- Water weekly if it doesn't rain.
- Stake or cage tomatoes and peppers before they flop over.
- Watch for insects eating the leaves of tomatoes and peppers. Pick them off and squish them.

When peppers, tomatoes, and squash are mature, children can hold a pizza party. Invite family and friends to help harvest and prepare the ingredients. Everyone can have a job, from kneading the dough to washing, slicing, dicing, chopping, snipping, and coring. Make one large pizza or divide the dough into small balls for each guest to flatten and decorate with the toppings.

Launching Lunch

As the countdown to the start of a new school year begins, parents are searching for creative ways to ensure their children eat healthy school lunches. Since many school-age children eat two of their three daily meals away from home, matching menus to the United States Department of Agriculture's Dietary Guidelines becomes a challenge.

The space program, which has brought many inventions and products to life on Earth, might provide thrust to the school lunch mission.

Explore with your child how gardening might be accomplished on a space voyage or at the international space station, where internal space is limited and payload weight restrictions discourage heavy cargo such as soil and water.

Space travelers and colonists need a continuous supply of fast-growing, nutrient-dense food, as does your child. Nutrient density refers to the amount of water, fats, carbohydrates, protein, vitamins, and minerals provided per calories of food. Vegetables provide the most nutrients per calorie.

How might you pack a nutrient-dense lunch in the confines of a lunch box?

One home venture to encourage consumption of fresh vegetables is to launch a series of space shuttle salad gardens in the kitchen or on the deck. Space shuttle salads will grow in a variety of miniature containers - seashells, detergent scoops, eggshells, bottle caps, dishes from a toy kitchen set, and even sponges.

Vitamin-rich greens such as arugula, burnet, chervil, cress, corn salad, leaf lettuce, chard, savory, sorrel, tatsoi, mizuna, pak choi, purslane, spinach, chives and parsley or a mesclun mix will grow on a window sill, under cool fluorescent lights, or on the deck.

One cup of greens in a zippered bag, flavored with lemon juice and olive oil or vinaigrette, fits easily into the lunch box and chalks up one serving of vegetables on the USDA MyPlate Plan.

Many of your child's favorite vegetables are candidates for space farming on the international space station. Since August is the time to plan and plant the autumn and cool-weather vegetable gardens, it's the perfect time to embark on a mission to create extraterrestrial beds.

Fast-growing, heat-loving snap beans, tomatoes, cucumbers, peppers, and summer squash can be sown in August for the fall lunch box. Slow-growing, cool-season vegetables such as beets, carrots, broccoli, Brussels sprouts, cabbage, cauliflower, collards, kale, and turnips may be sown in planting trays in the shade for future transplanting to sunny beds in September or October. Youngsters can print the names of the crops sown on tongue depressors or craft sticks to mark the trays.

Prepare out-of-this-world vegetable kabobs, soups, juices, slaws, ragouts, souffles, quiches, and ratatouille to fuel and propel children on a healthful trajectory throughout the school year.

Gateways to Gardening with Children

TRY THESE:

TRAVEL KABOBS
String a variety of fresh or marinated vegetables - cherry tomatoes, carrots, beets, squash, peppers, cucumber - on a bamboo skewer.

SPACE-WHEEL AMULETS
Cut wheels of fresh vegetables and string like popcorn on thread for lunch-box charms.

Growing a Healthy Family

Potting petunias, transplanting trees, digging dandelions, raking leaves, laying sod, turning compost, hoeing potatoes, pruning hedges, mowing a maze, sacking grass, pulling weeds, staking tomatoes, double-digging beds, mulching perennials, cutting bouquets. Quite a list, and we're just getting started! Almost everything we do in a garden is exercise.

Exercise and gardening complement each other. Gardening integrates important elements of exercise—stretching, resistance, repetition, stance, endurance, and movement. Your garden is a health spa minus the cost of club membership or purchase of treadmill, weights, or stationary bike.

Gardening engages all major muscles -- the calorie-burning muscles. Legs, arms, buttocks, shoulders, stomach, neck, back, and heart get a workout. Gardening promotes weight loss and maintenance. The stretching involved is not unlike yoga and increases physical flexibility, strengthening of joints, and mental relaxation.

Research suggests that thirty minutes of moderate daily exercise -- such as gardening -- lowers blood pressure and cholesterol levels, slows osteoporosis, and reduces the risks of heart disease and diabetes.

School garden programs are an excellent way to promote the physical and psychological benefits of gardening and to link families to home and community wellness programs.

Children benefit from gardens and exercise wherever they are exposed to them. When that place is at home or in the neighborhood, gardening exercise can be a family affair.

FITNESS the *Dynamic* Gardening Way

MODERATE EXERCISE — SOUND NUTRITION — PSYCHOLOGICAL WELL-BEING

A Health and Wellness *Lifestyle*

by Jeffrey P. Restuccio

To maximize a family workout in the garden, follow a few simple guidelines:
- Precede and follow each 30-minute workout by warm-up and cool-down stretches.

- Vary activities among strenuous (digging), moderate (transplanting), and enjoyable (harvesting).

- Avoid marathon gardening sessions.

- Tools should fit the person. Child-size tools are available at garden centers. Each tool has a rhythm for the task. Children easily exaggerate the rhythm to get maximum exercise value.

- Save your back by bending from the knees. Watch how toddlers bend their knees when they pick up pine cones. Alternate your stance to balance the muscles used. If the task can best be accomplished by kneeling or sitting, do so rather than bending the back.

- Listen to your muscles.

- Drink water before, during, and after gardening.

For a beginner's guide to family fitness in the garden, read *Fitness the Dynamic Gardening Way* by Jeffrey P. Restuccio.

Nutrition and Fitness Nuggets in a School Garden

Scattered out there somewhere are youngsters, now grown, who remember the Outdoor Learning Garden at their elementary school in Gadsden, South Carolina. We have no way to know whether the seeds planted in each of those individuals back then have gone dormant or have became an integral part of who they are today. What we do know is that most children benefit profoundly from growing up gardening.

Andrea Williams, the school nurse at Gadsden Elementary, believed children were able to learn and be responsible for their health, what they eat and the choices they make.

So she chose a garden as the best classroom to teach fitness and nutrition to the Gadsden Blue Jay Steppers and the Green Thumb Club at the Richland One school.

Gadsden's Outdoor Learning Garden started in 2004 with a set of drawings, big dreams, and generous donations. The garden used a large courtyard, and each classroom had its own gardening spot.

The blueprint included reading benches, raised beds, an orchard, an herb garden, a pond, a tree-shaded deck for outdoor instruction and programs, picnic tables, and walls for murals.

But school gardens need funding to become a reality. Since they are not part of district or state allocations for instruction, most are funded by donations and grants.

Area business partners stepped up for Gadsden Elementary, with Freeman's 3-in-1 and Big T's Bar-B-Q donating plants and soil. Lower Richland High School carpentry classes built the deck, benches, and picnic tables. Local churches donated money. A grant from International Paper in Eastover helped with garden maintenance. And a service grant from City Year provided volunteer labor.

At a City Year Workday in spring, parents, students, school staff, Lower Richland ROTC members, and community and City Year volunteers installed the pond and formed the beds.

Nurse Williams and students harvest collard greens.

The year-round garden grew plants for each season. In winter children would harvest and eat from the winter greens garden of collards, broccoli and mustards.

In the fall, after digging up a large bed of sweet potatoes, students enjoyed eating them baked and in sweet potato pie. They also made peppermint tea from the herb garden.

Students sowed seeds for the spring garden in a new professional seed table crafted by Gadsden custodian and carpenter David White. Their garden included starting peppers, tomatoes, watermelon, cantaloupe, yellow squash, and okra for the summer garden and two new features-a blueberry patch and an edible flower garden.

Students also learned about nutrition while they worked in the garden, harvesting their crops and preparing snacks and recipes.

Williams taught concepts of fresh versus processed foods, serving size, herbal seasonings, and the new food pyramid, along with gardening techniques and procedures. Composted leaves and pet rabbit manure were used to enrich the soil, and the young gardeners did not use chemical pest control.

The children took turns being chefs at school. The Blue Jay chefs made crunchy vegetable pita. They also learned juicing and made their own smoothies.

Williams observed students exercising, solving problems and thinking on their feet in the outdoor classroom.

"Children can mend out a lot of problems working in the garden," she believed.

Visit a Strawberry Patch or Grow Your Own

Spring is harvest time for strawberries in South Carolina. A visit to a local U-pick strawberry farm can plant the idea of starting a backyard or schoolyard strawberry patch.

The Cottle Strawberry Farm in southeast Columbia is a U-pick operation that by 2022 was heading into its fourth generation as a family farm. Joy Cottle, third-generation strawberry farmer, and her staff offer strawberry etiquette and education to families and school groups who come for the pleasure of picking quarts or buckets of fresh flawless fruit.

Out in the row-lined fields as far as the eye can see are strawberry plants with flowers and berries in various stages of development. The plants are grown on hills six-to-eight inches high and covered in black plastic that holds soil moisture, retards weeds, and keeps leaves and berries from touching soil, a risk for disease. The plastic also retains heat, which hastens ripening.

Although a back yard or schoolyard doesn't have the space for the long-row system of a commercial strawberry farm where as many as 15,000 plants cover an acre, strawberries fit many growing arrangements as long as there is full sun. Even an apartment dweller has space for a plastic bag of potting soil. Punch holes in the bag. Insert plant roots and a miniature strawberry patch is off and running. Some folks use strawberry pots, clay or plastic flowerpots with a series of holes around the sides, to grow strawberries. Hanging baskets, window boxes, vegetable gardens and raised beds work fine too. As strawberry plants mature, they start to flower. Pollinators, especially bees, visit flowers. Berries grow from the center of each fertilized flower. Berries, green at first, enlarge and turn red. U-pick farm visitors learn to pick only

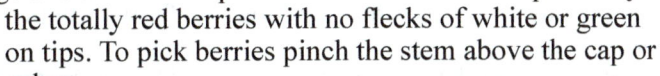

the totally red berries with no flecks of white or green on tips. To pick berries pinch the stem above the cap or calyx.

How many plants are needed per person? One plant produces about a quart of strawberries per 6-week season. A family of four should consider twenty-five to thirty plants.

Cottle grows commercial Chandler and Camarosa varieties of strawberry. Consult a Clemson extension agent for varieties best for small-scale production. If you live outside South Carolina, check with an agricultural agent in your state.

If berries are ready to pick, they are ready to eat immediately. Cottle recommends placing freshly picked strawberries in a plastic container with a dry paper towel on top to keep moisture and air off the berries.

Strawberries can be frozen if not used immediately or they can be refrigerated for up to three or four weeks in a tightly closed Mason jar. Whether fresh or frozen, strawberries should not be rinsed until just before eating. Then rinse with the cap on.

Although spring is picking time, strawberry farming is a year-long endeavor. To encourage communities to establish schoolyard strawberry gardens across the calendar year, the North Carolina Strawberry Grower's Association initiated the Schoolyard Strawberry Project with resources for parents and teachers. To find out how to get your strawberry garden started visit a local U-pick strawberry farm like Cottle's and investigate https://hgic.clemson.edu/factsheet/growing-strawberries/ for fruitful ideas on growing strawberries.

Fall is the Season for Planting

In South Carolina fall is the best of the four seasons for planting trees, shrubs and perennials, and food.

The months between September and December have advantages for establishing plants -- trees to provide shade and wildlife homes; shrubs and perennials for pollinators and birds; and other instructional theme gardens. Plant roots will have months to grow and become established before spring growth above ground begins and summer heat and drought arrives next year.

Why not consider a fall food garden on your school campus? It can be the hub for harvesting school-grown vegetables and seasonings. Growing herbs in the school garden can also be a means of support for the garden program. Herb plant sales are popular with the public.

Cool-season vegetables most common in the southern food winter garden are broccoli, Brussels sprouts, cabbage, cauliflower, kale, and the southern greens – collards, mustard, and turnip. Children are familiar with eating and even growing these at home.

Since roots tolerate fall and winter soil temperatures, beets, carrots, horseradish, kohlrabi, onions, radishes, and turnips are dependable root vegetables heading into spring. Cool-season herbs include chervil, chives, cilantro, garlic chives, mints, parsley, rosemary, thyme, and winter sorrel.

Chervil, French parsley

The fun of instructional gardens also is introducing new ideas to children and their families. Leafy greens are easy to plant from seed, fast to germinate, delicious in taste, and if planted in succession and harvested by cutting the leaf rather than pulling up, the plant will continue to produce salads, stir fry ingredients, and sandwich fillers until the heat returns in May. Introduce youngsters to arugula, celtuce (also known as celery lettuce), corn salad, mizuna, pac choi, radicchio, spinach, Swiss chard, and heirloom lettuces from around the world. What better way to teach geography than gardening with greens?

Bulbs are one of the easiest plants for children to grip when planting. Fall and winter flowering bulbs include colchicum, cyclamen, autumn crocus, fall snowdrop, sternbergia, and ranunculus. Of course, you will want to engage students in planting spring flowering bulbs: allium, bluebells, crocus, daffodil, hyacinths, and more. Old House Gardens at https://oldhousegardens.com, an heirloom bulb resource started by an English teacher, offers a historical perspective on bulbs to help integrate them into social studies.

Perhaps the easiest part of fall gardening is staging the fall annual flower display with alyssum, calendula, dianthus, larkspur, ornamental kale and cabbage, pansies, poppies, snapdragons, stocks, and violas.

Toss a Salad in the Garden

About the time quarterbacks start tossing footballs, families begin planting fall and winter food gardens. Fall gardening can be easier than at any other time of the year because there are fewer pests, lower humidity, and cooler temperatures.

The panoply of fall edibles is distinctively and refreshingly different from the hot season harvest. Fall and winter are the best times to grow salad greens in South Carolina. The assortment of salad green options for fall is as varied as choices for the summer tomato and pepper.

Salad gardening is a wonderful team endeavor. The easiest way to forge ahead with a beginner's garden is to purchase a mesclun mix. These seed mixtures usually contain lettuces, spinach, arugula, endive, chicory, and land cress. Simply toss the seed mixture over the prepared bed and watch a tossed salad erupt before your eyes. Well, almost.

Another method for initiating the garden is to have each family member select several different individual packages to trial in conventional rows, patches, or containers. Then when greens are harvested, they can be tossed in the salad bowl.

Salad greens adapt to the space you have available but a family of four will eat very well from a fifty-square-foot area. The area may include raised beds, edgings, a cold frame, green house, containers, hanging baskets, and annual flower beds in need of fill-in plants for fall. Even apartment dwellers with limited space can toss salads on the windowsill or patio or under light banks.

All salad greens need a well-prepared sunny site with fertile and well-drained soil.

Add four inches of organic compost to the surface of the bed and turn it into the soil to a depth of twelve to eighteen inches. Slow-release organic fertilizer pellets should be added before seeding. Regular watering is especially important for leafy greens. Start seeds well in advance of the first frost date, late October or early November in South Carolina.

SAMPLER OF GREENS

European	Asian	Southern
arugula	komatsuna	beet
chard	mizuna	cabbage
chicory	pak choi	collards
lettuces	red mustard	kale
mache	tatsoi	mustard
radicchio	tendergreen	turnip

SALAD SEED SOURCES
www.burpee.com
www.johnnyseeds.com
www.kitazawaseed.com
www.nicholsgardennursery.com
www.parkseed.com
www.seedsofchange.com
www.territorialseed.com

To keep greens growing vigorously, harvest as seedlings or when leaves are two to three inches long. Carefully hand pick or scissor cut the leaves to allow the crown to remain intact and assure continuous new growth. The cut-and-come-again method is in contrast to sacrificing the entire plant. However, to make sure of having plenty of greens on demand, sow seeds at intervals from September to December. Neglected plants will grow to maturity, produce flowers and seed, and take their final bow before ever realizing their salad days.

Coaxing children to eat salads is easy when they grow the ingredients, but leaf color, taste, texture, and shape add incentives. Remember greens are not always green! Swiss chard 'Bright Lights' is a collage of red, rose, cream, green, yellow, and orange.

Lettuces like bronze mignonette, lime green looseleaf, red Boston, and emerald oak leaf create salads with jewel-like qualities. When children mix colorful salad leaves together, the glowing greens are irresistible.

Experimenting with blending greens by taste takes time and practice.

The peppery flavor of land cress may be used sparingly. Sorrel leaves substitute for lemon dressing. Arugula is spicy. Tendergreen and red mustard have a mild mustard taste great for sandwiches and salads. Radicchio adds bittersweetness.

Unique textures and shapes catch children's eyes. Mizuna looks like feathers. Mache grows in tight green rosettes. Spinach 'Razzle Dazzle' is arrow-shaped. Lettuces can be crinkly, curled or ruffled.

The container for growing the salad garden can encourage interest. Young children can sow seeds in plastic play pails or peach baskets filled with purchased potting soil. The handles allow them to tote their salad around. Seashells or eggshells make unique miniature snipping planters for quickly sprouting cress and tendergreen. Even an outgrown pair of sneakers can be recycled into "salad shoes." Old wheelbarrows with drainage holes make nifty portable planters.

When you and your family start enjoying the salad days of winter, you'll have made it to the goal post.

Serve a Wild Dessert for Thanksgiving

Break with tradition this Thanksgiving by adding persimmon pie to the menu. Finding the fruit may be as close as your back yard.

The common persimmon tree, *Diospyros virginiana*, is a southeastern native found along fence rows, forest margins, empty lots, and in back yards. Its stoloniferous roots create thickets or groves often in association with sassafras trees. The graceful deciduous trees have simple, alternate glossy green leaves which turn deep purple in fall. By October branches of female trees sag from the weight of yellow and orange ripening plum-like fruit.

Unripe fruit is very astringent due to the concentration of tannin. To avoid making "pucker pies" select only sweet ripe fruit. The flesh of ripe fruit will be wrinkled and give way to light pressure like the skin on overripe avocados. Fruit must be soft and mushy to touch before one knows that sugar has replaced all the tannic acid. Ripe fruit may have skin that remains orange or varies to reddish purple

Persimmon Pie

2 beaten eggs
2 cups of persimmon pulp
½ cup of sugar
1 tsp. cinnamon or pumpkin pie spice
1 2/3 cups light cream

Preheat oven to 425°F. Mix filling ingredients in order. Pour into prepared pie shell. Bake at 425° for 15 minutes. Reduce temperature to 350°.
Bake an additional 45 minutes or until knife placed in center of filling comes out clean.

Persimmon Bread

2 cups of flour
1 tsp. baking powder
1 tsp. baking soda
1 tsp. cinnamon
½ tsp. nutmeg
2 beaten eggs
1 tsp. vanilla
1 cup persimmon pulp
½ cup nuts

Preheat oven to 375° F
Sift together flour, powder, soda, spices.
Cream together sugar, eggs, and vanilla and gradually blend in sifted ingredients.
Pour into well-greased 9"x 5" x 3" loaf pan and let set for 20 minutes before baking in oven for 55-60 minutes.

or bluish black. The flesh is orange.

The pulp of the fruit minus the skin and the brown seeds is used in cooking. A Foley mill is safe for children to use to separate seeds and skin from pulp. One cup of persimmon pulp equals one cup of pumpkin in your favorite pumpkin pie recipe.

Historically, persimmon fruit was an important food for Native Americans, European explorers, and early colonists. Natives made persimmon bread by mashing the pulp with crushed corn. They also dried and stored the fruit for long-term use like we do with figs, dates, plums, and grapes. Colonists prepared puddings, breads, and preserves with persimmons. Captain John Smith compared the taste of the ripe fruit to the sweetness of apricots. Early settlers brewed persimmon beer and used fermented juice to distill a brandy. Confederate soldiers made a coffee substitute with the dry, roasted, ground seeds.

Wildlife have appreciated and consumed persimmons for much longer than humans. Wild hogs, deer, raccoons, skunks, bobwhites, wild turkeys, rabbits, squirrels, bears, and opossums compete for ripe fruit.

While hunting for ripe wild persimmons, you will find green ones as well. The green fruit was once used to make indelible ink. Youngsters will enjoy doing the same today. Collect about a dozen green persimmons. Grind the green persimmons to a pulp. Place the pulp in a pan and pour just enough water to cover the pulp. Then boil the pulp down to about half of the original amount. Add a small piece of ferrous sulfate from a chemistry set or local pharmacy. The resulting indelible ink can be used to label children's school supplies and clothes.

Persimmons are fun to find, pretty in fall table displays, and healthy to eat. They are a fruit full of fiber, Vitamins A and C, magnesium, potassium, phosphorus, iron, and calcium. Welcome the common persimmon into your family's fall festivities.

Fresh, Fast, Fun Food Gardens to Go

Seed germination, plant propagation, and healthy eating become fun and easy for children with portable miniature gardening systems that teach and practice recycling, gardening, and nutrition simultaneously.

Bucket gardens. Fill one-gallon food-grade buckets with herbs, edible flowers, and vegetable seeds. Crops will depend upon the season and the region. The portability of buckets with handles allows children to carry the garden to different locations on campus as well as to tote it home. Bucket gardens transported between school and home and vice versa encourage intergenerational gardening and school/community-supported horticulture. One's personal bucket crop can contribute to a garden potluck picnic or fresh food festival.

MAKE A MINI-GREENHOUSE
- Use a hole punch to make two holes opposite each other on the top circular rim of a 1.25-1.5 oz. clear plastic portion cup.
- Measure and cut a 30" piece of thick yarn or twine for the necklace chain.
- From outside the cup insert the ends of the twine into each of the holes.
- Knot the yarn ends several times to keep it inside the cup.
- Fill the cup up to the holes with potting mix or compost.
- Sprinkle seed over the top of the soil.
- Sprinkle a thin layer of soil over the seed.
- Spray mist the soil.
- Put the cap on the cup to create a mini-greenhouse.
- Wear the necklace around your neck.
- Watch your cut-and-come again salad sprout.

Detergent Scoop Gardens. Plastic detergent scoops make convenient compact gardening systems for sowing microgreens, cat greens, herb garnishes, individual salad greens, or mixed green salad. They also can become cute dollhouse garden carts planted with edible flowers. The handle suggests giving a gift from the garden.

Juice Lid Disc Beds. Plastic lids from juice containers make circular disc-shaped beds for starting cut-and-come-again salad greens, microgreens, baby greens, grains, and cat greens. Gently scatter or shake seeds over the surface of the soilless potting mix or compost inside each disc. Press seeds lightly into the soil. Spray mist when dry.

Seashell Salads. Seashells make natural planters for seed like chia, radish, mung bean, cress, alfalfa, and mustards. Thoroughly wash seashells in dishwashing soap before using. Fill shells with moistened soilless potting mix or homemade compost before sowing seed. Mist soil with a spray bottle to prevent dislodging seed. Harvest greens with scissors for salads, snacks, sandwiches, and stir-fries.

Eggshell Planters. Eggshells are inexpensive seed starting planters plus calcium. Herbs, flowers, vegetables, and grains will sprout in eggshells filled with moistened soilless potting mix. Punch a drainage hole in the bottom of the shell with a carpet needle or awl. When the plant start is ready to transplant into the garden, gently squeeze the shell with the seedling inside and transfer both together. Decomposing eggshells add calcium to the soil, thereby moderating soil acidity and providing nutrients for plants.

Salad Necklaces. Clear plastic portion cups filled with moistened soilless potting mix or compost can start salad greens and microgreens quickly --

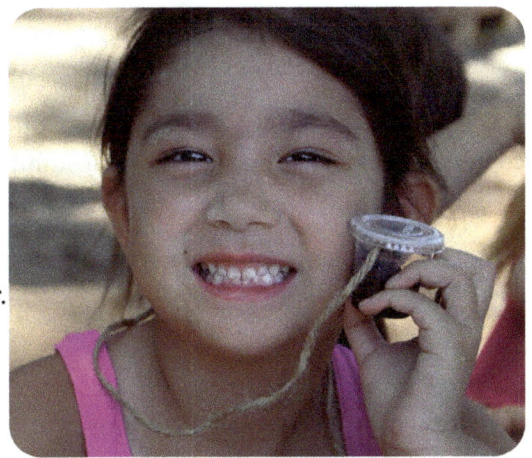

Salad Necklace

in as little as twenty-four hours. After sowing seed atop the soil surface and pressing seed beneath the surface, spray mist the soil. Then put the cap on the cup to hold in humidity and let the mini-greenhouse system water itself. When seeds sprout, transplant to the garden or harvest the cut-and-come-again greens. A salad necklace delivers fast fresh food while you watch it grow. And you can wear the salad necklace around your neck.

Involve your family and friends in "Fresh, Fast, Fun Food Gardens to Go" each season of the year.

Nutrition Gardens: Growing Healthy through Gardening

Condensed from Marturano, Arlene. (1997) "Growing Healthy Across South Carolina." *South Carolina Middle School Association Journal.* Vol. V No. 1, pgs.30-35.

Grow your way to a healthy life with theme gardens aimed at reducing risk for certain chronic diseases.

Nutrition gardens encourage health promotion through gardening. Nutrition gardening targets the prevention of diet-related diseases such as cancer, heart disease, high-blood pressure, osteoporosis, and diabetes. Theme gardens focus efforts on proactive plants for health.

Cancer-Prevention Gardens

The National Cancer Institute acknowledges the role of proper nutrition in preventing certain cancers. The cruciferous vegetables like bok choy, broccoli, brussel sprouts, cabbage, cauliflower, kohlrabi, and mustard greens contain a compound called sulforaphane which stimulates the production of cancer-fighting enzymes in the body.

Beta-carotene is a strong antioxidant that prevents cellular damage which can lead to cancer. Peas, spinach, parsley, carrots, cantaloupes, sweet potato, pumpkin, and other winter squashes are rich in beta-carotene.

Chives, garlic, leeks, and onions have compounds to thwart skin and stomach cancers.

Cholesterol Control Gardens

Although vegetables don't contain cholesterol, scientists believe foods rich in soluble fiber, like many fruits and vegetables, may help lower cholesterol levels and reduce the risk of heart attacks.

A cholesterol control garden grows foods rich in soluble fiber such as apples, barley, brown rice, carrots, corn, cow peas, garbanzo peas, collards, kale, lentils, romaine, leaf lettuces, oats, okra, split peas, winter squashes and zucchini.

Salt-Substitute Garnish Gardens

The American Heart Association recommends limiting salt intake to no more than 2300 mg per day and an ideal limit of less than 1500 mg per day for adults. High blood pressure may be aggravated by excessive salt in the diet.

Fresh herbs are an easy and flavorful salt alternative. For savory starters sow basils, chives, cilantro, dill, chervil, fennel, marjoram, mints, oregano, sage, rosemary, tarragon, thyme, and parsley.

Diabetes Control Gardens

Diet is one part of a diabetic's management plan to keep blood sugar levels at normal. Complex carbohydrates found in such garden-grown vegetables as dried peas and beans and brown rice raise blood sugar slowly over a longer period of time and contain a wide variety of vitamins, minerals, and fiber.

Diabetic children may need snacks between meals. Growing a snack-food garden of popcorn, peanuts, apples, grapes, and sunflower seeds encourages healthy snacking.

Diabetes experts note that low-fat foods high in fiber work well for diabetics. Fiber slows the absorption of sugar into the bloodstream. Low-fat and high fiber plants promote weight loss too. Weight loss reduces the severity of Type II diabetes. Alfalfa sprouts, artichokes, buckwheat, green beans, leeks, lentils, melons, okra, peas, squash, and tomatoes are high-fiber foods for a trial garden.

Bone Bank Gardens

Construction and demolition crews work side by side in our body. With osteoporosis demolition crews overtake construction of bone mass leading to loss of bone density and increased risk of fracture.

Calcium is the chief ingredient in bone. The National Institutes of Health recommends adults invest 1200-1500 mgs of calcium per day in their bone bank. Yet with the public consuming more caffeinated drinks than milk, calcium is leached from bones faster than being replaced. High sodium processed foods reduce the body's ability to utilize calcium.

The home garden can be a supplement center for high-calcium plants. Legumes are an excellent source of calcium: snap, adzuki, anasazi, black turtle, garbanzo, kidney, lima, pinto, and soybeans. Collard and mustard greens are good sources of calcium. Buckwheat, quinoa, and rice are high-calcium grains. A sunflower fence doubles as a calcium stockade providing seeds for salads and snacks.

While calcium is the main ingredient for strong bones, it cannot be absorbed without Vitamin D. Fifteen minutes of work in the sunny garden allows the body to manufacture and store the daily requirement of Vitamin D.

Growing food makes the gardener conscious of his power to pursue health.

MyPlate Inspires MyGarden

Originally published Marturano, A. (2011) "MyPlate Inspires MyGarden." *Eat Smart It's In the Garden.* South Carolina Department of Agriculture. 3(1)2.

MyPlate, the new USDA visual icon for healthy eating, can be a template for a garden, MyGarden and a bumper crop of well-fed Americans.

The new MyPlate icon of the five essential food groups unveiled at a press conference by the USDA's Center for Nutrition Policy and Promotion on June 2, 2011, translates the 2010 Dietary Guidelines for Americans into a familial and familiar visual image, the dinner plate.

MyPlate, two years in design, is the federal government's visual aid to promote health, lower risk of chronic diseases, and reduce overweight and obesity through nutrition and physical education.

Food Groups on MyPlate

The colorful plate graphic is easy to understand and remember as well as versatile in its use with preschoolers to geriatric populations.

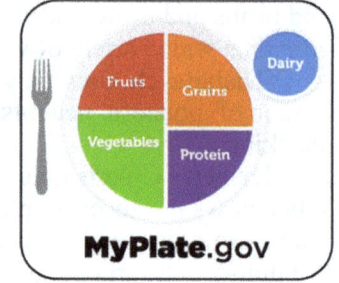

The divided circular plate, not unlike divided plates for babies and toddlers, has four unequal color-coded quadrants: red for fruits and green for vegetables on half the plate with brown for grains and purple for protein rounding out the other half. Portion size for each group is indicated by the size of the quadrant on the plate.

The dairy food group is a small blue circle off and to the right of the plate where the beverage usually is placed at the place setting.

The symbolic plate atop a place mat is a single place setting suggesting a sit down meal and a conscious intent to fill one's plate to match the model.

The USDA model plate follows the lead of several health promotion organizations like the American Diabetes Association and the American Institute for Cancer Research that use visual plate model images to direct meal planning.

Fruits
Blueberries
Currants
Cantaloupe
Grape
Strawberries
Watermelon

Vegetables
Beets
Carrots
Corn
Cucumbers
Onions
Spinach
Tomatoes
Zucchini

Grain
Amaranth
Barley
Buckwheat
Millet
Oats
Popcorn
Rye

Protein
Black beans
Edamame
Garbanzo beans
Lentils
Peanuts
Pumpkin
Sunflowers

Applying MyPlate

At the USDA's unveiling ceremony first lady Michelle Obama cautioned that although MyPlate is a simple icon for children to understand, the image alone will not stem the obesity epidemic and give all children access to fresh fruits and vegetables daily or to at least an hour of vigorous outdoor exercise each day. How parents, teachers, and caregivers integrate MyPlate into daily food experiences can make a difference though.

In considering the First Lady's initiative with the White House kitchen garden as part of her national Let's Move program to thwart childhood obesity, one of the strongest extensions and applications of MyPlate is the creation of MyGarden.

MyPlate converts concretely to MyGarden as fast as children can draw a circle on the ground. Backyard, schoolyard, or community gardening is one framework to transport the icon into exercise and healthy eating practices. Growing food develops an understanding of the relationships between agriculture, food, diet, exercise and health. And gardening involves exercise, lots of it.

From MyPlate to MyGarden

Using the MyPlate visual as the basic template for a garden implies a circular garden divided into the four sections represented on the plate. The USDA website provides lists of sample fruits, vegetables, grains and protein for each food group. From these lists garden planners can select seasonal crops.

One illustrative garden-plant selection plant list for a mid-western summer food garden follows:

MyGarden can have any number of themes depending on gardener inclination and imagination. For example, ethnic origin, favorite recipes, chronic illness prevention, or region may influence themes. All gardens will be influenced by seasonal conditions.

Bring Back Seasonality

Seasonal changes affect human activities. Just as we change our wardrobe for seasonal weather, growing food requires seasonal accommodations, which in turn affect diet.

The Slow Food movement, rise of local farmer's markets, seasonal chefs like Alice Waters and John Ash and four-season gardeners like Elliott Coleman and Barbara Damrosch celebrate seasonality.

The USDA's MyPlate has the potential to serve up garden-fresh food year round at schools across the country via MyGarden. Already the USDA Food and Nutrition Services has in place a Farm to School initiative to connect selected K-12 schools with local farms and farmers so seasonal local produce is prepared in school cafeterias. Some School to Farm programs break ground for school and community food gardens for local lunchrooms.

From MyGarden to MyPlate

The cycle of life in the garden is replicated on one's plate throughout the year.

When MyGarden fills MyPlate at mealtime, the US population can, in time, reverse the current diet-related chronic diseases.

MyPlate can generate a bountiful harvest of ideas for human health and nutrition education.

Sources

Coleman, Elliott. *Four-season Harvest*. White River Junction, VT: Chelsey Green Publishing, 1992.

Glover, Debbie, *MyPlate Simplifies Meal Planning*, St. Tammany News website June 4, 2011

Melnick, Meredith, *USDA Ditches Food Pyramid for a Plate*, Time Heartland website June 2, 2011

Nestle, Marion. *What Will USDA's Food Plate Look Like?* Food Politics website https://www.foodpolitics.com/

Seasonal Chef website Interview with Alice Waters July 1996

USDA MyPlate Press Conference video at USDA website

Eat Smart, Move More SC website https://www.wholespire.org/eat-smart-move-more-sc-announces-new-name/

USDA Choose MyPlate website https://www.myplate.gov/

USDA Farm to School website https://www.fns.usda.gov/f2s/farm-to-school

Chapter 4
RECYCLING

"If it can't be reduced, reused, repaired, rebuilt, refurbished, refinished, resold, recycled or composted, then it should be restricted, redesigned or removed from production." Pete Seeger

Turning Trash into Treasures

Trash, garbage, refuse, rubbish, discards--we all have mounds. In fact, we pay taxes so it will be disposed of. But a large portion of a family's discards can be converted to rich humus, garden plants, and even garden supplies.

Fruit and vegetable cores and peels, eggshells, tea bags, coffee grounds and filters, and wilted or spoiled crisper produce are select ingredients for the garden chef who views composting as cooking in the garden. The outdoor compost bin or heap is a hot oven of kitchen waste layered with leaves, hay, grass clippings, plant remains from flower and vegetable beds, wood ashes, sawdust, and garden soil. Add water to the consistency of a squeezed-out sponge and stir weekly to aerate.

A compost thermometer placed in the center of the pile allows the family to monitor the "cooking." The finished product is ready at 120 to 140 degrees. A small compost pile four by four feet and four feet high will yield a ton of humus. The process fascinates children. Kids love carrying out the bucket of kitchen waste to the pile, watching the transformation, and top-dressing the humus throughout the garden.

Some kitchen scraps convert into plants. Lemon, lime, orange, and grapefruit seeds pressed into potting soil surprise young gardeners when miniature tropical trees sprout in about a month. The seedlings transplant easily, making fragrant house plants and gifts.

Avocados have large, distinctive seeds, which produce attractive indoor trees. The first fun step in growing the trees is eating the fruit sliced in salads, on sandwiches, or mashed in guacamole dip. After washing and drying the pit, remove the outer brown seed coat. Press three toothpicks around the middle of the seed, making it look like a space satellite. Place the pit in a container of water with the flat bottom under the water and the narrow top above the water. Add water as needed.

In a month, a slender root will appear in the water and a stem will appear from the top. When two sets of leaves appear, transplant to a pot with soil and place in a sunny location. When the tree is a foot tall, pinch off the top to allow the plant to branch out.

Sweet potatoes are modified roots and can be easily sprouted in a glass. The emerging vine, a member of the morning glory family, will climb around the kitchen. Stick three toothpicks around the middle of the root. Put the root in a glass with the scarred and tapered end facing down. Toothpicks will rest on the edge of the glass. Add enough water to cover the bottom third of the root.

In three to four weeks, roots and shoots will appear. You may transplant into potting soil. To ensure home-grown sweet potatoes for Thanksgiving dinner, take cuttings from the sprouts of the indoor plant and root for the garden in spring.

The kitchen also can be a center for sorting and storing recycled garden supplies. Detergent scoops, 35-milimeter film cans, margarine and yogurt tubs, milk and water bottles, and caps make indoor systems for growing window-sill garnish gardens or for starting flower and vegetable seedlings for spring.

Plastic tomato and lettuce boxes, berry baskets, and rotisserie-chicken containers are miniature greenhouses.

Glass jars that once held pickles, mayonaise, jelly, peanut butter, or baby food can be saved to store seeds and root cuttings. They are also useful to sprout lentil, radish, alfalfa, and mung bean for the home salad bar.

Save popsicle sticks for multiple uses as mini-hoes, planting sticks, and row markers.

Converting garbage to gardens reduces waste sent to the landfill while increasing the amount of humus, plant material, ingenuity, and energy on the home front. Recycling is a valuable lesson and one of the best lifelong habits children can learn from gardening.

Kindergarteners compost garden waste in a bin.

Possibilities with Pumpkins

Within the cycle of the seasons in a garden, the pumpkin goes full circle. Seeds sown in spring produce a flowering bush or vine throughout the summer. Fruits harvested in autumn become decorations; food for wildlife, livestock, and humans; residence for rodents; and seeds for next year's garden. By winter remnants of the vine become organic matter for the soil.

Pumpkins, a North American native and member of the Curcubitaceae or gourd family, come in an array of sizes and colors – white, yellow, orange, and red. In autumn they can be found at grocery stores, garden centers, the farmer's market, and roadside stands. Picking a pumpkin is one of the joys of childhood.

And that's just part of the good times associated with pumpkins. Here are just a few more:

Pumpkin puree

Making fresh pumpkin puree is a fun and easy afternoon family project. Wash and quarter a small pie pumpkin. Remove loose fibers and seeds. Clean seeds with running water in a sieve and dry on paper towels for future use. Wrap each quarter in microwave plastic and place in the microwave for five to eight minutes or until the pulp is soft. Cool wedges before removing pulp from the shell. Puree pulp in a blender. Shuttle the shell to the compost pile.

Pumpkin pulp, high in potassium, fiber, and Vitamin A, can be used in recipes for pie, bread, muffins, cookies, soup, stew, flan, mousse, and souffle. Pulp can be frozen for up to six months.

Pilgrim pumpkin

Serve a slice of history with an authentic Plymouth Colony pumpkin dish this Thanksgiving. Start with a three- to four-pound pumpkin. Cut off the top and save it. Clean out seeds and fibers. Measure the hollow space by filling it with water and pouring into a measuring cup. For every cup of filling mix, ½ cup of milk; 1 large egg, beaten; ¼ cup raisins; 1 tablespoon sugar; ½ teaspoon cinnamon; and ¼ teaspoon nutmeg. Pour filling into hollow and cover with the top.

Place pumpkin in a round casserole to hold it upright. Add an inch of water around the pumpkin. Bake at 350 degrees for two hours until filling is set and flesh is tender when pierced with a fork. Let pumpkin set for fifteen minutes before serving. Slice in half and then into wedges.

Pilgrims ate pumpkin as a main dish, not as a dessert.

Pumpkin Seeds

Pumpkin seeds provide protein and iron. To prepare roasted seeds mix dry seeds with 2 tablespoons vegetable oil and a dash of salt. Spread the mix on a cookie sheet and bake at 250 degrees for about an hour, stirring the mix every fifteen minutes. Dry or roasted seeds are delicious solo or in cereal, trail-mix, muffins and salads.

Dried seeds can be saved for next year's garden or used in crafts such as necklaces, mosaics, paintings, and tambourines. Kids especially like noise makers. To make a seed tambourine, fill an aluminum pie pan with dried pumpkin seeds. Cover with an empty pan. Staple around the edges of the pans so seeds cannot fall out. Staple long ribbons to the rim of the pans and decorate the surface with stickers. Children can call family and friends to the holiday table with rhythm from pumpkin tambourines.

Growing Pumpkins

When weather starts to turn cool, the time is right to plan and plant a pumpkin patch. Provide a large sheet of graph paper for each family member to sketch out a rough plan before agreeing on a final draft.

Pumpkin plants grow in a loam or sandy soil with a pH of 6-7.5 in full sun. Ideal growing temperature is 65-75 degrees. Germination to harvest takes from 90-120 days. Pumpkins, 90 percent water, require space to grow and plenty of water and nutrients. To grow larger pumpkins remove all but a few fruits from each vine. Remove all but one fruit per vine to try for a record-breaking pumpkin. As of 2022 the American record breaker, grown in Minnesota, weighed 2,749 pounds. It also set a new world record, its grower's fourth, still unbroken in 2024.

Just be prepared to be happy with what you get through your own best efforts and care. Invite family and friends to pumpkin weigh-in guessing games at harvest time.

Pumpkin Planter
with Succulents

Black and White and Read All Over

Gardens are places to practice recycling, and newspapers are one of the most useful recyclables and a fun teaching tool as well. Playing the games of "It could become . . .," "It is used as . . ." and "It is used to . . ." with a newspaper in hand opens possibilities for children to be resourceful in the garden.

A newspaper could become a collar for bedding plants. A three-layer collar of wet newsprint around the base of each plant seals in moisture for the roots. Before the garden is planted in spring and weeds are rampant, a thick layering of newspaper (eight sheets) becomes a sun block and weed barrier.

Narrow strips of newspaper could become seed tapes. Tear 1-inch strips the length or width of a page. Space a dab of flour and water paste or glue stick on the surface, then place seeds atop the strip. Plant the seed tape in a furrow of soil shaped like a flower or your child's name. Cover the tape with soil and wait for sprouts to show.

Wider strips of newspaper could become seed starting pots. Roll a 3½-inch strip of newsprint onto a cylinder about 2 inches in diameter, - leaving a border of an inch over the edge. (Hairspray and shampoo bottles do just fine.) When finished rolling, press the border firmly under the container to make the bottom of the pot. Remove the cylinder and you have a paper container to fill with potting soil and your seed. Water and wait for the seedling to emerge in a few days.

You can make a smaller pot by rolling strips of newsprint around cylindrical 35-millimeter film canisters. Cluster pots close together on a planting tray. When you transplant seedlings in the pot directly into the ground, transplant shock is less likely to harm the seedlings.

Switching the game to "A newspaper is used as . . ." adds another dimension to utilitarian functions.

Shredded newspaper is used as mulch throughout the growing season. Today's black-and-white newspapers are printed with nontoxic soy ink. Avoid using glossy or colored newsprint, which may contain harmful chemicals.

When exchanging plants with others, **newspaper can be used as a moist wrap** before placing a plant in a plastic bag for transport. In the fall and early spring when frost is a threat, gardeners wrap tender plants in newsprint to insulate them from the cold. Gardeners have long used newspaper as a wrap to ripen fruit such as green tomatoes and avocados.

Newspaper is used as bedding for earthworms. To give earthworms their own garden bedding, add shredded newspaper soaked in coffee grounds.

For many a gardener the Sunday paper **is used as a cushion or kneeling pad.**

Let's change the game again to reflect what jobs newspapers can be used to do. For starters, **newspapers can be used to press flowers and leaves** for preservation when making collections or crafts.

In the days before offset printing, pressmen wore handmade newsprint hats to keep the oily ink out of their hair. Pressmen's hats are rarely used today, but **newspaper can be used to make a garden hat.** The gardener of any age needs shelter from the sun. Newspapers make good hot-weather hats because newsprint is cool like straw.

To make a newspaper hat, use two to three sheets of newsprint placed at different angles and centered atop the head. The edges will look like an eight-to-twelve-pointed star. Sculpt the crown over the head by pressing down and winding masking tape around the bottom of the crown just above the ears. After the crown is molded, roll the edges of newsprint tightly toward the crown to make the brim. Let children decorate their hats with markers, crayons, stamp pads, or paint and notions such as buttons, ribbon, and pompoms.

Newspapers also have been used to swat, smash, and trap insects in the garden. **Tight rolls of beer-drenched newspaper can be used to trap earwigs** by placing the bundles where earwigs congregate at night. By morning, throngs will have boarded the Titanic for your send-off. The garden is a great place to teach children which insects are harmful and which are beneficial and should not be smashed.

Here's the headline: Long after the news is old, newspapers continue to work for us in the garden.

Newspaper Seed Starting Pots

Turn the Christmas Tree into a Bird Bar

When the family Christmas tree is dismantled and taken outdoors, the evergreen is ready for a new mission as a tapas bar for birds in the winter garden. Once the crystal, porcelain, and cloth ornaments are placed in storage, a new assortment of edible ornaments can be hung and strung on the boughs.

Redecorate the tree with strings of unsalted popcorn, cranberries, peanuts, and raisins softened by soaking in water. Suspend stale donuts and bagels that have been smeared with peanut butter and dipped in bread crumbs, cornmeal, Cheerios, or crushed dry cat and dog food from the branches.

Tie to the dining tree seedheads from grains like corn, millet, and sorghum and dry seedheads from sunflowers, tithonia, coneflowers, coreopsis, and rudbeckia. Space bundles of Indian corn around the foliage.

After squeezing fresh orange juice and emptying grapefruit halves at breakfast, fill empty citrus cups with sunflower or niger seeds. Insert raffia or pipe cleaner handles for hanging. Abandoned bird nests filled with nut meats and seeds and anchored among the branches become "candy dishes" for nut-loving chickadees, titmice, cardinals, and nuthatches.

Cut mesh produce bags into squares and fill with a mixture of suet, peanut butter, dry cereal, cornmeal, and bird seed. Tie the bundles with raffia or twist ties and attach these edibles to boughs. Or smear the same mixture between the scales of pine cones and dangle from the branches.

Bamboo skewers used on the outdoor grill can be strung with chunks of fruit from apples, pears, oranges, and grapes to delight mockingbirds, orioles, bluebirds, waxwings, and even cardinals. Or slice the fruit and hang individual slices with aluminum ornament hangers.

If you decide to flock areas of the tree with crushed eggshells, sterilize the eggshells first by baking in a 250-degree oven for twenty minutes. Crushed eggshells offer grit for avian digestion.

The "skirt" beneath your tree can be a layer of acorns mixed with cracked corn to satisfy blue jays and grackles as well as uninvited squirrels. As with any eating establishment, keep food fresh and remove decaying food.

Returning Your Christmas Tree to the Wild

If your family resolved to live a greener life for the New Year, your Christmas tree offers an opportunity to get started. After giving weeks of enjoyment indoors, the post-holiday tree can be put to work in numerous ways outdoors on your property. Find the best fit for your family's green agenda.

Window Box Arrangements: Cut the conifer boughs to size and arrange them in empty window boxes along with other decorative garden plant material like holly or pyracantha sprigs and pine cones. Your Christmas tree will greet you when you arrive home and when you look out the windows.

Bough Blankets: Christmas tree boughs make a light weight and airy insulation for perennials. Gently place boughs over beds to protect plants from unseasonable dips in temperature and frost heave.

Log Feeders: The trunk of the tree can become log feeders for birds. Cut the branches away leaving short perches. Saw the trunk into twelve-inch lengths. Use a one-inch drill bit to make half-inch deep holes on the log's surface. Fill holes with homemade suet or peanut butter mixed with sunflower seed. Screw a hook onto the top for ease in hanging. Share feeders with neighbors and friends and compare notes on visiting species.

Mushroom Log Garden: The trunk of your Christmas tree could become a mushroom garden. Although most edible mushrooms grow best on hardwood logs, varieties that grow on conifer logs are lion's mane, cauliflower, chicken of the woods, and Phoenix oyster. Seek advice from knowledgeable mushroom growers for this unique project. Mushroom Mountain, a South Carolina resource is available at www.mushroommountain.com.

A Fish School: Families living by a farm pond or private lake can contribute their tree to the underwater world. A submerged tree provides a natural structure harboring aquatic insects and a place for fish to hide, spawn, feed, and "go to school." The S.C. Department of Natural Resources uses Christmas trees to construct fish attractor sites on public freshwater lakes like Lake Murray. DNR requests that the public not dump trees into public lakes but rather donate trees at designated drop-off sites across the state.

Brush Pile: One Christmas tree can initiate your backyard wildlife habitat. Wild species need places to escape from wind, harsh weather, and predators and to rest in protected surroundings. A Christmas tree propped up along a fence, garden shed, or compost bin or placed on its side in the corner of the yard will shelter birds, amphibians, reptiles, and mammals.

Bird Café: Keep the tree in its stand and place it on level footing in the back yard. Add edible garlands of apple and orange slices, cheese chunks, peanuts in the shell, cranberries, and popcorn and hang pine cone and gum ball ornaments coated with nut butters and bird seed. Your tree will be flocked with winter birds and their merry caroling.

Christmas Tree Fence: Beach residents can collaborate to gather large quantities of Christmas trees for dune restoration. The trees anchored in the sand collect the shifting sand and form the foundation for new dunes.

Y'all Mulch: Participate in the communal conversion of Yule trees into mulch through Grinding of the Greens programs. Spreading the fragrant mulch around your yard continues the cycle of life in your garden.

Returning your Christmas tree to the wild brings many happy returns for years to come.

The Days of Wine and Rabbits

The lazy days of summer are for making sun tea and sipping iced tea or chamomile. But at one special South Carolina school students used to brew another type of tea in partnership with the school's pair of pet rabbits, Toby and Ginny, who were nicknamed the Poo Masters. Students called themselves the Brew Masters for the magic mixture they made from the rabbits poo.

Poo? Ewww! Not really. This tea was an organic manure tea for plants to drink, made and sold by students at Barclay School.

Throughout the school year, until lack of grants and other funds caused the school to close, students at Barclay engaged in projects in a child-centered experiential approach to education. The curriculum was an organic outgrowth of student strengths, interests, and efforts. Learning took place outdoors just as much as it did indoors. Students and teachers developed a variety of instructional gardens and outdoor classrooms decorated with student-made art forms. Daisy, the resident dog, was always within reach.

The school modeled recycling, so the idea of recycling Toby and Ginny's rabbit droppings seemed a natural progression. Besides, when you have more than enough of a good thing, you want to share it. And rabbit manure is good for gardens. It is a rich source of nitrogen and phosphorus, two nutrients plants need for strong root systems, healthy foliage, and plenty of flowers. Hence, the enterprise of brewing and bottling rabbit tea was born.

Once a recipe for rabbit manure liquid fertilizer was created, students set to work processing manure by steeping it in pails of rain barrel water outdoors in sunlight. They needed containers to store the tea. Wine bottles seemed the best option not only because local restaurants could donate them in quantities but also because they catch the eye of consumers and connoisseurs.

To market and advertise rabbit manure tea the students needed a brand name and selected Bunnies' Brew.

Each student had a specific task in the production process. They all gathered outdoors once a week to wash and take the old labels off of the donated wine bottles.

When the used bottles looked like new, the children filled them with liquified rabbit manure and glued on Bunnies Brew labels with a signature cottontail rabbit tail. Labels included directions for use and ingredients without giving away any poo master or brew master secrets. Students hand signed tags to place around the neck of each bottle. Bottles were corked and sealed with wax. After the bottles passed quality control inspection, they were packed in cases for distribution by Barclay Green Goods, the official company name for the student-run business. Several Columbia-area garden centers sold the poo brew with profits going directly to the school's field trip fund.

Bunnies' Brew was just the cup of tea for local rosarians, who were particularly fond of rabbit tea for their rose beds. The tea could be applied to the soil around outdoor and indoor plants, sprayed on foliage, used as a dip for the roots of transplants, and sprinkled into vermicomposting bins.

Those were truly the days of wine and rabbits.

Bunnies Brew

Composting with a Wiggle

My compost bin had been effectively converting yard waste and kitchen food preparation scraps to crumbly, spongy, dark humus for over twenty years. I'd used the slow-cook method of layering plant remnants in a pile and letting the microorganisms, insects, and fungi decompose the ingredients with little human intervention. In the center of the pile a hotbed thermometer has monitored cooking temperature. (A reading of 140°-160°F indicates the compost is ready to be added to the garden.) Compost is available year-round

But a decade ago – about 2012 -- my slow-cooking compost operation took a dramatic turn when I joined an underground movement. I tossed a dozen red wigglers, *Eisenia fetida,* into the bin. These fellows –well, technically, they're hermaphrodites, but calling them fellows works for me -- knew just what to do and wasted no time in eating the garbage and gifting me with casting, the Cadillac of compost. The voracious feeders worked tirelessly around the clock outpacing but not ousting my long-term invertebrates, fungi, and bacteria decomposers.

The organic matter in the bin undulates with worm activity. These wiggling devotees of Starbucks grounds for the garden devour the coffee grounds and filters. They have accelerated compost creation while at the same time producing a population explosion. I have a breeding bin! With worms each partner produces offspring. One worm produces ninety-nine hatchlings in an 11-week period. A hatchling becomes a mature breeder in three months. At the same time the parents continue to mate and produce offspring.

Separating castings from worms is a challenge in a 27-cubic-foot bin. I use the "dump and sort" method. Spread a large tarp on the ground and place cone-shaped piles of compost atop it. Because worms are sensitive to light, they crawl to the bottom of each pile. I scoop casting from the top, reshape each mound and continue the tedious process until worms and castings are separated. Worms are returned to the bin. Castings are distributed to raised beds, flowerpots, seedling trays, and around shrubs and trees.

There are other ways to harvest castings. Garden writer Sharon Lovejoy describes in *Sunflower Houses* harvesting castings in a large worm bin eight feet long, four feet wide, and sixteen feet high – almost twenty times as large as my bin at home. She feeds the worms on one side of the bin one week and shifts to the other side the following week. The worms quickly learn where the fresh food is and move to the newest menu items. She harvests from the vacated side.

About ten years ago I met vermicomposter Billy Carson who had then been growing worms for fun and profit for ten years at Billy's Goat Hill farm in upstate South Carolina. He was 14

Red wiggler worms, *Eisenia fetida*, eat your garbage

years then! I asked for his ideas on separating castings and worms. He recommended the Can of Worms system, a stackable tower of trays. As worms finish eating organic matter on one tray, they migrate up to the next leaving behind a tray of casting for removal. Billy was selling red wigglers by the pound, approximately a thousand worms.

Composting and vermicomposting are wonderful ways to learn biology, ecology, and business basics. Open your own can of worms with your children and watch what happens.

Snip Seeds and Store for Planting Later

While the family is planting winter annuals and next spring's perennials, pause to discover the drying seedheads from summer's splendor. Fall is the time to harvest not only the fruits but also the seeds of our labor. Set aside time for a seed scavenger hunt in your garden. Seed saving is a form of recycling.

Annuals with seed ready for saving in autumn include cypress vine, balloon vine, moon vine, thunbergia, marigold, impatiens, zinnia, poppy, sunflower, cosmos, salvia, nigella, tithonia, and herbs such as basil, dill, fennel, and cilantro. Perennial seeds can be collected throughout the growing season and include platycodon, four o'clock, soapwort, rudbeckia, coreopsis, echinacea, milkweed, scabiosa, dianthus, stokesia, and baptisia.

Equipment for the hunt includes a pocket knife or scissors, gloves, brown lunch bags, marker, and hand lens. Close viewing with a hand lens lets one see the vessel design and the seed-dispersal plan. Nature's gifts come in a variety of dry fruit containers from long legumes and follicles to small capsules and siliqua. Some seeds explode from the capsule, some just drop out, and others depend on wind and animals to carry on their lineage. (That's why we leave seedheads on many plants so that birds and other wildlife can harvest the seeds.)

Collect seeds on a sunny, dry day. Snip seedheads and place inside the paper bags, labeling each bag with the name of the plant and date collected. Often seedheads collected in brown bags will shed seeds when you shake the bag. Some require opening the pod or capsule to remove the seeds. Thoroughly dry seeds on paper towel or newspaper before storing in labeled paper coin or glassine stamp envelopes, baby food jars, empty vitamin bottles, or spice tins. Some seed savers sprinkle one or two tablespoons of powdered milk between folded tissue paper and store this desiccant with the seeds.

Snip seed heads and place in a paper bag to dry.
Shake bag to release the dry seeds from the seed head.

Children enjoy designing seed envelope graphics along with planting instructions, signing, and giving the personalized seed packets to grandparents, teachers, cousins and friends for special occasions. A family can donate seeds to a local plant exchange, too.

Soon the habit of seed saving will become a hobby, and children ask whether they can save seeds from kitchen produce. Avocado, mango, and citrus seeds make attractive indoor plants. Pumpkin and gourd seeds will sprout on the compost pile, so why not save the seeds to share?

Can't Wait? Start Early from Seeds

When tree buds swell, birds begin courting, and daylight lengthens, our biological clocks respond with growing pains. Children seem especially sensitive to seasonal changeovers. They burst out of school to be invigorated by natural light and an abundance of fresh air in which to play on and in the earth.

For adults, the mere suggestion of spring summons agrarian inclinations. Seed catalogs and seed racks intensify the urge. We must plant. We must get seeds into the ground despite Punxsutawney Phil's prediction, the extension agent's advice, climatic data on the last spring frost date, and current soil temperatures.

To satisfy the natural need to sow seed, roll the dice, proceed to "go" and start your seeds indoors! Annual and perennial flowers and vegetable seeds all can be started indoors in late winter. Read the seed packets with your child to determine how to stagger seed starting dates to coincide with recommended outdoor transplant time, usually after the last spring frost date. (Where I live in the Midlands of South Carolina, that's mid-April.) Be sure to consider germination days.

Containers. Seeds can be sown in many kinds of shallow containers with good drainage and water retention. Margarine tubs, yogurt cups, Styrofoam cups, milk cartons, plastic salad-bar containers, aluminum loaf pans, and microwave dinner trays suffice for small batches of seeds. For large numbers of plants, use plastic pots, peat pellets or peat pots, or plastic flats. For individual plants that are difficult to transplant - cucumbers, melon, squash, eggplant, okra, and sunflowers - sow seeds in eggshells, peat pellets, or pots which can go directly into the ground without disturbing roots.

One preferred indoor seed-starting container is the self-watering Park Seed Bio Dome Seed Starter. The Bio Dome offers foolproof germination and seedling development. The system has four components: a white styrofoam planting block with 40, 60, or 120 cone-shaped cells, a green plastic water reservoir, Bio Sponge planting medium, and a clear plastic vented hood. The lightweight Styrofoam block sets inside the water reservoir. One pre-moistened porous Bio Sponge fits into each Styrofoam cell. The sponge is a plug with a pre-dibbled hole ready to accept one or two seeds. At transplant time the biodegradable plug is planted with the seedling eliminating transplant shock.

Park Seed Bio Dome is a mini-greenhouse.

Make sure to wash and sterilize any container before you use it. A solution of nine parts water to one part bleach is adequate.

Potting mix. The two best ways to obtain a superior potting mix are to buy a bag of potting mix such as Soil3 humus compost, Stout Ollie Compost, or Daddy Pete's Potting Mix. Or mix your own.. Children relish the latter. Here's how:

In a bucket, mix equal amounts of compost, perlite, and vermiculite. Use sifted compost made in your compost bin. Perlite, a volcanic rock, adds air space. Vermiculite holds moisture and lightens the mix. The mixture should be moistened just before it's used to fill containers. Do not use garden soil to start seeds - it is too heavy and not sterile. Fungal diseases in garden soil will prove fatal to seeds and seedlings.

Sowing seed. Success starts with fresh seed from good nurseries such as Park, Burpee, Johnny's, Landreth, and Seeds of Change or seeds you've collected yourself and properly stored.

When tiny seeds meet tiny hands, several methods can help make sure seeds get where they're intended to go:

Fine seed can be shaken from a clean salt shaker after sand, flour, or flavored gelatin has been added to carry the seed. Empty herb and spice containers make good seed shakers too. Shaking the mixture onto the soil is fun for toddlers and preschoolers.

Another method is to place the mixture in the crease of a folded piece of paper, then tap the paper gently over the soil. Tweezers can help tease some seeds out of the package onto the soil.

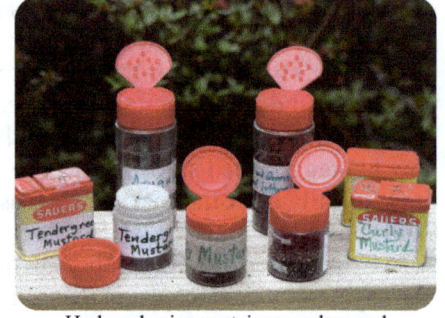

Herb and spice containers make good seed shakers for tiny hands.

But perhaps the most helpful tool is a No. 2 pencil. Dip the dull but sharpened pencil tip into the moist potting mix. Then dip the pencil tip into the seeds. Seeds will cling to the tip until you rub the tip into the planting site. Children delight in gardening from the tips of their pencils. Later, when seedlings are ready to transplant, the pencil will become a lever to lift the young plant from its birthplace to its outdoor bed.

The planting depth is on the seed package. If the package has no instructions, cover the seed the thickness of one seed. Make a furrow with pencil or chopstick, space seeds according to package instructions, and pinch the furrow closed. Once seeds have been planted, label the containers. Labels are a memory aid. Plastic or wooden stakes labeled with permanent marker or pencil work well.

Watering. Newly sown seeds are already in a moist mix, so gently mist the surface before covering with plastic wrap or greenhouse lid. Check the nursery several times each week to manage moisture. The mix should not become completely dry, and water is all you should add as it's needed. Germinating seeds do not need fertilizer. Start fertilizing when plants have been transplanted.

Light. Most seeds germinate in darkness. Once they have sprouted, they need bright light - but not direct sunlight. The best way to ensure strong and robust plants is to use artificial light from a fluorescent light bank such as shop lights or light from a grow bucket. Earlier in the chapter I told you how to make and use a grow bucket, which is like a miniature greenhouse.

At first, lights should be about two to four inches from the plants. Use the chains on the light banks to raise and lower the lights. For safety, place light-bank guards over the horizontal bulbs. Lights should be on for sixteen to eighteen hours per day. A timer is invaluable.

Before tender seedlings can be transplanted to the garden, they must be "hardened-off"--the process of acclimating them from an indoor protected environment to outdoor fluctuating temperatures, wind, water, and light. Gradually introduce seedlings to the elements by placing them outdoors in a shady, sheltered spot for several hours per day at first. Bring them inside at night. Over two to three weeks slowly increase the time outdoors until they become toughened tenderlings reared to live outdoors for the entire growing season.

Seed starting is just the beginning of an exciting season of gardening for you and your children. Soon the indoor cache of green will become an outdoor splash of splendor.

SEEDLING READING
Here are some children's books to inspire young gardeners:

From Seed to Plant by Gail Gibbons

From Seed to Pumpkin by Wendy Pfeffer

Miss Rumphius by Barbara Cooney

Seeds by Ken Robbins

Sunflowers by Miela Ford

The Tiny Seed by Eric Carle

Nature's Free Fall Podcast

The shapes, textures, colors, and designs of plant pods make them objects of art in the autumn landscape. Children enjoy collecting natural objects. The dry, fruiting body of a plant containing seed, its pod, is one collectible. Many plant families gift your family with pods. Searching for pods is a solo or family adventure.

Start in the yard, where you're apt to find among the ornamental and edible vegetables long, dangly pods of the legume family such as scarlet runner and hyacinth beans or pole, green, and edamame beans. The Japanese wisteria vine and mimosa tree, also members of the bean family, produce a beanlike pod.

Peanuts are the underground legume whose pod we remove to enjoy the protein-packed seed or groundnut. One of the fastest-growing members of this family is one you don't want in your yard. It's kudzu, a perennial vine and also a pod producer.

The milkweed family probably is present in your butterfly garden. Milkweed pods are among the most widely used plant parts in making dried decorations and ornaments or toys like milkweed mice.

Okra and cotton pods are decorative craft project pods. Make okra Santa and cotton boll angels for your holiday tree.

Pepper pods make longlasting, useful dried chili pepper wreaths, garlands and ristras to add flavor to cooking throughout the year. Distinctive chili pepper gift tags bring warm greetings.

In the final phase of the growing cycle, roses produce the rose hip, a pod containing seeds. After tiny fibers and seeds are removed, the ripened pod is used to make tea and jam. Hips add flavor to applesauce, soups, stews and syrups.

The poppy family has a ball-shaped seed pod with a flat top. Poppy pods dry easily and are long-lasting, so they are popular in dried-flower arrangements and crafts.

Asclepias syriaca, common milkweed pods

The soapwort plant from the carnation family yields a green soap when leaves are rubbed under water. The pink or white flowers bear a green capsule pod, which turns brown before releasing numerous seeds.

As you discover the podcasts in your garden and beyond, share the silent messages nature plays before our eyes. Gather the pods for holiday crafts and gift-giving. Celebrate the season by making pod bouquets for friends and neighbors.

Seed Saving in the Library? Check It Out!

Imagine returning books to the library and checking out seeds for this year's garden. That is exactly what is happening across the nation from coast to coast.

Seed libraries revive the notion of full-cycle gardening and provide the context for plant-based learning experiences for children and adults. Most seed lending libraries allow individuals and groups to borrow and grow heirloom and hybrid seed at no charge with the understanding they must return some of the seed from their harvest to the library at the end of the growing season.

Many seed libraries are located in school and public libraries, partly because antique card catalog cabinets convert readily from index cards to seed packets. Students learn older methods or devise new ways of cataloging via seeds.

Unlike seed banks, which store and hoard seed for catastrophic losses, the seed library is dynamic and changing with each borrower's donation. The seed library becomes a memory bank with the exchange of seed history and a way to build communities through shared interest in our native roots of gardening.

Seeds are a time capsule of genetic and cultural history. For thousands of years people have relied on saved seed as an investment to be recycled for the future food supply. The first settlers to America brought seeds from their homeland to grow on new soil and today's immigrants do the same. Neighbors traded seed over the garden fence and families passed down seed from generation to generation.

David Bradshaw, retired professor of horticulture at Clemson University, is an heirloom seed collector by family tradition. He has been gardening for over sixty years with vegetable seed passed down through generations of family. The willowleaf butterbean he grows has a 150-year heirloom history. Many of his vegetable seeds are offered by Heavenly Seed, a company in Anderson that encourages the use of heirloom, organically grown, open-pollinated varieties.

Since seed libraries may stock heirloom and hybrid seed, participants will become acquainted with the ongoing debate over the advantages and disadvantages of heirloom and hybrid seeds.

A seed library is a unique way to introduce seed-saving to students and to integrate science into the K-12 curriculum. Seed-saving encourages school gardening, the learning of plant scientific names and comparing plant families. Students will come to understand pollination, cross-pollination, self-pollination and the anatomy of flowers.

How might you start a seed library at your local school? Teachers who have done so recommend working with the school librarian for card catalog space. Students can write letters explaining their project and asking for donated seeds from seed companies that specialize in heirlooms, such as Baker Creek, Heavenly Seed, Seeds of Change, Native Seed/SEARCH, Seed Savers Exchange, and Southern Exposure Seed Exchange. They might also contact local farmers, longtime gardeners, and master gardeners for donations of heirloom seed and the stories behind them.

Find these folks at local spring flower and garden shows and farmer's markets. Invite heirloom seed growers to speak in the classroom. Set up the storage and filing system for the seeds and recruit growers who will "check out" seed to grow at their garden and agree to "return" seed after harvest time.

Libraries are making it easy to borrow, grow and share seasonal seed secrets in communities across the country.

The Poinsettia Project

Fifth-grade students in Dr. Sarah Burnham's class at Brockman Elementary School in Richland One are on a mission to save the planet one poinsettia plant at a time.

In 2021 the South Carolina students noticed the proliferation of poinsettias, *Euphorbia pulcherrima*, during the December holidays but also observed the disappearance of the festive flowering plants by January. They wondered, "Where did they go?" Through observation and research students discovered that many plant parents were perplexed about what to do with a decorative plant after the holidays. Should they plant it outside? If kept as a houseplant, how much water, light, humidity, and indoor temperature are required? Student research revealed that 34 million live-potted poinsettias ended up in landfills after the holidays.

Students decided to reverse the latter wasteful and detrimental practice and rescue poinsettias by keeping them as houseplants in classrooms and in their greenhouse. They produced a YouTube video on how to care for poinsettias as indoor houseplants. The video includes tips like removing the foil from around the pot to permit good drainage; keeping the plant away from drafts at heat vents, windows, and doors; providing cool room temperatures of 50-70°F; setting in bright, indirect sunlight for six hours a day; and watering with room- temperature water only when the soil surface is dry to the touch.

They challenged other classrooms to rescue poinsettias, properly care for them, and see how long the plants can survive. Rescue work is demanding whether it's focused on pets or plants. The students also requested the public to surrender their poinsettia plants to their project rather than to a landfill. Poinsettias could be surrendered at Brockman's school office in January.

In 2023 students worked on propagating poinsettias from stem cuttings and hoped to get their poinsettia population to rebloom for the next winter's holiday season just like greenhouse growers do.

Most of the poinsettias for sale in Columbia, South Carolina's big box stores come from Metrolina Greenhouse in Huntersville, North Carolina. They grow millions of poinsettias each year starting with cuttings from Ecuador and Guatemala. Cuttings root in three weeks. Pinching plants as they grow, fertilizing, and watering are part of the growing process. Since poinsettias are short-day plants requiring fourteen hours of total darkness from the first of October for an 8-10 week period to set flower buds, growers must manipulate day-length by using blackout cloth to create total darkness. Home and school gardeners can use dark closets or boxes. During the bud-forcing period plants need air temperatures between 60-70°F and no fertilizer. By December the poinsettia should bloom along with Christmas cactus, another short-day holiday plant.

These conservation-conscious youth live sustainably at school by sharing fruit peels with composting worms; retrieving pellets from two free-range rabbits, Soko and MaryBell, for the compost bin; and using compost in the raised-bed vegetable garden and in greenhouse six-packs for a spring herb sale. They test water quality at a nearby creek and clean and label neighborhood stormwater drains.

Brockman is a Green Step School, an initiative for students to model sustainable practices at school by learning, implementing, and teaching others.

Dr. Burnham and students

SECTION THREE

NATURE PLAY

*"Play is often talked about as if it were a relief from serious learning.
But for children, play is serious learning."*
Fred Rogers

Chapter 1
Playful Plants

"Play is essentially a research activity -- an adventure, an experiment, a transactional process. It is motivated by innate curiosity and enquiry. It is the expression of a child's urge to find out and discover for himself how to live, how to be. Play has the joy of discovery, the satisfaction of creativity." N.V. Scarfe

Props for Child's Play Abound in Nature's Toyland

Play is not the trivial pursuit of childhood. It is an essential component for growth and development.

Early childhood educators observe the effects of play on children's social, emotional, cognitive, and physical development on a daily basis. Members of the International Association for the Child's Right to Play consider play a basic human need along with nutrition, health, shelter, and education. The American Academy of Pediatrics advocates free and unstructured child-centered play to promote child development and sustain strong child-parent bonds.

A garden is nature's toyland and one of the best places for children to play. The open areas encourage gross motor activity including chasing, crawling, jumping, running, tumbling, and twirling in the turf. The abundance of plants provides play props.

Think back to your childhood days. What plants and plant parts stirred your imagination and encouraged exploration? Remember popping maypops, blowing dandelion heads, and tossing gum balls? My childhood playmates and I picked daisy fleabane flowers to make "fried eggs" for pretend breakfast. White snowberries were potatoes covered with mud gravy. Grandma's snapdragons became flower puppets. My strawberry plants competed to see which had the longest distance runners.

Plants and gardens can stimulate spontaneous and imaginative as well as developmental play.

Many trees provide play props. Acorns and their caps turn into make-believe dollhouse dishes and spinning tops. Hickory nuts are heads for Miss Hickory dolls. Children find leaf mittens on sassafras trees to match their hand size. Star-shaped sweet gum leaves simulate deputy badges.

Expressive faces on flowers spark children's imaginations for mime and verbal play. Good blooms for this are sunflowers, viola, pansy, snapdragon, nemesia, and torenia.

Children invent toys from plant parts. Blossoms of hollyhock, daylily, and nasturtium become floral dolls. They dress dolls and themselves with blossom caps of Queen Anne's lace and pink mimosa baubles or make chain necklaces from clover, daisy, forget-me-not, or rose hip.

Seed pods shake, rattle and float. Love-in-a-mist seed pod works like a pepper shaker. Poppy pods rattle. Nut shells and milkweed pods become a floating fleet with leaf sails.

Flat oval translucent lunaria seed pods stretch the imagination. Children pretend the pods are coins, jewelry, monocles, doll dishes, wafers, windows, mirrors, fairy wind chimes, and reflectors.

Gourds are pods with endless play potential. They grow in animal shapes like the penguin, snake, and swan. Small ornamental gourds become maracas. Birdhouse gourds bring avian families to your garden.

Some plants grow into play structures. Dense rows of corn become a "maize" of fun. A ring of sunflowers can become a sunflower house. Scarlet runner beans, hyacinth beans, gourds, or morning glory cover bamboo teepee frames.

Herbs are great sensory play props because of their texture and scent. Particular plants invite touch like wooly lamb's ear with its furry leaves. The tickle-me or sensitive plant, *Mimosa pudica*, mesmerizes those who touch its leaves and watch them close. Certain plant props make music, real and imagined. Children conduct bell choir concerts with the flowers of Canterbury bells and bells of Ireland. Tubular flowers like the trumpet vine, *Campsis radicans*, become mock musical instruments when not used as bubble pipes. Call an audience to your nature concert with grass blade whistles. The plant play improvised by children helps them manipulate the environment and transform it into their world. Take part in your child's play in the garden.

Mimosa microphylla, sensitive briar

Plants to Play With – and Maybe to Eat

Plants make responsive companions and playmates for all of us, but especially for children. Plants with kid appeal must be any combination of touchable, scented, colorful, flavorful, whimsical, useful, or playful.

Here's a top ten list of plants for kids:
Gourds. Children delight in growing a bird house, a bath sponge, or a speckled swan, penguin, or dipper. Gourds lend themselves to hours of anticipation as the vines twine, inspiring visions of fall and winter craft projects.

Popcorn. For snacking and sharing, popcorn is fun to grow and more fun to pop. Strawberry popcorn is a child's height and has red ears resembling jumbo strawberries.

Radishes. For sure-fire success, nothing beats the radish. Varieties mature in twenty to thirty days or sooner if grown for salad or sandwich sprouts. Easter egg radish comes in a rainbow of pastels. But there are French breakfast, white icicles, and Japanese daikon to sample as well.

Beans. There are many varieties, but the burgundy bush and purple pod pole change color when cooked. Scarlet runner beans make the best teepees, and the fiery blossoms attract hummingbirds. Asparagus yardlong beans thrive on summer heat. The edamame (soybean) is a sweet Oriental treat.

Sunflowers. Easy to grow, as well as heat and drought tolerant, sunflowers are universal favorites for children. Just as kids come in all sizes, so do sunflowers -- from toddler-high Sundance Kid and Teddy Bear, to towering giants such as Kong and Russian Mammoth, soaring ten to twelve feet tall. Build a sunflower fort, maze or fence. Harvest the seeds as snacks for you and the birds.

Berries. Whether in a bramble patch or in a patio planter, blueberries, blackberries, raspberries, and strawberries are a joy to pick and eat directly from the plant; sprinkle atop cereal, pancakes, and ice cream; or bake into muffins, tarts, and pies.. Stains on hands and faces make it easy to nab the berry bandits.

Sundial plants. Plants that tell time by opening or closing at regular times fascinate.

Grandpa Ott's Morning Glory

Morning glories, four o'clocks, the evening primrose, and the moon flower can be timepieces in a garden of hours. How many of us take time to watch flowers open and close?

Snapdragons. With faces resembling seahorses, butterflies, and dragons, this flower puppet encourages conversation. Impromptu playmaking is encouraged by many flower designs and faces, including the pansy, viola, nemesia, monkey flower, black-eyed Susan, and torenia. Why not sow a troupe of flower puppets?

Festive florals. Some flowers dance with color. Easy-to-sprout zinnias make cheerful cut-flower bouquets all summer. Ruffled portulaca, petunias, and nasturtiums are a chorus line of vibrant color for hanging baskets.

Herbs. Herbs stir the senses and the imagination. Basil,

SEED TAPES

To help little fingers and hands sow tiny seeds, consider making seed tapes.

Seed tapes use biodegradable paper and adhesive. The adhesive can be made with flour and water as in papier-mache.

Dissolve 1/2 cup of flour with enough cold water to make a thin paste.

Cut paper towels, bathroom tissue, or newspaper into long strips that are about one-half to three-quarters an inch wide. Dab the paste onto the paper using a Q-tip or craft brush, spacing at intervals suggested on the seed package. Children can measure and mark the intervals with a pen.

Place the seeds on the paste and let dry.

For very tiny seeds, place seeds in an old spice tin and sprinkle them onto the tape.

The dry seed tapes can be planted in endless designs. Children like seeing their names spelled in flowers or herbs.

chervil, chives, cilantro, dill, oregano, rosemary, sage, and tarragon expand a child's range of food flavorings. Parsley and fennel are shared with butterfly larvae. Doll tea parties need chamomile, lemon balm, lemon grass, lemon verbena, and soothing peppermint. Even the family cat appreciates catmint, catnip, thyme, and rosemary.

Seeds and plants are readily available at garden centers and nurseries or through mail-order catalogs.

Play Potential Can Hide in Gardens Unless You Seek It Out

Hide and seek was a favorite game of my childhood. There were wonderful hiding places in our family garden.

The pendulous boughs of the mulberry tree provided a shady reading nook. The arbor supporting Grandma's grape vines supplied snacks and security. We played chase between rows of sweet corn and paraded stealthily through a three-foot-deep corridor of hollyhocks separating neighboring lots. Braving the bees, we wedged among weigela, mock orange, snowball, and snowberry shrubs. Privet hedges made dense screens from the prairie winds and became white sculpted walls in the long winters.

Every garden has potential hideaway zones for children. In the Carolina Children's Garden we watched children gravitate to enclosed spaces like the big bird house, the three bears' vine-covered homestead, the cedar playhouse, the chinaberry umbrellas, the grape arbor, and the bean teepee.

Creating rooms, hideaways, and enclosures means considering placement of plants in space. Linear spaces of corridors, hedges, and fences allow for different activity levels than circular spaces of caves, teepees, and mazes.

A private reading room can be made with a weeping variety of tree like willow, cherry, or mulberry. Flower or bean teepees of all sizes can be made with five or more bamboo poles bound at the top and securely anchored into the soil. Underplant the shorter-poled teepees in sweet peas, morning glories, black-eyed Susan vine, or cardinal climber. Taller teepees can be planted in hyacinth bean, scarlet runners, pole beans, mini-pumpkins, small gourds, or cucumbers. Happy campers cluster inside the living tent.

Caterpillar tents are delightful outdoor rooms crawling with hungry caterpillars. The tents are framed with pliable branches and covered in plantings of passion flower vine, host plant for the gulf fritillary, or pipevine, host plant for the pipevine swallowtail. Plant dill, fennel, parsley, and rue around the sides of the tent to host other species of swallowtail. Brightly colored milkweed, verbena, phlox, zinnia, and bee balm clustered around the tent will attract the nectar-seeking butterflies. A soft carpet of chamomile, wintergreen, periwinkle, or bouncy mondo grass on the floor of the tent makes a comfortable observation spot for the life cycle of butterflies.

Screens encourage peeking through, up, and over. Hedgerows of hawthorn, juniper, holly, ligustrum, boxwood, and arborvitae can be linear or sculpted to create hiding places. The same shrubs can be used to create mazes. Berms, low hills of earth, function as screens to enhance privacy. They add the challenge of climbing over to find out what is on the other side.

Tall grasses are a refuge for children just as they are for other wild animals. Solo specimens of pampas or miscanthus can conceal a toddler. Ornamental millet, carex, panicum, broom sedge, or broom corn can make a fortress. The long stems, blades, and plumes of grasses easily become play props for children.

By letting a corner of the yard revert to its native flora without interference from human hands, a surprising retro room is added to the property. The spot would be like opening a time capsule of the past in the present and being able to walk right into the past.

We're 'All Ears' in the Garden

When we garden with children we often focus on flowers -- the pattern, shape, and color of their faces. What if we were to look instead at the "ears" of garden plants?

The most famous ears in the garden may be ears of corn. What are the "ears" on corn? Since they contain the kernels or seeds, the ears are considered to be the seed package of a grain. Suppose one were to grow corn with different sizes, shapes and colors of ears. You might include blue ears of Hopi flour corn, calico ears of Indian flint corn, Bloody Mary red ten-inch ears of dent corn, miniature strawberry ears for popcorn, yellow sweet corn, and white roasting ears.

Most "ears" in the garden are leaves. You may already have elephant ears (*Colocasia antiquorum*) in your back yard. If not, the tropical African native is easy to grow in a sunny location with soil amended with plenty of compost, organic material and water. Elephant ear stems grow from a few inches tall to 108 inches with "ears" from six to sixty inches in length. They are great fun to hide behind, to wrap yourself in, or to splash with water from a hose. The large leaves flapping in the breeze seem to cool the garden. Most elephant ears are shades of green but burgundy and black cultivars have been introduced recently.

Very colorful but smaller eared shade-loving relatives of the elephant ear are caladium. Grown from a tuberous root like the elephant ear, caladium ear color is green, white, red, or pink. A bed of caladiums looks like a family of elephants and might inspire you to find matching fabric and pattern to craft a stuffed elephant collection.

Lamb's ears (*Stachys abysantin*) are the shape and texture of real lamb's ears. They love sun and are drought tolerant. The soft silvery fuzzy leaves make them a wonderful candidate in a touch garden as a border or bedding plant.

Another silver foliage plant is the mouse-ear chickweed (*Cerastium tomentosum*). The four-to-six-inch white-flowered plant is useful in a rock garden or as a carpet for covering a steep slope or an edging along pathways.

Bunny's ears (*Opuntia microdasys*) are the small light green pads on ornamental prickly pear cactus. Although spines are not easily visible, they do exist, making this plant a touch-me-not. The yellow flower and dry fruits resemble those on our native prickly pear (*Opuntia compressa*) nicknamed "beaver tail" for the shape of the pads.

Donkey's ears (*Kalanchoe gastonis-bonnieri*) have long narrow leaves like a donkey's ear. The plant is a succulent shrub from Africa tolerating light shade and drought. The plant multiplies by forming plantlets on the edge of the leaf. A relative of the donkey's ear is pussy ears (Kalanchoe tomentosa) with white felt-like fuzzy leaves. The plant is often grown as a houseplant.

Pig's ear (*Cotyledon orbiculata*) is a succulent shrub growing to five feet tall. The glossy round leaves, two to three inches long and wide, resemble the flesh on a pig's ear. The plant is very drought tolerant.

Two tropical plants with flowers resembling ears are lion's ear and rabbit ears. Lion's ear (*Leonotis leonurus*) is a perennial flowering shrub that blooms all summer in rich, well-drained soil.

> **LOOKING FOR EARS**
> Here are some websites to check out:
> www.caladiumbulbs.com
> www.naturehills.com
> www.plantsdelight.com
> www.seedsavers.org
> www.toptropicals.com
> www.tytyga.com

The densely hairy tubular flowers are said to resemble a lion's ear. Bees, butterflies, and hummingbirds love the orange or white blossoms. The vine-like shrub rabbit ears (*Ruttya frutivos*) has orange or yellow flowers shaped like a rabbit's head with upright ears. The flowers ooze nectar, attracting butterflies and hummingbirds.

Young children enjoy introducing stuffed animals to their plant counterparts in the garden or making paper or felt stick and finger puppets of their plants with ears. Once you have established an "ear" garden, can you find any plants with "eyes"?

Caladium

Vines, Like Children, Thrive with Support and Training

Vines share a lot of characteristics with children. They are fast growers and great runners and climbers. They are gymnastic, twining or clinging, and tenacious, even seeming to be all over the place at times. They benefit from support and training. And they bring color to our lives each day.

It's no wonder that children have such a good time with vines. Here are some ways to get kids and vines together:

- Vines offer children the pleasure of hide and seek. Consider a brightly painted arbor for grapes doubling as a cave for kids. Or cover a bamboo pole teepee with scarlet runner bean (*Phaseolus coccineus*), hyacinth beans (*Lablab purpurea*), or morning glory (*Ipomoea tricolor*) to create a cool flowery getaway.

- Use the cooling effect of vines to create a welcoming playspace. Shade a patio pergola with hops (*Humulus lupulus*), American wisteria (*Wisteria frutescens*), Dutchman's pipe (*Aristolochia macrophylla*), or grapes (*Vitus* spp.). Vines like

Virginia creeper (*Parthenocissus quinquefolia*), creeping fig (*Ficus repens*), and English ivy (*Hedera helix*) reduce reflected heat from masonry walls or quickly cover ground with a durable carpet.

- Find unorthodox uses for plants to spark a child's imagination. Some fun and easy projects with vines are hiding the neighbor's yard, camouflaging the chain-link fence, making posts and poles disappear, building a living playhouse, secluding a swimming pool or outdoor shower, and obscuring the compost pile.

- The opportunity to eat fruits and vegetables fresh off the vine encourages children to try cucumbers, pole beans, squash, peas, pumpkin, melons, kiwi, and grapes.

- The anatomy of vines makes for an adventure as many blooms resemble floral puppets. Seeing moonvine flowers (*Ipomoea alba*) unfurl their four-inch flower and fragrance after dusk in about a minute is unforgettable. The yellow butterfly vine (*Stigmaphyllon ciliatum*) not only attracts butterflies but also is named for its seedpods, which resemble them. The tubular flowers of the firecracker vine (*Ipomoea lobata*) are red, orange, and yellow simultaneously, like a firework's display.

- The sweet-scented gnarled snail vine blossom (*Vigna caracalla*) is a conversation piece. Show children how primrose and lavender-pink flowers cluster like bunches of curly pasta or snail shells. Help them try to envision how a bee gets into the nectar-rich center of the flower.

- Stage a tea party with the cup and saucer vine (*Cobaea scandens*). The purple flowers resemble fluted cups sitting on a green saucer.

- No garden is complete without birds. Children are interested to find that some flowers look like birds or have names that sounds like birds. The canary creeper's (*Tropaeolum peregrinum*) bright yellow fringed upper petals resemble a bird in flight. Love-in-a-puff (*Cardiospermum halicacabum*) or balloon vine has diminutive white flowers that turn into puffy green pods like tiny birds.

- While the face and pods of flowers are fascinating, look closely at the "feet" of vines -- the stems, growth tips, tendrils and aerial roots. These structures direct the vine to a support or anchor.

- Experiment with vine behavior. What happens when you uncoil a vine? What happens when you coil it on a support in the opposite direction of its original twining? What happens to vines with no support? Which vines have tendrils and which have tiny suction cup feet for grasping?

Muscadine grape vine doubles as a cave for kids.

- A plant's response to a stimulus is called a tropism. A vine starts to twine when it touches an object. Thigmatropism is a vine's response to touch. Use that word while showing a child how vines grow, and enjoy the giggles as you go on to explain: One responsibility of a vine grower is to provide the searching vine with adequate support. A vine will inform a gardener if the jungle gym provided does not fit its needs.

- Recruit the whole family to stretch the garden to new heights by inviting eager and easy-to-grow vines into the landscape.

Planting Secrets

Two weeks into winter, gardeners' thoughts are on spring bulbs. Now is the time to introduce children to planting their secret garden under the influence of Dickon, Colin and Mary. Their garden at Misselthwaite Manor in the novel *The Secret Garden* followed several general guidelines for success.

Over the years, Ben Weatherstaff, the gardener, improved the entire garden with compost and manure, cultivating to a depth of at least six inches. Today we also tuck a bulb booster or bone meal feeding into the rooting area of each bulb at planting time.

Bulbs prefer well drained soil and well aerated soil to prevent fungal diseases. The spade, hoe, and fork are useful to aerate the soil and ward off fungus.

The secret garden grew bulbs compatible with England's climate. Select bulbs recommended for your climate zone to assure flowering success. In mine, aconite, allium, crocus, daffodil, dwarf iris, fritillaria, grape hyacinth, scilla, snowdrop, and Spanish bluebells offer a succession of color from early to late spring.

Snow Crocus

Bulbs are resilient and triumphant. Even though the secret garden had been closed and neglected for ten years, the bulbs naturalized and proliferated.

Most bulbs prefer sunny locations. Bulbs can be planted in perennial beds, around deciduous trees and shrubs, or throughout the lawn. Designers recommend natural arrangements for bulbs such as random cluster or drifts rather than soldiers marching in straight lines or grids. Let your child toss bulbs in your secret garden and plant them where they fall.

Plant bulbs at a depth two to three times their diameter. Which end is planted up? Have children investigate clues on the bulb. Sometimes roots still are visible or the shoot is pointing out. If top and bottom are questionable, plant the bulb sideways and nature will take over.

Immediately after planting, water the bulbs and mulch with compost, pine needles, or finely chopped pine bark to retain moisture and control weeds.

The awakening of life in the spring garden has a way of stirring life within each of us, as happened to the children at Misselthwaite. The garden was a place of magic, mystery and magnificence.

Give the gift of gardening to your children for the coming year with the simple offering of a bit of earth, a bag of bulbs and the same approval given to Mary in *The Secret Garden*: "Take it, child, and make it come alive."

Have Bushels of Fun Growing and Harvesting Potatoes

Potatoes are a popular food with families, but they are not a common crop in the home vegetable garden. Let's change that.

March is a great time to plant potatoes. The gardener's rule of thumb is to sow them anytime from six weeks to just before the last frost.

Potatoes like a sunny spot. Prepare a fertile, friable soil by mixing in well rotted compost. Potatoes need a fertilizer high in phosphorus for root growth (10-20-10 formula). As plants grow, you may add a side dressing with superphosphate. Clemson Extension recommends a soil pH of 5.8 to 6.5. An excellent draining soil is especially important for underground crops.

(You may want your soil tested to determine what it needs to produce a healthy crop. In my state we have that done by agriculture experts at Clemson University, which has "extension agents" in each South Carolina county.)

Seed potatoes are the stock from which you cut the planting pieces with "eyes." Garden centers and feed stores sell certified disease-free seed potatoes in ten- to fifteen-pound bags. Ask to buy a smaller quantity to fit the dimensions of your plot. A conventional home garden yield from a thirty-foot row is sixty pounds or a bushel of potatoes!

In Columbia the mid-season Red Pontiac and late season Kennebec are prevalent varieties available. With so many heirloom varieties of every imaginable skin color, flesh color, texture, size, shape, and flavor offered by online catalogs like Ronniger's, Johnny's, and Southern Exposure Seed Exchange, it is fun and easy to experiment with new varieties.

Cut the seed potatoes into ice cube-size chunks, each with two to three eyes. To reduce fungus and rot, dust chunks with sulfur. Place a tablespoon of sulfur in a paper bag with the seed chunk and shake to cover. Allow cut piece surfaces to dry for three to five days.

There are many systems for growing potatoes -- standard rows in the garden, raised bed, chicken wire cage, barrel, garbage can, bushel basket, fabric bag, and tire towers. If you plant in rows, plant each chunk, eyes pointing up, four inches deep, spacing twelve inches apart. Cover pieces with four inches of soil.

Deputize a potato posse to patrol for the first signs of green foliage and to pull any weeds that germinate. When the foliage is six to eight inches tall, begin mounding or hilling up soil and compost around the stems, leaving about two inches at the top. Mulch the entire growing area with six inches of straw or pine straw to keep soil cool and moist.

The potato posse should capture and squish insect pests invading potato plants. Post bug shots in the garden of the Most Wanted: wireworm, flea beetle, leaf hopper,

Colorado potato beetle, and aphids.

As the potatoes grow upward, tubers are forming underground. Anticipate hilling up compost three or four times during the growing period and up until flowers appear. The potato posse should then be on the lookout for vine death, a sign that potatoes are ready to harvest. Potatoes mature in sixty to 120 days depending on variety. The potato posse may use their hands to dig up surface potatoes through the layers of compost. Adults should use a spade fork to uproot the deeper tubers without bruising.

For those who have never sampled home-grown potatoes, they will taste like an entirely new vegetable. Your family may never touch store-bought spuds again.

Making Moveable Gardens and Landscapes for Children

Children are in motion from sunup to sundown. They need physical activity within the natural and built environment for optimal healthy development. Moveable gardens and landscapes are a teaching tactic to capture the kinetic energy of children and convert it to learning outdoors.

Children can grow food in the bed of a wagon or basket of a bike and wheel fresh produce right up to the kitchen door, tent, treehouse, or picnic table. Containers of all shapes and sizes fitted with casters on the bottom can move from sun to shade, carrying a fruit farm of strawberries and blueberries or a snack garden of cherry tomatoes, strawberry popcorn, and cucumbers. Depending on the season, snackable crops of snap peas, sprouts, lettuces, baby carrots, and radishes are easy seeds for children to sow in moveable buckets and pails.

Repurpose a wheelbarrow to be your children's moveable butterfly garden brimming with colorful zinnias, monarda, marigolds, pentas, tithonia, and gaura. Or help a child create a menagerie of plants so he can be zookeeper of the tiger lily, elephant ear, bear's breeches, cat's whiskers, skunk cabbage, and lamb's ears.

Moveable landscapes can hang from hooks, chains and wall-frame hardware. Consider building a simple or compound pulley system to apply a simple machine to water the hanging garden easily.

A moveable landscape garden project debuted the spring of 2012 at the Columbia Art Museum's Family Fun Day: Landscapes Great and Small. In conjunction with the museum's featured traveling exhibit of Hudson Valley School landscape painters from the 19th century, the Carolina Children's Garden at Clemson Sandhill Research and Education Center hosted a moveable landscape project designed by Amelia Cotty, kindergarten teacher and Richland County master gardener.

After viewing the landscape exhibit with parents, children drew and colored their own landscape on narrow strips of paper. Then they received a clear plastic cup in which to place a layer of pebbles under a layer of soil. Their landscape drawing was encircled inside the inner rim of the cup before they added sedum. Fillers like fern, mint and rosemary were added as finishing touches. This unique way to blend art and science traveled home with the children.

Growing up Gardening

Commercial moveable landscape planters specifically target young sprouts. The Woolly Garden is a vertical pocket planter made of recycled plastic bottles. Planters look like aprons with pockets for flowers, edibles, foliage, and succulents. The vertical planter can hang from wood patios, wrought iron rails, fences or gates. Fasteners allow for anchoring against wood, concrete, masonry, and chain link surfaces. The pocket garden could be mounted on a portable trellis or privacy screen and moved around for new play and make-believe spaces. Tuck into the pockets plant spillers such as verbena or nasturtium, thrillers such as balloon flowers and sunflowers, and sensory plants that include chocolate cosmos and silver sage.

Foodmap Container in Los Angeles County manufactures white plastic tubs made from recycled plastic milk jugs which accommodate a moveable edible garden. The caster stand can be wheeled on the driveway, sidewalk, patio or deck.

While gardening can keep kids moving, the activities are calming and focusing as well.

Growing Stones Instead of Throwing Them

Throwing stones and pebbles seems to come naturally to children. Why not divert throwing by interesting them in growing stones instead?

Living stones or lithops are one of the most bizarre plants on Earth. In fact, they look more like chunks from outer space than out of Africa, their native soil.

The dwarf succulents, just the right size for children, evolved to adapt to the harshest environments with temperatures of 120 degrees and rainfall as little as four to eight inches per year. Dire conditions produce minimalist plants containing the least number of parts to still be considered a flowering plant – a root, two kidney-shaped leaves, and one flower.

The two thick leaves are fused together in the shape of an inverted cone. At the narrow end is a taproot. A fissure or slit in the surface of the plant is the division of leaves. Leaves are thick water capsules and bear no resemblance to green foliage in our surroundings. Leaf colors mimic the soil or rocks in which they originated. Hence, they are earth tones from grey, brown, and red to blue and purple. Surface patterns may be marbled, mottled, or dotted, adding to the camouflage. In late summer one yellow or white daisy-shaped flower appears between the split in the two leaves. The leaves dry up in winter and two new leaves appear in spring. Leaves grow embedded in the soil, thought to be a protection against grazing animals and water loss.

Lithops or Living Stones

Children can grow living stones from seed as long as direct sunlight is available for six or more hours per day. Sprinkle a fine dust of seeds on moistened potting soil. No fertilizer is needed, but patience **is** required since germination may take from two to twelve weeks and plants grow slowly. And remember you are looking for stones not green leaves!

Once plants are established, they may be moved to a dish or container garden filled with cactus potting mix. Lithops like it dry so water only during the growing seasons of spring and summer and water only after the potting medium is bone dry. Overwatering will kill your stones. From fall to spring they need no water.

These miniature amulets have captured the imagination of plant collectors worldwide. On eBay one can find seeds and plants for sale. Scout for the displays of lithops throughout Riverbanks Botanical Garden in Columbia, South Carolina. Lithops are featured along with other Old World succulents in the Dorothy Chapman Fuqua Conservatory at the Atlanta Botanical Garden.

You and your children will delight in surprising family, teachers, and friends with a plant that rocks!

> **Seed Sources**
> https://jennysecretgarden.com
> https://www.cactusstore.com
> https://www.thompson-morgan.com

Hollyhock Days

A row of old-fashioned hollyhocks brings fond memories of childhood for many gardeners. Alan Armitage, professor emeritus of horticulture at the University of Georgia, recalls his mother's colorful hollyhocks along the stucco wall of the family garage. She stretched rows of white string horizontally across the line of plants to keep them standing upright.

Steve Bender, editor-at-large for *Southern Living*, remembers hollyhocks growing wild among the tall grass of the family farm and within the chaos of cottage gardens. The late Tasha Tudor loved, grew, and painted only the single heirloom hollyhocks. She wouldn't "look twice at the doubles."

Sharon Lovejoy, gardening author and illustrator, recalls encountering a "Hollyhock Hermit" in a California canyon where hollyhocks hugged the narrow trail and bordered the creeks. The hermit lived in a tent made of hollyhocks. Each colorful stripe in the tent was a cluster of hollyhocks of a different color. About eight feet up the stems, he had clasped the tops together with rope. Bee-decked hollyhock flowers spewed from the top of the tent.

Lovejoy learned about the edibility of hollyhock blossoms, seedpods, and buds as a child. She loved to eat hollyhock "cheeses," as the brown seedpods resembling small rounds of cheese are called.

Hollyhocks were ever-present in my childhood summers. They grew wild and free along our white picket fence, inside and out. Year after year they returned spontaneously. Little did I know back then about plant propagation, self-seeding, and naturalizing.

Hollyhocks were used to measure my height. Although I was outgrowing my clothes each year, hollyhocks continued to tower above the picket fence and my growth spurts. Hollyhocks six to ten feet tall challenge even basketball stars.

Hollyhocks provided me hours of enchantment. The bachelor buttons, zinnias, and marigolds around my playhouse garden had flowers at the top of the stems. These vertical giants bore flowers in long succession up and down a main stem.

Hummingbirds, bumblebees, and butterflies took turns flitting in and out of these high-rise flowers.

The hollyhock flower looked like a hoop skirt or ball gown for a doll. The green flower buds looked like doll heads. I liked to snip off a flower and a bud and attach the two with a toothpick to make a floral doll ready to dance throughout the garden, glide across the pond, or stage a puppet show.

Hollyhock seed was play money. The flat coins, half an inch in diameter, bought imaginary goods. For hollyhocks the coin-like seed is its investment in the future. The seeds germinate easily wherever they drop. The hollyhocks of my childhood assured plenty of descendants for adulthood.

On summer evenings we made colored lanterns by placing yellow, pink, and melon hollyhock blossoms in a Mason jar with fireflies.

When teachers explained the concept of "biennial", hollyhocks were used to illustrate. A biennial puts forth foliage the first year and blossoms in its second year. A biennial has a two-year life span but gardeners know the deep-rooted hollyhock often returns a few more than two years. Hence, hollyhocks are sometimes referred to as short-lived perennials.

While hollyhocks still grow along fence lines, I've seen them placed in front of garden walls, along narrow borders and pathways, tucked into corners, and stoically standing in alleys. They have been called alley-orchids for their propensity to escape cultivation and take off on their own journey.

The hollyhocks of childhood seemed as carefree as life itself was then. Only as an adult gardener did the world of disease and pestilence enter hollyhock days. I became aware that pests and diseases love hollyhocks too — Japanese beetles, leaf miners, spider mites, powdery mildew, and hollyhock rust. Despite the potential plagues destined for hollyhocks, archeological evidence puts the plant in perspective. Fossils of hollyhocks have been found at a Neanderthal burial site. They are survivors.

> **Hollyhock Data**
>
> **Family:** Mallow
> **Scientific name:** *Alcea rosea*
> **Close kin:** rose of Sharon, marsh mallow, hibiscus, okra, cotton
> **Colors:** white, crème, yellow, melon, pink, rose, crimson, maroon
> **Flower forms:** single and double

So that your children may experience hollyhock days, sow seeds in a sunny spot with compost rich well-drained soil in the fall garden. Mulch the young plants over the winter. During the winter the taproot will grow and by spring foliage will shoot forth.

Party Favors in One Perennial Plant

Blue, purple, pink, or white bells, balloons, and stars are packaged in each flower of *Platycodon grandiflorus*, the old-fashioned balloon flower. The hardy ornamental perennial is like having party favors growing in the garden. The plant is named for the flower buds. As buds grow they inflate until they unfold like an origami floral bell cut into a pentagram or five-pointed star.

Balloon flowers are in the bellflower family, *Campanulaceae*. Like other family members they exude a white milky sap when buds or stems are pinched and bear scentless flowers with petals fused to form a five-lobed corolla, single or double.

While balloon flowers are slow to erupt in spring, once they appear, the cultivars reach thirty-six to fifty inches in height. They thrive in light shade and sandy acidic soil but the species are suited for full-sun and alkaline soil as well. Clusters of flowers are borne at the tip of stems. Tall-stemmed varieties tend to lean so staking may be necessary. Dwarf cultivars have been introduced to remedy the problem. Balloon flowers can be grown in hardiness zones three through eight.

The plant, an Asian native, may be found under the common name Chinese bellflower or Japanese bellflower. Traditional Chinese medicine considers the herb to have medicinal properties. In Japan the balloon flower is one of seven plants of an ancient autumn festival.

The clump-forming perennial perpetuates itself by self-seeding. Gardeners propagate the plant from spring cuttings or seed. Division is rarely necessary and not easy to do because of the plant's tap root.

The carefree balloon flower produces a pest and disease free abundance of floral displays from summer into fall. They are a favorite for children's gardens. Deadheading is about all that is needed to keep them tidy but snipping the tan dry seedpods to collect seeds to share and sow is a favorite option for children.

Balloon Flower

Balloon flowers make interesting cut flowers for the dining table and are conversation plants for both adults and children. Bring stems with both buds and blossoms indoors for the delight in watching or contributing to the grand opening. The swelling bud, which is the developing corolla, becomes turgid just prior to opening. Touching the turgid bud can cause it to pop open.

Let this stalwart party favor perennial become the life of the party for a children's birthday party.

Walking with Wildflowers

Blue-eyed grass, bouncing bet, maypop, pokeweed, spiderwort, sneezeweed, and rabbit tobacco are a few of the captivating common names of wildflowers native to South Carolina.

Wildflowers appear in all four seasons but are especially showy in spring and fall. Whether growing between cracks in pavement, along roadsides, in ditches, in woodlands, on lawns or in schoolyards, children are attracted to their blossoms, foliage, seed pods and behaviors.

In the not-so-distant past, wildflowers were as prevalent as children playing outdoors. With the loss of green space due to construction and urban sprawl, wildflower populations decreased.

How might you and your children at home or at school contribute to the health and wealth of wildflower communities? A survey of what exists is a starting point. Using field guides on Southeastern Wildflowers, magnifying lens, note pad, pencil, and camera document the population of wildflowers in a given area. As you identify them, note characteristics of location. Is it sunny, shady, moist, dry, open field, wooded? Does the wildflower appear solo or in colonies?

On subsequent excursions into the field change your mind-set to vary what is noticed. Approach wildflowers with an artist's eye by capturing the line, shape, color, and texture with a pencil sketch of the plant in its habitat. In the field, watercolor pencils make it easy to tint the sketches. Over a series of days accrue a collection of wildflower portraits for your own field guide, for a deck of wildflower playing cards, or for note cards.

Coordinate the photographer's eye with the macro lens feature on a digital camera to frame wildflower images for slide shows and nature prints.

Most wildflowers have stories pertaining to their use by native peoples. Stories add another layer of understanding to wildflowers. For example, the Cherokee had many uses for the evening primrose. Its roots were boiled and eaten like potatoes and the leaves were boiled as greens. A poultice made from the entire plant was rubbed on the muscles to increase strength.

Wildflowers are used by wildlife too. The same evening primrose valued by the Cherokee supplies nectar and insects to hummingbirds and nectar for nocturnal insects like hawk moths.

Once established, wildflower gardens are low maintenance. Wildflowers look best when planted en masse in meadows, patches or ribbons of land. They adapt to soil pH of from 5.5 to 7.0 and do not require fertilization. Select drought-tolerant plants and water regularly during seeding and seedling periods.

Commercial wildflower mixes of Southeastern plants are available as loose seed or in mats. Seed mixes contain annuals, biennials and perennials. Spring seeding brings late summer and fall plants. Fall seeding yields spring and early summer wildflowers. Of course, you may want to buy container-grown wildflowers from local or mail-order nurseries. By all means include South Carolina's state wildflower, tall goldenrod, *Solidago altissima*, in your garden.

Here are some sources for wildflower seed and plants:
www.carolinawild.com
www.edenbrothers.com
www.ernstseed.com
https://roundstoneseed.com
https://www.woodlanders.net/

Growing Sunshine and Smiles

Sunflowers have universal appeal. This healthful, happy, native composite has over seventy varieties available from mail-order catalogs such as Burpee, Johnny's and Park Seed.

Native Americans domesticated the sunflower 4,000 years ago. The sunflower permeated their lives. Some tribes grew sunflower fences around the three sister crops of corn, beans, and squash. Natives used the seeds as nuts and as meal in cakes and bread. The oil flavored food and lubricated their skin and hair. Hulls were recycled into dye for baskets, cloth, and body paint.

Spanish explorers took the sunflower to Western Europe in the fifteen hundreds. By the sixteen hundreds English cottage and kitchen gardens included sunflowers. Eastern Europe learned of the sunflower from Peter the Great who brought seeds to Russia from Holland in the seventeen hundreds. Van Gogh's three-year fascination with the sunflower through painting started a horticulture renaissance for the plant in the eighteen hundreds.

Sunflowers thread their influence throughout our lives. Birders purchase black oil seeds in fifty-pound bags. Bakers include sunflower seed in cookies and breads. Chefs are experimenting with sunflower oil as an alternative to olive oil on salads and in stir-fries. Roasted or raw seeds are a high protein snack. Sun butter, approved by the USDA for the school lunch program, is marketed as an alternative to peanut butter and other tree nuts known to cause allergic reactions. The motion picture industry used French and Italian sunflower fields as the backdrop for the 1969 film *Sunflowers* starring Sophia Loren and Marcello Mastroianni.

Plant breeders have manipulated the color, head size, height, maturity date, and pest resistance so the gardener has the opportunity to grow bouquets Van Gogh never imagined. The expressive face of sunflowers contains two sets of florets-- ray and disc. The outer ray discs may be gold, yellow, white, orange, bronze, red, or burgundy; the hundreds and thousands of center disc florets may be black, chocolate, purple, beige, or green. Each center disc floret has the potential to become a seed.

Flower buds are heliotropic and follow the sun from east to west daily.

However, once the flower bud opens the flower head faces east. Just as people come in all sizes, there is a sunflower variety to match each member of the family. The small ones range from infant size Sunflower Elf to toddler-high Sundance Kid, Solar Babies, and Teddy Bear. Elementary-age children come face to face with Happy Face and Bashful. Adult-sized sunflowers at five to six feet high are Van Gogh and Soraya. Mammoth Russian, Cyclops, and Paul Bunyan are for the towering tall.

Help bees and butterflies hit the jackpot with pollen-rich varieties: Mammoth Greystripe, Black Russian, Lemon Queen, Arikara, Autumn Beauty, Chocolate Cherry, and Sonja. Pollen-free and perennial varieties are also available.

Growing sunflowers in South Carolina requires six to eight hours of direct sun, warm soil temperature of 50°F, adequate moisture, and soil pH from 6.0 to 7.5. Sunflowers like nitrogen so work a two-inch layer of composted manure into the topsoil before seeding. Seeds germinate in seven to ten days. Plants grow fastest in the heat of summer and continue flowering until the first frost. Dry the seed heads and harvest seeds for the birds, yourself, and next year's garden.

Whether you plant sunflowers as a fence, fort, house, or maze; in a container, bed, or meadow; as a nectar source for butterflies and hummingbirds; as a pollen feast for ladybugs; or snack food for the family, you will be growing sunshine and smiles all summer.

The National Sunflower Association provides educational information for growers, educators, and the general public at www.sunflowernsa.com . A coloring book for elementary age children, *The Story of the Sunflower*, is available at their website.

Chapter Two
Indoor Gardens

"Like people, plants respond to extra attention." H. Peter Loewer

Houseplants Sprout Lessons for Healthy Living in Every Pot

Houseplants are green furnishings, and like furniture, they need dusting and periodic washing. Just as children sponge bathe their skin, they may use cotton balls, soft cloths, or paper towels to wash the epidermis of leaves (top and bottom) and stems. Wipe plants with a mild soapy solution before rinsing with water. Use a dry toothbrush to brush fuzzy leaves on African violets. The fuzz on African violet leaves deters chewing insects and also keeps water from running down the stem and causing crown rot.

Sometimes houseplants and their owners are afflicted with similar problems in the winter. For example, if a family member notices dry flaky skin, most likely plants are suffering, too. Most houseplants are native to the tropics, where humidity levels are much higher than our homes. Try relocating plants to high-humidity areas such as the bathroom, kitchen or laundry room. You can also give plants a steam spa treatment by taking them to the shower.

If houseplants show signs of insect infestation, first identify the culprit to determine the correct prescription. Children enjoy "nursing" sick plants back to health. Mealy bugs and scale can be treated with a cotton ball or Q-tip dipped in rubbing alcohol. Mites can be eradicated with a forceful water spray. Some insects can be handpicked off.

Overwatering is the Number One cause of planticide. Houseplants in good health may need watering only once every ten to fourteen days. Many plants prefer to dry out between waterings. Soil should never be soggy.

Houseplants Sprout Lessons for Healthy Living in Every Pot

Try asking your children to perform a finger test to determine the moisture content of the potting soil. Insert the index or "pointer finger" into the soil up to the first joint. If soil is dry, water the plant. If the soil is wet, hold off. To establish a plant's watering schedule, conduct the test for ten days.

Houseplants multiply easily, making for the creation of an indoor plant nursery. Leaf and stem cuttings propagate in water or potting media. Some houseplants such as the prayer plant and chrysanthemum form clumps just like perennial flowers and can be divided by root division. Other houseplants that can be propagated by root offsets include sansevieria, aloe, dieffenbachia, and hen and chicks.

Winter propagation gives way to spring plant sales for the classroom or gifts from the growers throughout the year.

Whether for personal enjoyment or the joy of selling or gifting to others, gardening is a commitment. Children may be happy taking care of house plants until one droops or seems sickly. That's a learning opportunity about the commitment gardening requires in sickness as well as health. This can become a game at home or an interesting part of the year at school.

Call Plant 911

Are your houseplants threatening to uproot themselves? Do you see listless leaves, sagging stems, pitiful pots and scaly soil? Are your plants on a starvation diet? Sounds like you need Plant 911. Children love the idea of deciding whether a plant needs an emergency room, intensive care, or just more love.

Plant 911 is a pretend hospital designed to get your ailing houseplants under control. Plant doctors and nurses administer first aid to plant patients. Initial consultations with patients include a check of leaves for dust, color, and turgidity, stems for rot and growth habit, soil and pots for diseases, insects, crusts, and drainage. Dead and dying leaves should be removed. Leaves should be washed with water using a cotton ball. Check stem and leaves for mealy bugs, aphids, thrips, scale, and spider mites. Wash infestations with cotton balls dipped in soapy water or rubbing alcohol.

Stunted stems with small leaves may mean a lack of light, water, or nutrients. Spindly growth often means a lack of light. White-crusted soil and pots indicates a buildup of salts. Scrub pots and replace the soil with new potting medium.

The environment of the houseplant can affect its health. All houseplants require light but few require direct sunlight. Nurses will have to determine if lighting is adequate for the particular patient. Patients need periodic rotation to get equal exposure of light to all sides of the plant. Seasons provide changes in light, heat, cold, and humidity for houseplants as well as their outdoor kin. Winter brings dormancy for most houseplants.

The intensive care unit feeds, prunes, aerates soil, transplants, and propagates. Propagations from stem or root cuttings, leaf slips, root divisions, and runners reside in the plant nursery. In the tissue lab nurses prepare slides of stomata, cells, root hairs, disease biopsies, pollen, and soil for better understanding the growth and development processes of the patient. Patient progress can be monitored by sketching progress over time or by setting up a digital photo lab where a series of progress visuals are made.

Houseplants can suffer from dehydration just like animals. Placing them in the bathroom during shower time is one way to add humidity. Your plant's original habitat dictates its water needs. Overwatering is a common cause of houseplant death.

When watering use water at room temperature and let chlorinated water stand for a day before using on plants.

When plant emergencies arise, the ER nurse prepares an emergency room report and calls the doctor for treatment.

As children experience how their actions affect plants, they are becoming aware of the effect of humans on the environment. As plant patients recover and thrive, the family will take pride in rescuing another life.

Plant Hospital
Emergency Room Report

Observed Problems:

____ yellow leaves	____ insects on plant	**Diagnosis:**
____ scale on stem or leaves	____ wilting leaves	
____ holes in leaves	____ leaning stem or trunk	
____ soggy soil	____ dust covering leaves	
____ compacted soil	____ leaves folded up	
____ salt deposits on pot	____ splitting stem	**Treatment(s):**
____ mold on pot	____ spindly stem	
____ root rot	____ fails to flower	
____ roots exiting drainage hole	____	

The Plant Hospital.

This classroom version is a school year context for experimentation. Here's the concept:

The occupation of gardening is a vital experiential and experimental method encouraging children to solve problems pertaining to life while learning botany, soil science and entomology. Gardening has the plot interest of a good drama by including the old and the new, the familiar and the unexpected, and the routine and serendipitous. As the new school year begins, consider adopting or adapting the plant hospital indoor gardening experience as part of the instructional program.

Houseplant nurses

The plant hospital is a year-long project for elementary and middle school students designed to introduce science concepts through continuous close observation and care of potted plants.

The first week of school each student brings an ailing indoor or outdoor plant to class for a physical exam. Student nurses work under the direction of a plant doctor (teacher or visiting horticulturist) to conduct a thorough inspection of all plant parts, potting media, and pots. Hand lenses aid in looking for evidence of pests and diseases and signs of environmental or nutritional deficits and digital cameras document the physiognomy of the patient.

Each patient has a clipboard holding chart data. Nurses measure and chart vital signs like height, width, and weight in pot. They post observed signs of illness on patient's chart. The common name of the plant is printed on a craft stick placed into the soil. The common name gives the nurse a starting point to research the plant's history. Patients with infections that could spread to other plants are placed in the ICU, isolated care unit.

All patients are given a sponge bath upon admission. Student nurses use small sponges with warm water and mild dish detergent to bathe the plant leaves, stems, and buds. Patients are rinsed to remove the soap. Fuzzy-leaved plants like African violets are cleaned with an old toothbrush rather than soap and water. Plants with scale or mealy bugs are treated with cotton balls dipped in rubbing alcohol before the sponge bath. The sponge bath is the opportunity to introduce the 'epidermis' of the plant, the outermost cellular layer covering the entire plant structure and the first line of defense against diseases and pests.

The doctor and nurse establish a treatment plan for each patient. The plan may be as simple as placing the patient near a sunny window or pruning a gangly fruit tree to encourage branching. Sometimes surgery is scheduled. A transplant operation may be needed for root rot or root bound conditions.

Light, water, humidity, and temperature must work as a harmonious quartet to support health of plants. Nurses adjust these four factors for each patient's needs. Sometimes a light bank is used for certain patients. Misters can increase humidity. All patients need water but the amount varies greatly for different species and requires restraint and close observation by nurses. Identifying the microclimates in the classroom allows nurses to place patients in the best temperature zone for each species.

Student nurses follow orders which might include feeding of liquid fertilizer, pruning dead branches, aerating the soil, transplanting to a larger pot, deadheading, propagating, preparing plant tissue or plant pest slides to view under microscope, sketching and photographing patient over time, and recording observations and progress on patient's chart.

Plant patients are recruited for lessons on such concepts as "plant cell," "cell wall," "chlorophyll," "chloroplast," "photosynthesis," "respiration," "reproduction," "epidermis," "stomata," "guard cells," "phototropism," or "geotropism." Some patients become subjects in science fair experiments.

In time a plant nursery wing is added. Healthy patients become parents through vegetative propagation of leaf, stem, and root cuttings; root divisions; offsets; and air and soil layering. With an expanding crop of healthy young plantlets, the plant hospital adds a gift shop. Income purchases hospital supplies.

Throughout the year healed patients are sent home and new patients are admitted. Nurses are on call throughout the school to administer first aid to plants in

the main office, front entranceway, media center, and classrooms..
  Students look forward to plant hospital labs and take pride in their nurturing capabilities. They recognize how their actions can affect plants and become increasingly aware and knowledgeable about the effects humans have on plants.

A Lesson in Beauty in Wake of Tsunami

  In midwinter as poinsettias fade and only the leaf tips of daffodils are emerging, a sun-shy demure houseplant is in full bloom. The velvety dark burgundy leaves beckon, "Touch me." The striking red and gold veins suggest graceful line drawings, and gemlike rosettes of leaves surround foot-high spikes of white, fragrant flowers. For an IMAX image, slowly scan the plant with a magnifier.
  Content to live as a houseplant in a plastic pot or a terrarium, the terrestrial Jewel orchid, *Ludisia discolor*, is easy for a child to grow at home or for school terrarium and science projects.
  Beautiful as a solo specimen or clustered in colonies, *Ludisia* prefers a soilless potting mix, low to medium light on or near window sills, and warm room temperatures of sixty-five to seventy-five degrees. A native of tsunami-swept Malaysia and Indonesia, *Ludisia's* tropical temperament requires moisture in the air. Household activities adding humidity - showering, washing dishes and clothes, and cooking - should suffice.
  Houseplants depend on us for nutrition. You may use fish emulsion and liquid seaweed, liquid houseplant fertilizer, or fertilizers labeled for orchids, according to label directions. Have your child keep a calendar of application dates.
  The Jewel orchid is easy to propagate from stem cuttings anytime of the year. Place cuttings in water or directly into potting mix. Single plants are inexpensive and available from online mail-order nurseries such as www.carterandholmes.com, www.orchidsbyhausermann.com, www.evergladesorchids.com, and www.foxvalleyorchids.com.
  Profiling the family orchid to record changes in its growth and development can occur in a variety of formats--a journal describing observations by each family member; video, 35mm, or digital images dated and sequenced over time; index-card sketches or watercolor drawings; or flip books.
  To learn more about *Ludisia*, place a "wonder board" next to the plant so people can write questions and compete to see who finds the answers first. Questions might include, "How did the recent tsunami affect *Ludisia* populations?" or

Jewel Orchid, *Ludisia discolor*

"Where is the nearest orchid nursery?"

The satisfaction experienced in raising *Ludisia* will make you feel that growing houseplants is like growing winter jewels.

A Terrarium Is a World unto Itself

One of the best ways children learn ecological concepts is by constructing a terrarium. The miniature world under glass contains a balanced environment modeling the water cycle. Water in the soil is absorbed by plant roots, released into the air through plant leaves, and condensed on glass to "rain" back to the soil, thus continuing the cycle.

Often teachers have students build a variety of terrariums to simulate contrasting ecosystems or biomes -- desert, grassland, tropical, alpine, woodland. Some terrariums feature single kinds of plants, such as terrestrial orchids, carnivorous plants, African violets, or a citrus grove. More imaginative themes might be fairy or elfin gardens, Lilliputian gardens, or Thumbelina's garden.

Terrarium containers are as numerous as themes. Cookie jars, large Mason jars, gallon pickle or mayonnaise jars, brandy snifters, sun-tea jars, fish bowls, aquariums, and Wardian cases have been used. So have clear plastic liter soda bottles standing eight to ten inches tall after the narrow top is removed.

Pre-service teacher making terrarium

Terrarium construction follows these basic procedures:
- Line the bottom of the container with an inch of gravel or pebbles for drainage. Spread one-half inch layer of crushed activated charcoal over the gravel to filter impurities in the system and keep odors pleasant.
- Place a nylon stocking, nylon mesh fabric, or sphagnum moss over the first layer as a barrier to keep the potting soil mix from entering the drainage area.
- Add moistened soilless potting mix (minus fertilizers) to fill one-third of the height of the container. In a desert terrarium use one part soilless mix with one part sand.
- Use spoons, chopsticks, or fingers to make holes for plants or seeds. Insert plants and/or seeds into holes, gently firming soil.
- Use a bulb baster or paintbrush to remove soil from glass or foliage. Add decorative items if appropriate to the theme, for example, shells, stones, acorns, ceramic frog, mushroom or snail.
- Mist plants lightly with spray bottle only if necessary. Cover container with glass or plastic. Leave desert terrariums uncovered to maintain a dry microclimate.

The terrarium should be placed in indirect light, never direct light. The one exception is a desert terrarium which prefers direct sunlight and heat. For most terrariums twelve to sixteen hours of artificial light per day, as in a classroom or office, is fine too.

Moisture control is crucial to success. If too much water builds up inside, remove the top for a few hours to allow evaporation. If no water builds up on the glass, add some.

Fertilizer is not necessary in the first year of a terrarium. Plants need to anchor themselves and grow slowly. After the first year, add a dose of liquid houseplant fertilizer in spring. Maintenance is minimal, but pinching plant tips, pruning overgrown vines, and removing dead foliage is important.

Terrariums don't have moving parts or bells and whistles, but they have a fascinating quality of their own. Children become engrossed peering into miniature worlds created under glass.

Budding Botanists Trick Winter by Forcing Blooms

While winter continues to surprise with temperature fluctuations and precipitation quandaries, children will enjoy plotting to trick winter in the classroom and at home.

How might they sneak up on winter by surprise? Gardeners take on winter by creating an early spring indoors. When deciduous trees and shrubs go dormant in fall, they spend a period of leafless, flowerless dormancy through winter. Light and temperature changes in spring break dormancy, sap starts flowing, buds swell, and leaves and flowers burst on the scene. Almost overnight a fantasia of flower appears.

Steps to a successful spring simulation
- Use a sharp knife or pruning shears to cut branches twelve to twenty-four inches long from selected trees and shrubs. Staggering the pruning of branches over a period of weeks produces an extended "springtime."
- Place branches in lukewarm water for the first day to launch the forcing.
- On the second day replace the warm water with cool and cut the stems at an angle to better absorb water. Place the container (pop bottle, vase, jar) in a cool place with indirect light.
- Take turns changing the water daily and cutting an inch off of the stem once a week. A drop of Listerine® in each container retards bacterial growth.
- Mist the branches several times a week with "spring rain" to keep buds moist.
- When buds open in two to six weeks, move the cuttings to brighter light but avoid direct sun, heat, and heat vents. The time of bloom depends on the types of branches and when they were cut.
- Continue to change the water daily as you enjoy this early touch of spring. Once blossoming is flourishing, children can experiment with arranging the branches into spring bouquets.

- Patience is a necessary ingredient when working with children and with plants. Drawing daily progress of branches on index cards, a calendar, or flip book can nourish wait-time. Daily digital photography can also capture subtle changes over time.
- Add serendipity to the simulation by taking children on a walk to gather from unidentified trees and shrubs bare branches for forcing. By closely observing and comparing the different arrangement of buds, leaf scars, and bark with the aid of a winter twig guide, they will learn how to identify the plants before they burst forth.
- Children enjoy tricking Mother Nature as much as grown gardeners do.

Branches to Force		
Almond	Elderberry	Pear
Apple	Forsythia	Plum
Azalea	Hawthorn	Pussywillow
Buckeye	Hazelnut	Quince
Cherry	Lilac	Redbud
Crabapple	Magnolia (saucer, star)	Spirea (bridal wreath)
Dogwood	Mulberry	
	Peach	

An Avocado Plantation

Avocados are a readily available and inexpensive educational resource whether demonstrating monoculture agriculture, seed starting without soil, seed structure, roots versus shoots, dicot development, ripening of fruit, healthy fats, garbage gardening, pruning trees, biogeography, recipe writing, economic botany, or the concept of from-plant-to-plate.

Since many families make guacamole, avocado pits can be saved for growing a plantation. The following activity introduces children to growing avocado trees, a mini-plantation similar to those in Mexico or groves in California and Florida.

- Remove the pit from the fruit and wash it with water.
- Dry the pit.
- Peel off and compost the dry brown seed coat. You will see a crème colored seed.
- The broad bottom or root zone of the seed is flat. The top of the seed is rounded.
- Insert three toothpicks half an inch deep around the center of the seed about one inch from the bottom.
- Fill a small plastic cup like a yogurt cup with water.
- Place the bottom of the seed suspended by toothpicks in the water.
- The seed will start to show a root in three to six weeks. Be patient.

Growing up Gardening

- Mark a calendar on the date you started.
- Place the cup in a secure place out of direct sunlight. Replace water as it evaporates.
- Watch for the seed to crack, a sign the stem is sprouting.
- When the stem is six inches tall, cut it back by three inches. This will promote branching and prevent the plant from becoming a spindly stalk.
- When roots are thick and stem has leafed out, transplant into a rich humus soil in a ten-inch-diameter pot leaving the upper half of the seed exposed.
- Water frequently but do not saturate the soil.
- Place the potted tree in a sunny location.
- When the stem reaches twelve inches high, cut it back to encourage branching.

    Although South Carolina's climate is not conducive to growing avocado fruit plantations outdoors, your homegrown evergreen avocado will become a subtropical indoor houseplant in winter and an attractive outdoor patio tree the rest of the year.

Seedling

Seed

Sapling

Chapter 3
Holiday Gifts from the Garden

"Flowers always make people better, happier, and more helpful; they are sunshine, food and medicine for the soul." Luther Burbank

Gifts Grow in Every Garden

The garden as a resource for holiday gift giving lends a refreshing perspective to the world around us.

For families desiring to minimize consumption as a way of life, the natural world supplies materials for an economically and ecologically sound holiday season. Table and tree trimmings, house and package decorations, and gifts are in your back yard.

The entire family can participate in being green. Scout the back yard, farm, woods, and roadside for possibilities -- flowers, leaves, vines, herbs, pods, evergreens, bark, grasses, nuts, fruits, berries, lichen, dry seed heads, cones, and late-season vegetables

Brainstorm as to how the materials might be used and combined. What can a pine cone become? A miniature tree, a recipe or business card holder, a photo stand, a mistletoe frame, a fire starter. A bunch of pine cones glued together could become a picture frame, a basket, a wreath. Ingenuity, a good glue gun, craft glue, sewing scraps, fabric paint, colorful ribbons, and cord go a long way in creating charismatic crafts.

A family assembly line setup works best with certain tasks like a broom factory. Gather pine straw or dry grasses into bundles two-to-three-inches thick, and bind with rubber bands and holiday ribbons before adding a handle. This creates door decorations or whisk and hearth brooms that will warm the heart of any grandparent.

A circle of acorns, hickory nuts, or pecans glued together become napkin rings. Or add holly branches and berries to the circle and insert a candle. Children enjoy looping flexible daylily leaves or the blades of grass or chives around napkins, making simple but attractive napkin rings.

If the family has an active compost pile, a labeled bag of "Johnson family compost" and a bag of divided bulbs or flower seeds are personal gifts from your home that recycle your garden to someone else's. Package garden seeds in one-of-a-kind origami envelopes, or deftly painted or labeled 35mm film canisters.

Enlist a berry brigade to make stunning sprays from holly boughs, pyracantha, French mulberry, or tallow tree and juniper sprigs.

The pod squad can transform okra, honeysuckle, mimosa, magnolia, cotton, and milkweed pods into tree ornaments and rattles with spray paint, a dash of glitter, and colorful cord. A string of peppers adds a festive feel to the kitchen and cuisine. Dried gourds become birdhouses, ladles, painted Santas, or vessels for dried arrangements.

Wreath materials are everywhere beckoning to be chosen for the circlet. Honeysuckle, grape, and wisteria vines make firm natural frames, but so does a coat hanger bent to the desired diameter. Add pine boughs, holly branches, dried magnolia leaves, bay leaves, boxwood, rosemary, wax myrtle, ivy, or pine cones. Floral wire, floral tape, and a hot glue gun are supplies used to attach the natural decorations.

Lonely leaves blowing in the wind can be captured for a variety of uses. Large magnolia leaves become tree ornaments and bookmarks. Pressed leaves become immortal as leaf prints on note cards, bookmarks, greeting cards, muslin pillow cases or place mats, and white canvas garden gloves. Brush the underside of leaves with fabric paint and firmly press the painted surface onto the paper or fabric using a rubber roller or rolling pin. Card stock or index cards can be used as printing surfaces for leaf identification card game gift sets.

Time is a gift of nature, too. Coupon books to perform garden tasks encourage children to think of others. Coupon entries might offer to pick up pine cones, sweep the driveway, turn the compost, rake the leaves, hoe the vegetables, clean the birdbath, or weed the lawn.

Where I live chances of a white Christmas in the Midlands are slim. But the forecast for a green Christmas is but a step into the garden. Harvest happiness from the garden this holiday season.

A Flamboyant Flower for the New Year

One single plant can open the world of horticulture to youngsters. The bold fast-growing amaryllis received at Christmas provides an educational IMAX drama for the whole family.

The amaryllis is a world wanderer with contemporary cultivars hailing from South Africa, Holland, and Israel. This tender traveler makes its home indoors in six-inch pots. Plant the bulb in moist potting soil mix with one-third of the bulb protruding above the soil. Place the pot in a warm, well-lit southern exposure and do not water again until the first leaf or flower bud appears, indicating roots have become well established. Overwatering leads to bulb rot.

Once your adventurous amaryllis has established its roots, apply a slow-release fertilizer such as Osmocote that lasts for several months or a liquid fertilizer like Miracle Gro every two weeks. Soon gargantuan flower stalks reach two feet in height and produce two to six flamboyant trumpeting flowers in variations of red, purple, pink, and white. To extend flowering, move the blossoming plant to cooler, less sunny quarters.

Your newly blooming companion designed its flowers to show off, inviting investigations of flower parts, pollination, and seed production. Flowers have six petals and six stamens surrounding the pistil. Watch for the sticky three-pronged pistil to open upward, a sign the flower is ready to accept pollen. Family members become "indoor bees." Using a cotton swab, eye shadow applicator, or watercolor paintbrush, dab pollen from the stamens of one flower to the pistil of another.

When pollination occurs, the ovary (seed pod) containing seeds emerges at the base of the flower and matures in four to five weeks. When the amaryllis tires of blooming, it's on to the next adventure - reseeding. When seed pods turn yellow and begin to break open, seeds should be removed, dried for a few days, and planted immediately in a shaded well-drained seed bed. Following germination, increase the light. It can take from two to three years to grow a flowering plant from seed.

Your adaptable amaryllis has several more ways to make sure it continues its lineage. Vegetative propagation is the more common method of producing new amaryllis. Bulbs two or more years old produce offset (daughter) bulblets, which can be removed from the mother bulb, and each planted in its own pot.

Cuttage is another method of vegetative propagation. The large bulb can be cut vertically into as many as sixty wedges, with each wedge needing a portion of stem tissue attached to it. Wedges can be planted immediately in moist soilless potting mix or a mix of peat and sand.

Children can capture each stage of the growth cycle of the amaryllis by photographing or sketching the changes as they unfold. The children's book, *A Flower Grows* by Ken Robbins sequences the beauty of amaryllis ontogenesis and serves as a tutor to the nuances of the process.

If you plant your amaryllis now, you can celebrate a floral show by Valentine's Day. If you care for the bulb, it can be a winter bloomer for as long as a quarter of a century.

If you live in hardiness zones 8-10, after the last frost date in spring, you can plant the bulb outdoors in the ground, leaving one-third of the bulb above ground. Mulch around the bulb to control weeds and conserve water. It should rebloom in time for Christmas in July.

Amaryllis

Picking and Preserving Poinsettias

By December 12, National Poinsettia Day, garden centers, nurseries, and farmer's markets are displaying holiday poinsettias, *Euphorbia pulcherrima*. Each year the selections are more distinctive than ever since breeders have added many new features including new colors and variegations, earlier bloom times, extended flowering, and uniquely shaped bracts. 'Christmas Mouse', one popular variety, has bracts shaped like mouse ears. 'Alaska' is the brightest and whitest poinsettia on the market with holly-shaped leaves and bracts for a unique holiday presentation.

What are bracts? The colorful red, white, burgundy, salmon, or pink blooms are not flower petals but rather bracts, modified leaves just like native dogwood with white bracts. The small yellow flowers in the center of the bracts, known as cyathia, should be closed when purchasing. Why? Closed flowers indicate the plant has not yet bloomed and is fresher than if the blooms are open. If the center flowers are missing, brown, or wilted, the plant is past its prime.

Inspect the green leaves and bracts. The lower leaves should look healthy. The bracts should look fresh and full. Drooping leaves and bracts are a sign of poor hydration. Water only when the soil surface feels dry. Never let the roots rest in wet saucers. Remove the decorative foil packaging around the pot because it can hold water at the root. Experts note that overwatering is a common cause of problems with poinsettias. In the typical home or office a poinsettia will need watering only every 5-7 days. Room temperatures of 60°-70°F are ideal. Place plant in indirect bright natural light of a window away from drafts, cold panes, or heat vents. Fertilizer is not necessary while in bloom.

With careful shopping for a fresh plant and proper care at home, your Christmas poinsettia can reward you with three months of vivid natural color right up to Valentine's Day.

Poinsettias, originally known as *"flores de nochebuena"* or "Christmas Eve Flowers" in their native Mexico where they grow to heights of six to eight feet tall, were introduced to the U.S. by South Carolina ambassador to Mexico, Joel Poinsett. An amateur botanist, he sent specimens and cuttings to plantsmen and botanical gardens in the early 1800s. A century later the tropical poinsettia became a potted plant marketed for the home at Christmas. The Ecke family in California bred and selected the first portable poinsettias in the 1920s. Today a select number of floriculture companies around the world -- Selecta One, Dummen Orange, Syngenta, and Beekenkamp -- compete in commercially breeding the floral star of Christmas. In 2015 the Ecke farm merged with Dummen Orange, the European market leader for poinsettia cuttings and young plants.

The Christmas Eve Flower - Poinsettia

Poinsettias add warm festive feelings to the winter holidays.

The Best Flowers for Giving Their Hearts

Valentine's Day is the perfect time to show your love through gardening. A heart-shaped planting bed is easy to design, measure, and prepare in a sunny or partly sunny location. Once you have the heart, you are ready to fill it with home-grown love.

Children enjoy searching in garden catalogs for plant names signifying love, affection, and friendship. Love-in-a-mist, *Nigella damascena*, caught my curiosity as a child. Once I had planted the seeds, the flowers returned faithfully in abundance each year in shades of blue, pink, white, rose, and violet. The lacy green foliage appears like mist surrounding the blossoms. Love-in-a-puff, *Cardiospermum halicacabum*, has tiny white, inconspicuous flowers, which become pods that resemble green balloons, shaped like paper globes. I give pods as presents. The three black seeds in each pod contain a message. When you grow them, you will receive the message too.

Express playfulness with fast-growing Kiss Me Over the Garden Gate, *Polygonium orientale*, a fast-growing old-fashioned cottage-garden plant standing five feet tall and with gently drooping pink flower clusters.

Solidify friendship by giving a bouquet of homegrown Forget-Me-Nots, *Myosotis sylvatica*. The tiny plants are covered with dark blue topaz jewels in spring and early summer.

Heartsease, *Viola tricolor*, was the love charm in Shakespeare's *A Midsummer Night's Dream*. Ancestor of the pansy, the cream- and purple-tinged flower adds serenity to the winter garden. The plant has a long and interesting history of herbal use.

Make a new friend by planting lovage, *Levisticum officinale*, a culinary herb taking only a small space in the garden. Its celery-like taste will enhance the flavor of salads, potato, and poultry dishes.

The most romantic flowers come from the tropics. The Mexican native "Exotic Love," *Ipomoea lobata*, is a radiant flowering vine growing ten to twenty feet tall. Tubular flowers change from red to orange to yellow as they enlarge. Hummingbirds will be your valentines when they drink the nectar. The vine needs sun and an arbor or trellis to climb like its close kin--the sweet potato vine, morning glory, and cypress vine.

Some Valentine plants help convey the pain of lost, distant, or unrequited love. The spring-blooming perennial Bleeding Heart, *Dicentra spectabilis*, has a petal formation that resembles broken hearts. The outer petals are shaped like one-inch hearts colored rose, pink, white, or red. The inner petals are white. Plant the Fringed Bleeding Heart, *Dicentra formosa*, for blossoms all summer. Love-Lies-Bleeding, *Amaranthus caudatus*, a poignant Victorian garden favorite, produces foot-long chenille-like red tassels that make long-lasting cut flowers.

The Best Flowers for Giving Their Hearts - Hearts-a-burstin, *Euonymus americanus*

If your heart garden is spacious consider a shrub or grass. Hearts-a-burstin', *Euonymus americanus*, is a modest deciduous shrub with green stems reaching a height of four to six feet. Inconspicuous spring flowers produce a warty red capsule resembling a strawberry. In fall, the ripe capsule bursts open, revealing orange-red seeds inside heart-shaped husks. Purple love grass, *Eragrostis spectabilis*, is a native American grass growing two feet tall with a spray of reddish-purple seed heads.

and Love-in-a-Mist, *Nigella damascena*

Once your hearts-and-flowers garden gets growing, you will have new flowers, seeds, and memories to share with your valentines.

Fireworks from Flowers

Fourth of July can be the start of a sparkling summer. As families look for safe ways to celebrate at home, they are including gardening as part of the festivities. Along with flying the flag, families are growing their own colors in liberty landscapes, patriotic plantings, and freedom flower beds and containers.

Head to nearby garden centers and nurseries to select an array of red, white, and blue floral fireworks. Annuals will provide instant color for this season. Perennials will become the framework for future celebrations.

Some flower heads look like skyrockets exploding at yard level. Cleomes are a safe substitute for sparklers, and mixed with red, white, and blue bachelor buttons and nigella, provide bouquets for the picnic table.

A border of liberty red rocket snapdragons, blue delphiniums, and white hollyhock unites three singularly dramatic plants into a marching band of color.

Red hot pokers, *Kniphofia uvaria*, stand as flaming sentinels. A fence or trellis of red, white, and blue morning glory sings "You're a Grand Old Flag."

A surprising and fun firecracker for evening is the gas plant, *Dictamnus albus*, which releases miniature explosions when seed pods are brushed with a lighted match. Your garden may already contain specimen sparkler shrubs like red rocket crepe myrtle and purple chaste tree.

Here's a shopping checklist of Fourth of July floral fireworks:

- Red flowers for sun: geranium, salvia, canna, verbena, monarda, zinnia, celosia, snapdragon, *Amaranthus candelabra*.
- Red flowers for shade: coleus, impatiens, caladium.
- White flowers for sun: alyssum, cleome, petunia, cosmos, zinnia, nicotiana, verbena.
- White flowers for shade: begonias, impatiens, browallia, caladium.
- Blue flowers for sun: petunias, morning glory, salvia, bachelor button, balloon flower, blue-eyed grass, delphinium.
- Blue flowers for shade: lobelia, torenia, forget-me-not.

Thinking ahead to next year's celebration, consider an alternate to this year's herbaceous tribute to independence by planting famous and historic trees from the "roots of freedom."

American Heritage Trees Project offers saplings propagated by seed or cuttings from parent historic trees across America that have been silent witnesses to momentous events: George Washington tulip poplar, Mark Twain Cave Bur Oak, Henry David Thoreau red maple, Franklin D. Roosevelt Hickory, Helen Keller southern magnolia. For information on historic trees, visit https://americanheritagetrees.org/.

When you spark a child's imagination with a Fourth of July garden this year, you may have fireworks forever.

Celebrating Christmas with Cats

Cats gift us with affection, humor, warmth, and companionship throughout the year. Show appreciation for their attention with homemade holiday gifts from the garden. Whether making presents for the family cat, the neighbor's cat, or shelter cats these projects can be shared by all the hands in the family or classroom.

Grazing green grains
A bowl of fresh grass is a favorite cat snack and a healthy vitamin and mineral source. You will need to sow the seed at least ten to fourteen days before Christmas to have the green gift ready for cats to sample. Purchase quantities of organic rye, wheat berry, barley, or rice seed from the health food store. Germinate seed in small plastic bowls filled with potting soil on the windowsill or porch, one tablespoon per crop. Grass is best eaten when four to six inches tall.

Catnip yule log
A log-shaped catnip toy sends any cat into fits and frenzies on the floor. Cut colorful cotton fabric or felt into five-by-three-inch pieces for each log. Fold fabric pieces lengthwise and inside out before sewing a half-inch seam along two side seams, leaving one small seam open. Turn log right side out to show pattern. Alternately stuff log with a pinch of dried catnip and an inch of fiber fill or cotton balls until the log is full to the opening. Stitch the seam closed. Let the good times roll!

Stocking catnip toy
The holiday stocking catnip toy is a variation of the Yule log. Use baby stockings instead of fabric pieces. Fill the stockings alternately with fiber fill or cotton balls and dried catnip. Close the stocking with a bright ribbon or yarn or stitch closed. Dangle from the branches of a cat's Christmas tree.

Catnip rolling ornament
The rolling motion of the ball and its contents drives cats wild. Use recycled clear round plastic knee-high containers or one-and-a-half-inch plastic globe ornaments from the craft store, colorful foil spangles, and dried catnip. Make a hole in the sphere with an awl so scent is released. Sprinkle one tablespoon each of dried catnip and spangles inside globe and snap closed tightly. Cats will take it from there.

Feline sleep pillow
A chamomile dream pillow placed in the cat's bed to deter fleas can assure everyone of pleasant dreams. Cut two five-inch squares of cotton fabric for each dream pillow. Sew the two pieces of fabric squares together face to face, leaving a two-inch opening for stuffing. Insert a three-quarter-inch layer of fiberfill

Ferdi found his yule log and catnip globe ornaments.

inside the pillow. Sprinkle a quarter cup of dried chamomile onto the fiberfill and shake to distribute. Sew the seam closed. Place pillows in the cat's many napping spots.

Rosemary tea rinse
Your cat will contribute herbal essence to holiday events with a rosemary rinse. This natural bath rinse serves as a conditioner and flea repellent for cats. To make rosemary tea bath rinse pour two cups of boiling water over two or three sprigs of rosemary or one teaspoon of dried rosemary. Allow the tea to cool to room temperature. Use as a final rinse after the cat's regular bath.

Cat kisses
Mix one can of cat food and a pinch of dry catnip in blender or food processor to consistency of frosting. Place mixture in plastic bag or cookie press and squeeze "kisses" onto cookie sheet. Bake at 300 degrees for approximately fifteen minutes or until set. Cool and refrigerate until treat time. Enjoy the sensory delights of the season along with your feline friends.

Ms. Slither Trims a Holiday Tree

Students and teachers in the midlands are familiar with Ms. Slither, the captive-bred corn snake, a red rat snake. The education snake visits classrooms and nature camps answering questions about reptilian anatomy and physiology. How can a snake hear with its body, smell with its tongue, and climb without arms or legs? She demonstrates how snakes swallow prey larger than their heads and keep the rodent population under control in school and home gardens.

Ms. Slither's vivarium, a repurposed aquarium with screen cover, simulates her natural habitat. Rather than leaf litter, the floor is aspen bedding. A heavy water dish large enough to submerge her body mimics a pond. A Y-shaped limb provides a climbing gym and a faux hollow log offers a hideout.

In the wild Ms. Slither and rat snake kin are found in woodlands, rocky hillsides, meadows, farm fields, and residential gardens. These carnivores may enter corncribs, barns and abandoned buildings where prey like mice and rats can be found. In the garden they pursue frogs, toads, and lizards too. Snakes often live underground in the tunnels of rodents but they are good climbers and can easily slither up trees.

At holiday time Ms. Slither uses natural objects found in her native habitat to make decorations for her tree and encourages students to do the same for animals housed in their classroom.

What natural ornaments come from Ms. Slither's habitat for her holiday tree? Deciduous and pine woodlands provide raw materials for ornaments. Start with oak acorns. Take off the cap of six to twelve acorns and place them in a wreath-like circle. Use carpenter's glue between each cap. After the glue dries, wrap the acorn cap wreath around a bough on the tree. Similarly, make wreath rings of acorns, pecans, or hickory nuts dotting glue between each nut. When all dries, add the nut wreath to the tree.

The dry pods of many summer annuals and perennials are decorative, needing only a ribbon or raffia to fasten to the tree: milkweed, love-in-a-mist, money plant, Chinese lantern, heart vine, rose hips, cotton bolls and okra. Dry flowers of globe amaranth, yarrow, bachelor button, strawflower, lavender, tansy, and celosia add everlasting multi-colored lights. Trees and shrubs contribute pinecones, popcorn tree pods (tallow tree), magnolia seedpods, sweet gum balls, and hearts-a-burstin' seedpods adding shape and textural variety to Ms. Slither's natural tree ornaments.

Corn snake dorsal scales are red-orange and match the color of pine needles and autumn leaves. Rake up a pile of pine needles to make miniature pine needle dolls or pine straw brooms. Press and hang colorful autumn sweet gum, pistache, dogwood, and maple leaf ornaments.

When the limbs of dead trees are cut into thin slices, they make ornaments called tree cookies. Drill a quarter-inch hole in the top of the tree cookie, thread with colored yarn and its ready to hang on Ms. Slither's tree.

Leaf litter isn't the only groundcover a snake encounters. In some areas reindeer lichen covers logs or the ground in oak-pine litter. Reindeer lichen looks like moss but is a fungus and algae composite. The spongy blue-green lichen can cover Styrofoam balls if attached with dressmaker pins making lightweight spheres to tuck among the evergreen boughs.

Ms. Slither has made a garland for her tree. She's been working on it all year. As snakes eat they grow; as they grow they shed their skin. The outer skin is made of clear keratin, the same material as our fingernails. Starting at the head she slithers out of her old skin revealing a bright and shiny new one. At forty-four inches long Ms. Slither has shed her skin four times this year, enough skins to make a silvery-scaled garland for around the holiday tree.

What natural ornaments come from the native habitat of critters in your classroom for their holiday tree?

Ms.Slither molts her skin as she grows.

Gateways to Gardening with Children

SECTION FOUR

RECREATION IN THE GARDEN

*"Happy hearts and happy faces, Happy play in grassy places--
That was how in ancient ages, Children grew to kings and sages."
Robert Lewis Stevenson*

Chapter 1
Games

"We do not stop playing because we grow old; we grow old because we stop playing." Ben Franklin

Circling Around the Yard in a Maze

Going around in circles is a familiar complaint of adults. In contrast, children delight in running around in circles, especially outdoors in the garden. So as a symbol of the hurried life of parents and a celebration of the wild abandon of childhood, join hands with your offspring in designing, building, and using a maze garden.

Mazes have a 5,000-year history. Their serpentine circuitry satisfies human desires for security, surprise, exploration, enclosure, meditation, exercise, problem solving, and happy endings.

The first recorded mazes were in Egypt and were made of stone. On the isle of Crete stand the remains of an ancient maze resembling the prison of the Minotaur in Greek mythology. In the Middle Ages monks wandered along mazes as they read. During the Renaissance, European gardens had hedge mazes of yew, boxwood, and privet.

Louis XIV of France commissioned the *avant-garde* of maze gardens at the Palace of Versailles to be used in the education of his oldest son. Passageways, arbors, and alcoves illustrated the fables of Aesop with thirty-nine fountains and over three hundred animal statues.

Your maze can be scaled to fit your "palace" and can be made of stone, trees, shrubs, herbs, flowers, grass, and even farm crops such as corn. Corn mazes are popular in rural areas where farmers cut pathways through the fields, carving a maize maze. Large lawns and wildflower meadows can be mowed into meandering mazes. Mazes require adequate space to combine concentric passageways with plantings. The smallest size maze recommended for a home landscape is a diameter of eighteen feet with three concentric pathways with paths two feet wide and planting beds one foot wide.

To sketch out the maze design on your property, select a sunny spot. Attach a nine-foot clothesline or string to a pole set in the center of the maze. As you walk the string in a radius of nine feet, have a helper sprinkle flour along the curve. You will have outlined the outer rim of the maze. Open an entrance and exit opposite each other by brushing away or wetting the flour.

Roll up the string to six-foot and three-foot lengths to create smaller circles and mark each of them with flour, too. White rings are the outer edge of a one-foot planting bed. Allow one or two openings in each bed to walk from section to section. Prepare the beds by digging up and pulling out weeds and unwanted grass. Loosen the soil to a depth of at least a foot. Work a two-inch layer of aged manure into the bed before planting.

Evergreen shrubs such as boxwood, holly, cleyera, azalea, and even camellias create enduring mazes. These plants can grow large in height and width, something to consider when planning the project.

A flower maze is well suited to back yards. Which flowers are the best maze-makers? Look for tall study stems and bright long-lasting blossoms hardy for your garden zone. Cleome, cosmos, marigold, monarda, snapdragon, sunflowers, and tithonia meet the challenge. Produce a swirling pinwheel of color and texture by alternating seeds or bedding plants. Add scent surprises by infusing turning points or alcoves with herbal fragrance from sweet Annie, lemon verbena, or creeping thyme.

Corn Maze

The center of the maze should be an open area for resting, reading, sketching, writing, and observing. Surprise those who make it to the center with pots of strawberry and blueberry plants from which to pluck a snack. Some centers have space for a fountain, birdbath, or gazebo while others have thick grassy carpets with stepping-stones or stump chairs.

In times of unrelenting demands on family time and energy, mazes are a wonderful respite for the whole family and for children, perhaps a great place for hide-and-seek and other games.

Explore Nature with Garden Games

Games are a fun way to engage the entire family in outdoor adventure. Nature games stimulate joy and energy toward the beauty of Mother Nature. Here are some games that families can enjoy together:

Firefly Lanterns: After dark in the summer my sister and I would challenge each other to catch the most fireflies, place them in a Mason jar, and create the brightest lantern. After each night's play we released the fireflies, only to play our lightning-bug game night after night. Sometimes we would lie in the grass with the jar up to our faces, watching our glowing captives.

Seasonal Color: Each season has its distinctive colors found among the flora and fauna. How many orange objects can be found in your autumn garden? Who can find the most? Play the game each season with a new color.

Finger Puppets: The cups of acorns come in many sizes, colors and shapes. Collect a variety to put on fingertips as hats or hair. Use washable markers to create faces on each finger and stage impromptu puppet shows from the porch, patio, deck, or hedge.

Whistle from Grass: Find a long, flat piece of grass. Place the blade between your thumbs, holding the blade tightly together at top and bottom like a violin string. The curve of the thumbs leaves a small opening in the middle. Put lips to the opening and blow hard. Crabgrass does well for this game, but different types of grass will make different sounds. As a family, create a grass band.

Leaf Hopscotch: Collect a variety of fall leaves--persimmon, blackjack oak, sycamore, tulip poplar, sassafras, loblolly pine, mockernut hickory, dogwood, sweetgum, magnolia, and white oak, for example. Draw enlarged leaf shapes on the driveway or sidewalk with chalk making a leaf hopscotch board. Players must name the tree as they hop and find the matching tree in the landscape.

Scavenger Hunt: Make a list of natural objects to find in the yard or playing field. Twenty-five items is a good start and could include feather, stone, solar trap, bone, male pine cone, petal, five different seeds, thorn or tendril. Provide bags for collecting items. Who can find the most items in a set period of time?

A variation of this hunt is the **Alphabet Scavenger Hunt.** Lists are not provided, only the number of items needed, say three for each letter of the alphabet. A child might collect an acorn, apple, aster, bud, berry, burr, cattail, corn, cone, and so on.

Greet a Tree: This game requires partners in pairs. One will wear a blindfold, and the other will be guide in the yard or forest. The guide walks the blindfolded partner through the area to a tree and helps him explore it. First he should put his arms around it and hug it. Can he put his arms around it? Is the tree larger than he is? Is this tree older or younger than he? Is the tree alive? Are plants growing on the tree? Are animals on the tree? How does the bark feel to his cheeks? When your partner is finished exploring the tree, lead him away from the tree in a circuitous route before taking off the blindfold. Remove the blindfold and let him hunt for his tree.

Music in the Garden: In the garden, forest, or park, all but one member of the family lie down on their backs with eyes closed and both fists held to the sky. The standing family member gives them a listening task. For example, "Every time someone hears a new bird song, lift one finger." Who has the best hearing? Can they count to ten without hearing a bird? Extend the game by identifying the bird from its call. Vary the game by listening for sounds of water, mammals, wind in the trees, or humans.

Parents are the first and sometimes the only nature guides in a child's life. Sharing your observations and insights with children through games opens their hearts to nature. These family times also create lifelong memories like mine, catching lightning bugs with my sister.

Challenge Your Family with a Puzzle Garden

We all love playing with puzzles like crossword, jigsaw, Sudoku, and various versions of Wordle. Gardens share many characteristics with puzzles. They involve strategy, recall, spatial perception, logic, and luck. Play a garden puzzle with the entire family this summer.

Since the 1980s and '90s, the most popular garden puzzle has been the square-foot garden proposed by retired engineer Mel Bartholomew, who said families could grow a food plot in as small an area as four feet by four feet.

To create this type of garden, measure off your space and build a raised bed six inches high around the perimeter. Fill the bed with a mix of vermiculite, compost, and peat moss. Section off one-foot-square planting zones using twine or narrow wood strips. In this space, a family could grow a variety of vegetables, herbs, and flowers.

One large plant, like a tomato, would take up one square foot. Eight to sixteen smaller plants like lettuce or carrots could fit in a square cell. Runner plants such as cucumber, melon, and squash could grow upward on vertical supports.

The close-encounter cropping had numerous advantages. Plants could be watered by hand, which conserves water. Dense foliage prohibited weeds getting the upper hand. Plants could be tended outside the bed to avoid compaction of soil. Yield for the space was much higher than for row gardens. And when one crop expired, new soil was spread on the surface of the square and another crop was sown.

The 21st-century modification of the square-foot garden is the Sudoku puzzle garden. This garden is laid out in squares, with or without raised beds. A nine-by-nine-foot plot must be sectioned into eighty-one planting cells. The prerequisite to planning the garden is having played Sudoku as a family. The family selects one of their completed puzzles as the garden game board or an incomplete Sudoku that can be solved as the garden is planted.

Brainstorming sessions can help determine the criteria for placing plants in certain cells. Setting out the number of plants in each cell according to the puzzle's solution is one factor to consider.

To make the game more interesting, try a pancake Sudoku using nine cereal grains, such as oats, corn, barley, rice, buckwheat, quinoa, millet, wheat, and rye. Assign each grain a number from one to nine. Plant the crops to play out according to the numbers in the puzzle. Of course, you will eat your puzzle pieces as you harvest and grind the grain into flour for pancakes, cookies and muffins.

A colorful cut-and-give-away bouquet garden might include snapdragons, larkspur, marigold, cosmos, alyssum, bachelor buttons, zinnia, nicotiana, and globe amaranth. A child's garden of doll-sized bouquet flowers for make-believe could include candytuft, linaria, alyssum, violets, viola, forget-me-nots, signet marigolds, lobelia, baby's breath, and dianthus.

Planting a garden puzzle will be a mental, physical, and social challenge for the whole family. And in the garden, one can always pick up the pieces and start again the next day, the next season, or the next year.

Spelling and Vocabulary Grow with Scrabble® Gardening

Whether used for rainy day recess, review for a spelling test, or to assess understanding of vocabulary, school children will dig Scrabble® Gardening.

Scrabble® Gardening, a crossword board game with a garden theme, adds a new dimension to indoor and outdoor plant study and gardening with children. With the integration of gardens into school curriculum, the game is a perfect vehicle for practicing spelling, word meanings, prior knowledge, and understandings about plants and their environment.

The Game Plan

The game, recommended for ages eight and up, is played on a flat surface with a traditional Scrabble® game board framed around the edges with a garden scene. As many as four players can play with the wooden letter tiles and tile racks in each game. Letter tiles are stored in a brown gardener's tool tote bag.

As in the original Scrabble®, players compete for the highest score by making and linking words onto squares with letter tiles marked with different points. Some squares give bonus double and triple letter and word scores. Children enjoy the competition and score keeping too.

Seed Packet Cards and Bonus Point Cards

Along with traditional letter tiles, the game adds two new features: twenty-six seed packet cards and four bonus point cards for the use of gardening words.

At the beginning of the game each player selects seven letter tiles for spelling words. He also receives three seed packet cards to place upright in the letter rack. The card is divided into three horizontal zones.

At the top of each card is a garden vocabulary word including propagate, biennial, and drought. A picture illustrates the word in the middle of the card. The bottom zone of the card states a move the player can choose to make--for example, "Extend a word on the board. Get a Double Word Score."

Cards are replenished as used so there are always three in a player's rack. A teacher and class could create sets of seed packet cards with the three zones and gardening tips targeting their specific plant and garden program.

The back of each card gives a Gardening Tip pertaining to the vocabulary word.

The bonus point cards list the number of points earned if a gardening word is spelled on the board. Word length determines points received.

Relaxing the Rules

Scrabble® Gardening relaxes the rules of traditional Scrabble®. Players may use common and Latin scientific plant names. Garden tool and garden technique words like spade, tiller, prune, and compost earn extra points depending on the length of the word. Names of public gardens like Chicago Botanic Garden or Winterthur are acceptable as are proper names of famous gardeners, horticulturists, and plant scientists like Carver, Burbank, or Mendel.

If the students decide on it prior to playing, local garden centers or local garden experts and extension agents could be named on the board. Even acronyms for gardening societies like ARS for the American Rose Society and products like NPK on fertilizer get extra bonus points.

Scrabble® Gardening grows more than academic knowledge. The crossword game fosters camaraderie, collaboration, and conversation among participants.

Some schools may consider adding a concrete outdoor Scrabble® Gardening game board to the playground near hopscotch and shuffleboard courts.

Inclement weather may dampen your outdoor school gardening plans, but Scrabble® Gardening provides an indoor forecast for growing fun, friendship, and facility with words.

Weather Detectives

The results of weather and atmospheric elements and events are everywhere in the garden affecting animals, plants, soil, and the sky.

Erosion, die-back of vegetation, seed-pod formation, dewdrops on leaves, leaf color, decay, germination, photosynthesis, and dormancy are weather dependent. Gardeners use weather-related vocabulary such as "heat zone map," "hardiness zone," "last frost date," "drought tolerant," and "pruning time." Weather includes air, soil, and water temperature, as well as humidity, air pressure, cloud cover, precipitation, and the direction and speed of wind.

Our senses are basic instruments used to detect weather phenomena. Skin feels temperature and moisture in the air. Ears respond to air pressure. We observe the rate at which clothes dry outdoors because of relative humidity. Cloud cover signals changing conditions. We smell rain and comment on the scents of the season. We observe, feel and sometimes, taste precipitation.

Add a few weather instruments to enhance sensory acuity and you and your child can become weather detectives in the garden year round. Finding and monitoring elements of weather have the added benefit of supporting school skills of observing, questioning, measuring, recording, graphing, comparing, analyzing, predicting, and interpreting data.

A backyard weather station might include an outdoor thermometer in Celsius and Fahrenheit, soil thermometer, rain gauge, wind vane or weather sock, cloud chart, and blank calendar or journal for recording measurements.

Use the outdoor weather thermometer to measure the air and water temperature at various times of day, in sun and in shade, and at different locations. Over time, you may find microclimates in the garden.

With a soil thermometer, compare the differences between solids (soil) and fluids (air and water). Soil temperature is important when planting seeds. By graphing the differences in soil, water, and air temperatures over time, you will have the data to compare with local forecasts and the farmer's almanac, and for drafting science fair experiments.

The rain gauge should be mounted on a post with open access to the sky but no runoff from roof or trees. Monitor the gauge within a twenty-four-hour period. Post rainfall amounts on your calendar or bar graph. Compare your rainfall readings to those of local meteorologists. The variance may surprise you and lead to further inquiry. What happens to the precipitation in connection with the wind, temperature, clouds, and pollution is a clue to the water cycle in your back yard.

Windsocks measure wind direction at ground level. Cone-shaped ground-level socks are used by airports, at rail yards, oil and gas refineries, and on farms. Windsocks are easy to make from patterns and nylon fabric. Since changes in wind direction signal approaching weather systems, windsocks are good indicators of impending changes. Record wind directions and changes in a journal.

Observing cloud types and cloud cover give clues to current and future weather. Cloud charts and field guides are useful in cloud study. Stretch out on the lawn to observe cloud choreography. Hold up a picture frame to view a cloud video. Contrails from airplanes are considered clouds, too. Sketch clouds in your journal. What correlations exist between air temperature and cloud-cover data? What correlations exist between rain-gauge readings and cloud type and cover?

Compare local weather forecasts to what you and your weather detectives observe happening in your garden.

Cloud Choreography

Chapter 2– Crafts

"The hand is the instrument of intelligence. The child needs to manipulate objects and to gain experience by touching and handling."
Maria Montessori

Branching Out with Trees

Neighborhoods where I live are fortunate to have trees as the backdrop for the drama of daily life including an abundance of tall and stately trees that have seen the city's history as it happened. The onset of tree planting season officially begins in South Carolina on Arbor Day, the first Friday in December.

Trees provide children with the raw materials for making a variety of gifts and decorations, especially during holiday seasons:

- Pine straw whisk brooms for the car or hearth are simple to make. Gather pine straw into bundles about two inches in diameter at the sheath end. Tightly wrap a wide rubber band around the sheaths to secure. Add holiday fabric bows. Short brooms can become longer hearth brooms by inserting a dowel handle into the sheaths.
- Persimmons hang from branches like orange drop earrings. Collect persimmon fruits to prepare persimmon bread. Wash fruit and extract the seeds from the pulp by hand or with a foley mill. One cup of pulp substitutes for pumpkin in your favorite pumpkin nut bread recipe.
- Walnut and pecan shells can become Christmas mice. Fill half shells with fiberfill or cotton balls and cover with holiday fabric. Glue felt ears and nose to the front of the shell and a yarn tail to the back. Use a marker to make eyes. Glue a gold or silver loop of string to the shell and hang as an ornament.
- The *Liquidambar* tree commonly known as sweet gum has star-shaped leaves of red and amber in the fall. The gumballs are seed pods, which can be transformed with glitter, glue, and spray paint into tree and wreath ornaments.
- Leaves from most deciduous trees such as oaks, maples, dogwood, sweet gum, sycamore, and river birch can be used in crafting holiday cards or leaf identification game cards. To work with leaves, first press and dry them between pieces of newsprint. To spray paint a design you will need a toothbrush, tempera, and a screen tacked to a frame. Arrange the dry leaves on card stock paper or parchment, and place the screened frame over the leaf arrangement. Then dip the toothbrush into the tempera and rub the brush across the screen to spray around the edges of the leaves. A leaf silhouette remains.
- To make leaf prints, brush the underside of dry

Pine Straw Whisk Broom

leaves with tempera and firmly press the painted surface onto craft paper with a rubber roller or rolling pin.
- Bark shed by the river birch tree can be used for table menu scrolls and place name cards. Children can decorate the dry bark with magic markers, then use gel pens and calligraphy pens to list the menu inside the scroll and print guest name outside. Scrolls may be tied with longleaf pine needles.
- Pignut and mockernut hickory leaves are bright yellow in autumn. Beneath the trees are hundreds of fallen hickory nuts. After reading *Miss Hickory* by Carolyn S. Bailey, children want to make Miss Hickory nut dolls. Here's a simple version. The nut is the doll's head; the point on the nut is her nose. Collect forked twigs for the arms and legs. Use a hot glue gun or carpenter's glue to attach the twigs to the nut. Dress the doll in calico and felt remnants. Miss Hickory can hang from your holiday tree, live in the dollhouse, or dance with holiday guests. She is a prized favor for children's holiday parties and just one of many ways children can celebrate the character they met in a book about a real nut.

While Away an Afternoon with 'Miss Hickory'

Each fall while walking among brilliant yellow leaves of the hickory trees and watching squirrels snatch fists full of nuts, I am reminded of the nature fantasy *Miss Hickory*, by Carolyn S. Bailey. With a little imagination, children can relive the story among the hickory trees in your neighborhood. November is the ideal time to read *Miss Hickory*. The story opens in the season of autumn as Miss Hickory, a country doll with a hickory nut head and apple twig body, prepares for a New Hampshire winter. The adventures of Miss Hickory and her wildlife neighbors -- Squirrel, Crow, Bull Frog, Ground Hog, and Mr. T. Willard-Brown -- take place outdoors from fall to spring.

The author's keen descriptions allow children to visualize and recreate the world of Miss Hickory. Many of the natural objects in the story are underfoot in back yards, schoolyards and woodlands. Excerpts from the Newberry Award-winning book inspire these craft projects:

Miss Hickory dolls

"Her head was a hickory nut with an especially sharp and pointed nose. Her eyes and mouth were inked on. Her body was an applewood twig formed like a body. She wore a blue-and-white checked gingham dress."

Materials needed for this version: hickory nuts, felt-tip markers, assorted twigs, pressed fall leaves, hot glue gun, fabric glue, carpenter's glue, gingham fabric, scissors, pieces of bark, moss or lichen.

Directions: Children draw facial features on the nut using felt-tip markers. Glue nut onto twig's neck to form the doll. Use fabric or carpenter's glue to attach dry pressed leaf skirt or gingham fabric dress to twig body.

Miss Hickory Dolls

Glue small pieces of bark to tips of the feet for shoes. Glue moss or lichen cap onto doll's head. With a roomful of dolls, children can retell the sequence of the story, re-enact Miss Hickory's conversations with her friends, or introduce Miss Hickory to their outdoor world.

Corncob house

"Miss Hickory's house was made of corncobs, notched, neatly fitted together and glued."

Materials needed: dry corn cobs, hot glue gun, nails, wire, plywood, balsa and natural roof shingles.

Directions: After defining the dimensions of the corncob house to accommodate Miss Hickory and sizing the cobs, glue the cobs together, strengthening them with nails and wire. Children can find suitable natural scraps such as bark, pine cone scales, or flat pods for roof shingles to glue onto a balsa platform. Display the house atop a plywood base.

Miss Hickory's dishes

"Her acorn cup and saucer, neatly washed, stood on a shelf above the stove."

Materials Needed: Variety of acorns with caps, MOD-PODGE™, paintbrushes

Directions: On walks in the schoolyard, back yard and woods, collect acorns from a variety of oak trees. Clean acorns with a damp sponge to remove surface dirt and dry thoroughly. Brush a thin layer of MOD-PODGE™ on the surface of the caps and nuts to give a ceramic shine. Children should arrange Miss Hickory's dishes for different social events pertaining to the story--for example, a doll's tea time, a Thanksgiving dinner, or a Ladies' Aid Quilting Bee.

Quilting

"A bright quilt of patched sumac leaves was ready for pleasant dreams."

Materials Needed: a variety of colorful fall leaves, newspapers or telephone books, laminating contact paper or film, craft glue, scissors.

Directions: Press leaves between newspaper or telephone book pages, applying pressure. Paper may need to be changed several times to dry leaves thoroughly. Arrange dry leaves overlapping each other in the shape of a bed quilt for Miss Hickory. Use craft glue to attach overlapping leaves to each other. When glue is completely dry, laminate the leaf quilt and cut with scissors to reshape. Display individual quilts on bulletin board or refrigerator or group together to form one large autumn leaf quilt. Individual quilts may be hung on windows as sun-catchers or used as place mats or doilies.

Write this Lesson on a Leaf

Teachers and parents can collaborate to get children to rake autumn leaves while participating in imaginative projects that encourage writing and language development. Children are intrigued by things like writing on leaves.

There are messages to be made with leaves. Magnolia messages. The large waxy evergreen leaves of Southern magnolia, *Magnolia grandiflora*, have a leathery undersurface covered in rusty fuzz. This undersurface makes an ideal writing surface for brief messages in the form of invitations, birthday and get-well greetings, thank-you notes, riddles and limericks, memos, and poems. Magnolia leaves preserve well if pressed and dried between absorbent material such as newspapers or pages in telephone books.

Leafy letters. While raking leaves, look for the large specimens from sycamore, sweet gum, yellow poplar, maples, and oaks, including white, southern red, swamp chestnut, post, and blackjack. Press and dry the leaves as with magnolias.

Leafy letters are personal letters written on leaf stationery, either directly on the leaf, around the perimeter of the leaf, or atop a leaf rubbing. If the leaf is the stationery, the child prints his final proofed copy of the letter directly onto the leaf's surface. Sometimes the leafy letter is a science project about the leaf. Words describing the leaf's color, size, shape, and texture can be printed around the edges of the leaf or upon a template of the leaf. Children trace the shape of a leaf onto construction paper, cut out the construction-paper leaf, and print the leaf's description on the paper model.

A leaf rubbing is a representation clearly showing the vein pattern and leaf margin. Placing the undersurface of the leaf face up on a solid surface and covering the leaf with newsprint or copy paper, children use the side of a crayon to rub over the leaf's surface to see an imprint of the veins and edges of the leaf. The rubbing becomes the stationery, and the veins can be used as lines for the leafy letter.

Pine straw poetry. The loblolly pine contains three needles per sheath, making it an ideal leaf for creating haiku and other descriptive poems. Longleaf pine also has three needles per sheath, and each needle is almost twice as long as the needles on the loblolly, offering a longer writing surface. If pine needles' clusters can be anchored upon marker boards or magnetic walls, children can use portable words to fashion poems. Otherwise, have children make crayon rubbings of the needles and form poems on the needle lines. Initial poems might describe the pine tree from which the needles came.

Leaf-printing on muslin. A leaf-printing activity leads to a particular type of procedural writing. The project calls for a collection of pressed dry leaves and pieces of muslin cut into fifteen-by-twenty-inch pieces. Children paint the undersurface of leaves with tempera or acrylic paint. After they position the painted leaf surface upon the muslin, they lay a sheet of dry newspaper over the leaf and firmly roll the leaf with a brayer. This procedure continues until the entire muslin surface is patterned with leaves.

Pine Cone Dictionary

Hang fabric pieces to dry thoroughly before laminating both sides to create a place mat for the child's home table. Trim the edges of the place mat with a paper cutter or pinking shears. Children can sew yarn fringe along the edges. After the place mat has been created, ask each child to write "How to Make a Leaf Print

Place Mat" so someone else could follow the directions.

Filling a pine cone with words. Pine cones are useful in many ways, but for the teacher and parent, they can be a resource for helping children compile a repository of words for use in writing. Pine cones make excellent portable word holders. As children sort, classify and describe autumn leaves, their words can be printed on three-by-five-inch index cards and inserted between the scales on the cone to be used later in story writing and message making.

Painting with Colors from Earth's Palette

Right under our feet is Earth's rainbow, the first pigments used by early man to represent his world on cave walls, tree bark, animal hides, and human skin. These natural iron oxide pigments have been used for centuries as coloring agents and are mined commercially worldwide.

Take students on a soil safari to collect samples of the many different colored soils on and beneath the surface of the schoolground. Use a soil auger to obtain a vertical soil profile. Students will be surprised at the range of earth tones they find from tan, brown, yellow, grey, and black to mauve, orange, and red.

Soil colors found on a South Carolina school campus

Soil colors are clues to the mineral content and the chemical processes acting on soil including weathering of geologic materials, oxidation-reduction actions upon the minerals, and decomposition of organic matter. The samples are the raw materials needed to launch an investigation of the science and history behind the artist's palette of paints.

In the children's book *Benjamin West and His Cat Grimalkin*, author Marguerite Henry tells how Native Americans taught America's first portrait painter how to grind soil to fine powder with stones and then pour the pigment into seashells. Bear grease, the best binder of the time, was stirred into the powder to form a painting paste. Indians used twigs and grass stems to apply the paint to birch bark.

Today's students still use stones to grind the soil and transfer the stone ground powder to a mortar and pestle for refinement. Sifting in soil sieves or flour sifters can reduce particle size further. Color quality depends on the grain size. Finer grain size usually yields more intense color.

What simulates bear grease? Binders like bear grease hold soil particles together and the paint to the surface receiving the color. Prehistoric and primitive man tested binders from their surroundings – plant saps, vegetable glues, and animal and vegetable oils. Children can experiment with cooking oil, solid Crisco, lard, egg, and nonfat

Earth Pigment Resources

http://forces.si.edu/soils/
http://nrochre.com/
http://www.c-blyth.com/
http://www.webexhibits.org/pigments/
https://naturalearthpaint.com/earth-mineral-pigments/

dry milk as well as craft glue, MOD-PODGE™, and contemporary artist's acrylic.

Mix the binder into the powder with fingers, spoon, craft stick, palette knife, or spatula. If seashells are used to hold and mix pigments, have on hand enamel palette butcher pans to compare mixing platforms. Coated paper plates make inexpensive palettes. Just as purchased paints have color names, students can name the colors on their palettes.

Children can apply earth pigments with their fingers, twigs, grass stems, feathers, bones, and brushes made of hair and fibers just like early man. Brown butcher paper or paper bags can simulate tree bark, and muslin can serve as faux hide. Watercolor paper has a good surface for soil painting too.

Subjects of the paintings are left to the imagination. Some teachers combine soil painting with social studies units on prehistoric man and early civilizations. Others use the earth tone paints in murals or maps of the schoolyard. Making soil color collections can intersect with rock collections from the same area.

Students mapped the schoolground with soil found on campus.

Invite a soil scientist to introduce the Munsell soil color charts, the special standard set of color charts used to name and identify soils worldwide. Students can examine and identify the schoolyard soil samples using the Munsell charts

In South Carolina, when Earth palettes are a project, older elementary and middle school students can explore the commercial mining of earth pigments in nearby states of Georgia, Alabama, and Virginia. Teachers in other states can use similar localized details to enhance students' experience and add relevance to the project for them.

Digging deeper into earth pigments can prompt students to make drawing instruments like chalk and crayons or to tint handmade paper with soil. Encourage children to mine and utilize the rainbow of school supplies right under their feet and at their fingertips.

Peeking Inside Nature's Closet

Fashion designers learn how to create beautiful color combinations by studying nature's flowers, leaves, grasses, bark, clouds, and animals. Each season, the garden and sky above provide inspirational colors, patterns, and textures that suggest how we can complement and coordinate clothing and accessories with our surroundings.

Dressing with nature heightens a child's observation of the surroundings and awareness of how humans fit right into the natural world. A few simple activities can turn daily dressing for play, school, work, and other occasions into an adventure in nature's closet:

Wardrobe in a pile of leaves. After raking leaves, gather a handful to examine the colors against the tops, slacks, sweaters, socks, hats, and shoes in your closet.

Put together outfits that mimic fall leaves. Often by dressing paper dolls in fall-leaf clothing, a child can see a model for assembling his own wardrobe.

Dress like a nut. On a walk, collect a variety of nuts, such as acorn, hickory, walnut, and pecan. Observe and compare the shades of brown on each, along with the texture and patterns. Compare eye, hair, and skin color to the shell. Find and blend clothing and accessories to dress like a nut. Take an excursion to the fabric shop to find fabrics matching nutshells. Make twig dolls with nutshell heads and dress them in tree leaves for a fall-fashion show down the garden path.

Look like a fall flower. Chrysanthemums give crisp, clear colors to the landscape in a wardrobe you can mimic -- orange, purple, yellow, burgundy, and bronze. Or glow like a ruffled marigold in tones of yellow, gold, crème, and orange. Pansy faces experiment with mixtures of purple, blue, orange, yellow, and crème. Green kale leaves fringed in magenta suggest a green sweater with magenta scarf or belt.

Animal apparel. Young children readily imitate animals, so the idea of dressing like animals found in the garden sparks added enthusiasm. Wearing clothing with colors and textures of different species and genders increases awareness and knowledge in a fun way. Wear the colors of a male towhee, female cardinal, eastern cottontail, or gray squirrel.

Nature's closet is always open to us. Just peek outside.

Tie-Dye from the Garden

When a teacher asked me to lead a tie-dye class with her kindergarteners during their study of cotton clothing, she was surprised when our first class took us traipsing through the woods, garden, and schoolyard picking leaves, flowers, fruits, herbs, nuts, and bark to test as potential dyes just like early man did. But home and school grounds have dye gardens waiting to be discovered, to stain your hands, the knees of your jeans, and your garden gloves, and to make indelible marks on your life.

The teacher had expected me to use Rit™, the fast synthetic fabric dye manufactured since 1910. I chose the slow natural dye version because children in an industrial and technological society grow up blind to the processes underlying the products that surround them. My slow method was to foster perception, appreciation, and understanding of scientific processes by replicating production rather than merely making an end product.

Since childhood is a phase viewed by some as paralleling early civilizations and the growth and development of children recapitulates the history of civilization, replicating processes of early man comes naturally to children.

As far back as the first century Roman naturalist Pliny the Elder described plant sources of dyes--indigo from indigo, blue from woad, red from madder, yellow from saffron, and golds and browns from acorns and walnut shells. Many common weeds, wildflowers, and trees found on school grounds today yield parts for the rainbow of colors desirable for tie-dye. Dandelion roots and goldenrod shoots produce brown dye. Sassafras leaves and bloodroot create orange. Red comes from hibiscus flowers, pokeweed berries, and sycamore bark. Fruit of the Oregon grape and sweet gum bark give purple. Dock root, dandelion flowers, and willow leaves produce yellow. Oak galls and walnut hulls make black.

Culinary and medicinal herbs including yarrow, Queen Anne's lace, peppermint, chamomile, sorrel, onions, and fennel exude colorful fabric dyes. Cutting flowers like zinnias, sunflowers, dahlias, and marigolds double as dye flowers. There are the obvious cultivated garden plants that yield wonderful dyes--carrot tops and roots, red cabbage, spinach, and beets. And don't forget edible berries like strawberries, blackberries, blueberries, grapes, and mulberries.

The leaf, flower, or fruit color you see isn't always the color you get when the dye is cast. This makes dying a magical and mysterious process which children love. They are experimenters, and the surprises and suspense build with each new and different plant part added to the dye vat.

The second class involved brewing the dye. Children shredded the plant material into small pieces, exposing more surface area to release color. In this method, shredded plants are placed in a heavy enamel pan and covered with water. Bring water to a boil before simmering for an hour. Strain the dye bath to remove plant material.

Our third class was devoted to preparing cotton muslin to hold the dye. Dyers use a mordant to bind the dye and fibers. The safest mordants for children are alum, a pickling spice, and vinegar. Vinegar is easy to use with young children. Add one tablespoon of white vinegar to every two cups of water. Bring vinegar water to a boil before adding presoaked fabric to simmer for an hour. Lastly, cool and rinse fabric to remove vinegar.

For a tie-dye effect bind the fabric with rubber bands to achieve the desired designs keeping in mind the rubber banded area blocks the dye. Place the rubber-banded fabric in the dye bath for thirty to sixty minutes until the desired color is set. Then rinse fabric in cool water and hang up to dry.The dying process and tie dying introduces elementary chemistry concepts to kindergarteners without formulas and foreboding.

The Asiatic dayflower petals make a true blue pigment

In our classes in South Carolina, older elementary children enjoy planting a dye garden as one phase of learning about the textile industry in South Carolina.

Keeping Fresh Colors Through the Fall

As summer slips into autumn, families who've enjoyed summer gardens seek ways to preserve favorite floral furnishings. Here are some ways to hold onto the colors we love:

Safe and simple preserving strategies prepare flowers, petals, pods, and foliage for their next lives as a table decoration, window or wall hanging, fashion accessory, or stationery. It's as easy as pressing, drying, or waxing.

Children can collect and press plants from the garden. Place the plant between two sheets of absorbent paper such as newsprint or blotter paper, flatten under pressure, and keep in a warm, dry location so moisture is absorbed. Change the paper often. Once specimens are dry, store them in a box or container until ready for use on such projects as stationery, gift cards and boxes, a garden journal, framed floral portraits, or costume jewelry.

- Why not masquerade as a flower from the garden? Children enjoy making and wearing masks or giving them as party favors. Flower and leaf masks are easy and fun to make with half-masks from the craft or costume shop. Replace the elastic tie with a ribbon thirty-six inches long but cut in half. Sew or knot the ribbon onto each edge of the mask before gluing leaves or flowers to the front.

- Air-drying preserves plants in three dimensions to be enjoyed as bouquets, wreaths, or swags; in memory boxes; as borders around frames, jewelry, or ornaments; and garnish around dessert trays. Cover single flower blooms with hairspray or petal porcelain to prevent damage. Air-dry plants in a warm, shaded, dry environment with good air circulation to allow moisture to evaporate.

- Four common air-drying techniques are hanging bundles of banded plants upside down; flat drying on screens or racks; upright drying in containers with two inches of water that is allowed to evaporate; and garden-drying, which occurs as plants reach the end of their growing cycle, set seed, and die back naturally.

- For lifelike flowers that retain color and shape, many gardeners use a drying agent such as sand, kitty litter, borax-cornmeal mix, or super-quick silica gel. Dry flowers face up in the agent and sprinkle the drying agent to barely cover the flower. Check daily for degree of dryness. Once the flowers are dry, shake off the drying agent and store the flowers in a covered box in a dry place.

- Flowers that dry easily and make long-lasting arrangements include globe amaranth, everlasting flower, hydrangea, starflower, statice and strawflower. Pods on balloon vine, Chinese lantern, milkweed, and monkey plant contribute interest to dry arrangements.

- Waxing is a quick way to keep flowers. Specimens are encapsulated quickly so color and shape remain. Fresh and dry flowers may be waxed. Miniature roses, tea roses, sunflowers, and calla lilies wax well. The process utilizes hot paraffin, so an adult should supervise. Melt wax in a double boiler and dip specimens into the liquid wax, then into a cold-water bath to set. Place finished flowers on a baking rack with wax paper or newspaper beneath. When they have cooled, wax flowers make pretty still-life displays and centerpieces.

Grow a Garland, Braid a Chain

When was the last time you sat in the grass linking dandelions into chains? Certain weeds, wildflowers and garden flowers bring out the child in each of us, and before we know it, our hands are weaving, chaining, and braiding fabulous portable strands of fragrance and color. These are pleasant pastimes that are worth sharing with our children. And they afford times to sit and talk while hands and minds are not occupied with things electronic.

Flower Chains. Pick a bouquet of dandelions or long-stem clovers. Slit a stem with your fingernail just below the flower head. Insert a new flower stem into the slit until the flowerhead reaches the slit. Repeat until you have the desired length for a crown, headband, necklace, bracelet, or maybe even a jump rope! For young children the repetition of chaining promotes concentrated effort and also provides practice with fine motor skills and eye-hand coordination.

Among the garden flowers that make longer-lasting chains are clover, marigolds, zinnias, daisies, tithonia, black-eyed Susan, chrysanthemum, asters, globe amaranth and bachelor buttons.

Flower chains are worn by children and adults in Scandinavian countries in celebration of the summer solstice, Midsummer Eve. Females wear circlets of clover and daisies in their hair and males don chaplets of flowers and leaves around the head.

Floral Garlands. Garlands are circles of flowers stitched together for a variety of purposes. Quite naturally, children make them while playing outdoors. Garlands are made to be worn, to decorate for special occasions, to honor a teacher, or to give to a friend.

Whereas chains use flower stems, for garlands we snip off stems at the calyx.

To make a garland, use a tapestry needle and heavy-duty thread (measured to ensure extra for knotting the ends). Divide the flowers into two piles. The first pile is threaded from the flower petals through to the stem end at the calyx. The second pile is threaded from the stem end to the flower petals. Gently press the flowers together while threading to form a compact garland. Knot the ends together securely and your garland is ready to wear.

More elaborate and elegant floral garlands are fashioned into wedding regalia --headbands for the bride and bridesmaids and tiaras for flower girls. Roses and carnations are commonly used. However, in the world of children's play, many flowers suffice for make-believe pageantry. Children can bring their flower garlands indoors as napkin rings, circular centerpieces, and circlets around candles or bowls. And, like flower chains, flower garlands may be worn as jewelry, but also as ponytail holders, belts, and in an assortment of ways only children can invent.

At your child's next birthday party, offer guests a contest making floral chains or garlands. Divide guests into teams, each with the same ingredients. Demonstrate the procedure. Allow time for practice. State the rules for winning, for example, "the first team to thread all their flowers, knot, and wear a daisy necklace chain is the winner." Turn the "chain gangs" loose to have fun collaborating.

The lei. The lei is the floral garland of Hawaii. Leis are circles of natural materials including flowers, ferns, seeds, and leaves. Commonly used flowers are those growing on the islands -- among them, plumeria, orchid, mock orange, hibiscus, bougainvillea, and roses.

Garland ingredients depend on the lei's purpose. The handiwork involved in making the lei is more detailed than in chaining or threading. Different types of leis require diverse skills, including twisting, knotting, basting, pierce stitching, and coiling. The intricate handiwork is especially good for fine motor skill development.

In Hawaii, May Day is Lei Day. Young and old enter the lei competition. Your family will enjoy reading, *A Lei for Tutu* by Rebecca Nevers Fellows. It's about a Hawaiian girl who loves making leis with her grandmother. Follow-up with a family lei-making event.

Time's a-wasting! Much handiwork waits in the garden. Get out into the grass and start stringing floral chains and garlands with your children. And discuss planning a chain link or garland flower garden next spring.

Joining Hands for Wreath Making

Naturalist Chanda Cooper teaches children how to make grapevine wreaths

If the holidays have you going in circles, why not make the most of it?

Give the family circle and the classroom circle an energy outlet for holiday spirit by fashioning festive wreaths. Making wreaths comes naturally in an environment rich in resources. Consider crafting wreaths outside on a deck, patio, picnic table, or lawn for easy clean-up and quick access to nature's finishing touches.

Planning for wreath making with children involves several steps. Selecting the appropriate foundation form is basic. The choice will be determined by available natural resources and size and skill of the crafters' hands. Grape and honeysuckle vines work well.

Searching the back yard, schoolyard, and woods for a variety of materials should involve the children. They will find pods, seeds, cones, berries, evergreen boughs, bark, dried flowers, shells, and nuts to use and to share. The theme of the wreath may determine what is collected or vice versa. Selecting a theme prior to collecting helps focus and organize collecting, but surprises along the way may reframe a theme.

Finally, acquire adequate tools to hold all together. Items needed may include glue guns, craft glues, scissors, floral tapes and wires, wire cutter, twine, raffia, fabric swatches, ribbon, and hangers.

Here are four wreath themes to try:

The Wilderness Wreath

This wreath is a mosaic of natural forms found outdoors. The base is an inexpensive corrugated cardboard donut eight to ten inches in diameter with a four- to-five-inch inner hole. Children use craft or carpenter's glue to adhere treasures like pine cones, acorns, hickory nuts, mimosa or crepe myrtle pods, sweet gum balls, and dry oak leaves onto the cardboard. When the glue is dry, spray the wreath with clear varnish. Add a picture hanger on the back.

Grapevine Wreath

If you have been putting off pruning the muscadine, wreath making is an incentive. After pruning the vine and removing leaves, soak the vine in warm water for at least thirty minutes.

Parent and child create a holiday wreath.

Children will enjoy circling the vine around a coffee can, bucket, or other cylindrical object. Twelve wraps should do it. Tuck in loose ends or tie with floral wire.

This basic wreath is a form for myriads of wreaths. Decorate to your heart's content.

Holly and Ivy Wreath

Reading aloud the classic children's book *The Story of the Holly and the Ivy* by Rumer Godden will inspire a wreath blending two garden evergreens. With ivy being a plentiful, if not invasive, groundcover and hollies a favorite foundation shrub, the greenery for this wreath is easy to acquire. Use a grapevine wreath for the base. Wrap solid or variegated ivy around the grapevine, tucking ends into gaps. Tuck springs of holly into the vine and secure with floral wire if necessary. Tie a bow at the top and add a hanger to the back. Mist the holly and the ivy periodically to keep fresh.

Bird Wreath Feeder

Create a decorative and delectable holiday bird feeder. Using the grapevine wreath as the base, tuck bird edibles into the base, including clusters of berries, acorns, nuts and pine cones, grass seed heads, sunflower and thistle seed heads. Suspend the wreath horizontally with three thirty-six-inch lengths of heavy twine spaced equidistant from each other around the wreath. Alternately, set the wreath on an outdoor table or platform feeder for birds to feast. Replenish supplies as they disappear.

As family and friends visit for the holidays, engage them in making a wreath from your garden to take home to theirs. Homemade garden wreaths make interior and exterior decorations, ornaments for special occasions, and great gifts in any season.

Eggshell Garden Crafts: Useful and Decorative Projects for All Ages

Oysters on the half shell can't compete with camellias on an eggshell. Explore the potential of eggshells in garden crafts for children and adults.

Eggs comes wrapped in a container equally remarkable for the variety of useful and decorative products it can become. Empty eggshells await imaginative forces to fill them up again. Gardeners find eggshells to be an ever-present, lightweight, inexpensive, and green resource.

Eggshell Vases

Eggshells make petite personalized floral vases for individual place settings at formal or informal meals. An eggshell vase of fresh flowers brightens a breakfast-in-bed tray and the recipient. Save eggshells for vases by opening them at the narrow end. Wash and air-dry the shells. Decorate eggshells using your favorite techniques: beading, coloring, collaring, or collage.

Mount eggshells on dime-sized pieces of putty or modeling clay or in egg cups. Just before the occasion fill shells with water and arrange one seasonal blossom or a bouquet of tiny flowers atop each shell with stems in the water. In springtime crocus, daffodil, and camellias work well but there are blossoms for every season.

An alternative to individual eggshell vases is to make an eggshell floral centerpiece by mounting a dozen eggshell vases in a muffin tin or clustering eggshells filled with flowers in the center of the dining table.

Eggshell Ikebana

Introduce children to the culture of Japan by creating miniature contemplative floral arrangements through the art of Ikebana. Fill eggshells with sand or floral foam. Select three main branches of different lengths according to the minimalist line principles of ikebana to arrange in the sand or foam. In late winter children may force flowering ornamental shrub and tree branches to bloom as part of their arrangements. Ikebana may be given as gifts or used as decorations for special occasions.

Eggshell Seed-Starters

The thrifty gardener finds multiple uses for everything. Eggshells happen to make wonderful bio-degradable seed-starting containers. For each of the projects listed below crack eggshells on the narrow end to make the largest pot possible. Wash and air-dry shells.

Pierce a drainage hole in the bottom of each shell. Fill eggshells with moistened soilless potting mix. Add only a few seeds per eggshell unless desirous of a dense effect. Use a spray mister to water when soil is dry. When transplanting eggshell seedlings into the garden, simply crush the eggshell and plant it too.

By starting each season's vegetable garden (tomatoes, peppers, squash) with seedlings grown in eggshells, you'll never have to buy bedding plants in six-packs again.

Eggshell Salads
Cut-and-come-again greens are easy to grow in eggshell planters. Sprinkle seeds of tendergreen mustard, arugula, mizuna, pac choy, mache, leaf-lettuce, or a mesclun mix onto the surface before covering with a thin layer of soil. Regularly snip and sample salad greens to keep them growing. Reseeding may be needed.

Eggshell Edibles
Sow popular sandwich greens like alfalfa sprouts and cress in eggshells. Cut sprouts for sandwiches, soups, and salads.

Eggshell Herbs
Start herbal seasonings like basil, thyme, sage, parsley, chives, and oregano in a windowsill egg carton eggshell planter before transplanting to the outdoor garden.

Eggshell Herbal Tea Garden
Start mints, chamomile, bee balm, lemon grass, lemon balm, and lemon verbena seeds in eggshells. Snip the herbs to make relaxing summertime beverages.

Eggshell Cat Grass
Treat feline friends to nutritious organic wheat, oat, barley, and rye grass snacks grown in eggshells. The curvy eggshell may become a cat toy.

Eggshell Rooting Containers
Root three-to-four-inch stem cuttings from herbs like rosemary, oregano, and basil or houseplants like philodendron, pothos, and African violets. Place cuttings in eggshells filled with water. Cuttings will develop roots in eggshells if water is added and changed regularly.

Eggshell Lilliputian Garden
Creating miniature replicas of nature in an eggshell can be an imaginative journey for children. What might Thumbelina's world look like in an eggshell? What plants work well in minuscule spaces? A carpet of moss might support a seedling pine or citrus. Find tiny succulent terrarium plants like hen and chicks, string of turtles, or lithops for your eggshells.

Eggshell Fertilizer Tea
Wash and dry two dozen eggshells. Crush shells and place in a large temperature-safe container like a cooking pot. Cover eggshells with boiling water. Steep overnight or until the water reaches room temperature. Strain the liquid off to use as a calcium fertilizer tea when watering the vegetable garden. Tomatoes, eggplants, and peppers can benefit from the calcium boost.

Add the eggshell shards to your compost pile or scatter them around the base of plants visited by snails and slugs to deter the slippery slimy creatures from reaching their destination.

SECTION FIVE

ETHNOBOTANY

"Ethnobotany is the study of the interaction between plants and people."
Gail Wagner

Chapter 1
Intergenerational Gardening

"Gardening is an activity that connects people with their families."
Mary Pipher

Reconnect Nature and Your Child

How did you spend your free time in childhood? Many adults recall riding bikes, climbing trees, building forts, walking in the woods, fishing, exploring vacant lots, plucking and eating blackberries, digging a garden, camping, swimming, and stargazing. Will your children have similar memories when they become parents?

Research from sociology, public health, and education reveals contemporary youth are disengaged from nature and estranged from their immediate environment. The Kaiser Family Foundation presents research indicating a preponderance of electronic screen media, including television, computers, and videos, is reaching children as young as six months to six years, a time span necessary for sensorimotor and language development. In a typical day, eighty-three percent of children under the age of six use screen media for two hours.

Older children (age eight to eighteen) spend seven and a half hours per day observing electronic screens.

Parents put TVs in children's bedrooms to keep them occupied, free up other TVs, help children fall asleep, and reward good behavior. Parents use TV during mealtime, too.

Naturalists and fathers Gary Nabhan and Steve Trimble describe the importance of sharing nature with children in their book, *The Geography of Childhood*. As fathers they discuss how human growth is rooted in wilderness.

Journalist Richard Louv characterizes today's children as suffering from a

"nature deficit disorder" compounded by schools reducing or eliminating outdoor recess time and parental fear of abduction of children who play outdoors. In his book, *The Last Child in the Woods,* Louv encourages parents to take their children outside to "nearby nature" in the back yard or neighborhood.

Researchers at the Landscape and Human Health Lab at the University of Illinois found that outdoor play after school and on weekends increased focus, concentration, and productivity of students with Attention Deficit Hyperactivity Disorder. For children whose ADHD symptoms don't respond to medication, the "green dose" from Mother Nature may be the elixir for a good night's sleep, too.

Teachers and parents can make an informal inventory to gather environmental data on their child --

the pocket survey. Ask your child to empty his pockets for you. Do you find feathers, shells, stones, acorns, berries, earthworms, honeysuckle, or pine cones? Or action figures, Happy Meal toys, electronic pocket-size games, gum wrappers, and trading cards?

To restore children's playtime and interest in nature, the National Wildlife Federation has introduced a "Green Hour" for families. NWF recommends parents and children engage in unstructured outdoor play and interaction in a garden, the back yard, a park, or any safe green space where children can learn and play at least an hour per day. A Green Hour website, https://thegreenhour.org/, supports parents by offering activities, explorations, and a blog to share ideas and experiences with others. Unplug the electronics and reconnect with the natural outlet.

Gardening Binds Generations

Many gardeners associate early memories of gardening with a grandparent who seeded their interest by growing fruits, flowers and vegetables outdoors or houseplants indoors.

Grandparents are a significant learning resource for families, schools, and communities. Capitalizing on knowledge of grandparents may be as easy as encouraging student-grandparent scrapbooks on joint garden ventures or reserving a parcel of the schoolyard or community park for "gardening with grandparents."

In recent early childhood research on families with three to six year olds from diverse cultural backgrounds living in England, gardening surfaces as one of the important shared learning activities between grandparents and grandchildren. One case study of a five-year-old girl illustrates how grandparents transmit gardening knowledge to her.

Sumayah lives in a house with her extended family including her paternal grandparents, parents, siblings, uncles, aunts, and cousins. Their fruit and vegetable garden is an essential part of the family's food supply. All family members contribute to the garden overseen by the grandparents.

Through Sumayah's scrapbook, interviews, and videotapes, we can see clues to how she learns garden savvy from her grandparents.

Identifying plants: When harvesting produce alongside her grandmother, Sumayah appears to know the difference between useful plants and weeds. Her scrapbook contains many plant names. She has planted trees with her grandparents and identifies their names by the leaves. She identifies apple and pear trees and pumpkin, tomato, and potato plants.

Understanding conditions of growth: Sumayah surveys plants and knows which need water. She and her grandmother hold the watering can together, so that Sumayah learns how to position the spout and how much water to pour on each plant. Grandmother informed her of plants not to water and why. Sumayah experiences firsthand the effects of sunlight, soil type, and temperature on plant growth.

Stages of plant growth: When watering a patch of bare ground, Sumayah indicated knowledge that seeds will sprout if watered, by saying, "These are gonna grow." She observed two pumpkin seedlings of different sizes and commented that the shorter had stopped growing. She pointed out "new" leaves on the lemon tree. She noted color changes of apples growing on the same tree.

Garden maintenance: Sumayah cares for her plants and for those of family members. She and other children in the family take turns using the watering can as they learn to work as a team to achieve goals.

Sumayah's story of intergenerational learning resonates beyond the home garden to the school and community. The study found that the intergenerational learning activities in a family garden supported and extended the national school science objectives in England without and beyond the limits of an indoor classroom.

Reference:

Ruby, M., Kenner C., Jessel, J., Gregory, E. and Arju, T. "Gardening with Grandparents: An Early Engagement with the Science Curriculum." *Early Years - An International Journal of Research and Development.* 27, no.2 (2007): 131-144.

Jozefine's Catering Garden

Step out the back door of Jozefine Mikolajcxyk's brick bungalow and be greeted by grapes. A backyard vineyard supplies enough grapes to make fifty or more bottles of grape liqueur annually.

Step down into the back yard and you are in a central European potager garden of vegetables, herbs, and fruits. Plants nestle tightly together like passengers on rush hour trains. The biointensive organic method produces high yields and minimal waste. No doubt Jozefine learned and practiced intensive gardening in her native Poland.

Kohlrabi becomes coleslaw.

Small space is bountiful on harvest. A plot no larger than fifteen feet on all sides contains cucumbers, tomatoes, green and yellow beans, kohlrabi, dill, and sorrel.

Every plant has a culinary commitment. Kohlrabi becomes cole slaw. Tomatoes are sliced fresh, stewed, or served as a sauce. Josephine uses dill in making pickles and for flavoring and decorating food. But dill is her companion gardener in controlling pests too. Dill not only attracts a number of beneficial insects to the garden, but it also provides beneficial growth nutrients to cucumbers, kohlrabi, and tomatoes. Conversely, the beans support the growth of dill. Sorrel, an herb with a lemony tang, is used in soups, stews, salads, and sauces, as well as with fish.

Fruit weaves throughout the garden. Black and red currant bushes form a fence. The black currants are eaten fresh and coated in sugar. Red currants are made into jelly. Several different strawberry cultivars are grown. When I saw them the raspberries had fruited out for the season but the pear tree was heavy with fruit for fall.

I had fun hearing the names of foods in Polish such as *poziomka* for wild strawberry, *winogron* for grape, *szczaw* for sorrel, and *kalarepa* for kohlrabi. Jozefine imports seed from Poland. There are numerous Polish heirloom seed sites on the Internet.

While Jozefine is devoted to growing a food garden to feed her immediate household, she caters fresh-from-the-garden cuisine to extended family and friends for parties and special occasions.

Jozefine nurtures a large cut flower container garden too because she loves being surrounded by beautiful flowers…begonia, datura, geranium, cleome, impatiens, vinca, coreopsis, petunia, verbena, and torenia. And flowers keep insect pests away from the food garden.

One of the best fruits of Jozefine's gardening is a new generation gardener. When I was there her granddaughter, Annette, then eleven years old, was an understudy in the garden and a major fan of her grandmother's work both there and in the kitchen. Jozefine had just received a bouquet of sixty roses for her sixtieth birthday. Annette was drying the bouquet so her grandmother will be able to enjoy the roses for many years to come.

The biointensive organic method produces high yields and minimal waste.

Jozefine and her granddaughter Annette grow food and flowers together.

Annette proudly reported that her grandmother had 11,000 social networking friends reading and testing her recipes. Josephine's website is part of Nasza-klasa.pl, a Polish social networking service similar in concept to Classmates and Facebook. Her posts are only in Polish but she is considering publishing a book of recipes, which should be printed in many languages.

The pleasures of Jozefine's catering garden feed the senses, body and soul of family and friends near and far.

Grow A Family Floral Clock

Add a new dimension to the family timetable by living on flower time and growing a floral clock.

The idea of floral clocks emerged in the eighteenth century. Carl Linnaeus, Swedish botanist and father of modern taxonomy, observed that flowers opened and closed under three sets of different circumstances. Some open and close in response to weather. Some open and close in response to length of day. Some have set times for opening and closing unaffected by weather or day length.

Growing up Gardening

Intrigued by the observation that some flowers adhered to a clocklike fixed schedule of opening and closing, Linnaeus introduced the idea of floral clocks in *Philosophia Botanica* in 1751. He researched the opening and closing times of native wildflowers he observed in landscapes around Sweden and illustrated a circular living clock placing the flowering plants at the hour of the day they opened.

Schedule an evening primrose party to watch the flowers open.

Over the centuries scientists have discovered much more about the circadian rhythms of plants first noticed by Linnaeus. A complex set of factors combine to signal a flower's opening and closing. They include cell biology, light, temperature, weather, and evolutionary adaptations.

Setting Your Floral Clock

Select a sunny location for your clock. In essence you are creating a sundial with flowers. Many clock flowers keep time only with exposure to sun.

When making the family's first floral timepiece, place plants in portable pots to make easy adjustments for latitude and seasonal changes in light. After carefully watching and recording the opening times of flowers and fine–tuning placement of plants the first year, specimens can be installed permanently the second year.

Morning Glories open at 6 a.m. and close by noon.

Join hands and form a circle in the site selected. The circle could be three to six feet in diameter. Mark the circle with a garden hose or flour before preparing the soil.

Divide the circle into twelve sections like the face of a clock. Place a post, birdbath, or sundial at the center of the circle. Edge the perimeter of the clock in rocks or low growing non-spreading plants like alyssum, candytuft, or thyme.

Floral Clock Flowers Shopping List

Flower selections for your clock will depend upon your area's USDA hardiness zone and the close observation of flowers in your yard, at botanic gardens and nurseries, and along the roadside. Times in the chart below are approximate flower opening times and should be attuned to your latitude.

Below is a list of flowering plants in sequence of the approximate opening times of blooms:
3:00 a.m.   convolvulus
4:00 a.m.   blue flax, salsify, spiderwort, umbrella milkwort, dogrose

155

Time	Flowers
5:00 a.m.	buttercup, chicory, corn poppy, goatsbeard, Japanese morning glory
6:00 a.m.	cape marigold, catmint, dandelion, daylily, morning glory, Iceland poppy
7:00 a.m.	African marigold, balloon flower, catnip, St. Bernard's lily
8:00 a.m.	fringed pinks, scarlet pimpernel
9:00 a.m.	catchfly, marigold, moss rose, mullein, sandwort, yellow gentian
10:00 a.m.	California poppy, gold star, strawflower, gazania
11:00 a.m.	calendula, passionflower vine, Star of Bethlehem, sweet pea
Noon	ice plant, wild daisies
1:00 p.m.	carnation
2:00 p.m.	acanthus-leaved thistle, rock pink
3:00 p.m.	vesper lily
4:00 p.m.	English plantain, four o'clocks
5:00 p.m.	jimson weed
6:00 p.m.	evening primrose
7:00 p.m.	evening campion, flowering tobacco, fig marigold
8:00 p.m.	evening catchfly, night blooming stock, night phlox
9:00 p.m.	dame's rocket, moonflower, schizopetalon Milky Way
10:00 p.m.	night blooming cereus

Creating a floral clock requires planning and persistence but the finished timepiece can be an heirloom. Share the seeds with others who wish to customize their own floral clocks.

How accurate will the floral clock be? Only time will tell.

To celebrate the family's accomplishment and to dedicate the floral clock garden, host an evening primrose party commingling family and friends face to face with flowers.

Sources

- Gaber Solar Clock Garden https://photos.truman.edu/gallery/gardens-gaber-solar-clock-garden/
- Koukkari, Willard L. and Robert B. Sothern. *Introducing Biological Rhythms: A Primer on Temporal Organization of Life*. New York: Springer, 2006.
- Lerner, Joel M. "A Garden of Blooms You Can Set Your Clock By," *The Washington Post*, February 9, 2008.
- Linnaean Society of London https://www.linnean.org/
- Linnaeus Garden in Sweden https://www.botan.uu.se/our-gardens/the-linnaeus-garden
- Lovejoy, Sharon. *Sunflower Houses*. Loveland, CO: Interweave Press, Inc., 1991.
- Swedish Linnaeus Society http://www.linnaeus.se/en/about-us/
- Truman State University's Solar Clock Garden at Botanical Society of America
- https://newsletter.truman.edu/article.asp?id=709

Hope Grows in Your Back Yard

It's spring and soon children will be home for summer vacation. Have you made plans on how the family will spend the summer? If not, a children's book has done so for you. *Nature's Best Hope (Young Reader's Edition): How You Can Save the World in Your Own Yard* by Douglas Tallamy, entomologist, ecologist, and grandfather summons the naturalist intelligence in children into action by bringing nature to outdoor spaces at home.

In fifteen chapters eight to thirteen year olds will eagerly invite native flora and fauna to their yard. Tallamy gives a brief history of conservation in America through the eyes and actions of Theodore Roosevelt, Rachel Carson, Aldo Leopold, and E.O. Wilson. He introduces the Endangered Species Act and notes how human actions like biocide and synthetic fertilizer use, deforestation, urbanization, invasive plants, and lawn lunacy have contributed to the decline of biodiversity across the globe. He explains the concept of earth's "carrying capacity" for species like white-tailed deer and humans.

The author's grandchildren provide illustrations too. In his granddaughter's Portland, Oregon, neighborhood, Tallamy and Sofia listed 1,156 trees. Ninety percent were from Asia or Europe. Why does that matter? Native animals need native plants as food. Non-natives don't provide the right food for the native butterflies, bees, and birds. Sofia's surroundings had many trees but very little wildlife. When Tallamy's son was concerned that the red fox and kits denning beneath their porch in suburban Washington, DC, would eat his two-year old son, grandpa reassured that foxes don't eat people and to enjoy sharing the natural entertainment in their own yard.

How can your family feel part of nature in your yard? Tallamy proposes sharing the yard with other species of plants and animals by planning and planting a Homegrown National Park in their back yards. The public High Line wild gardens in New York City built on an abandoned elevated rail line and a homeowner's native plant garden along Chicago's Kennedy Expressway near O'Hare Airport are cited examples. I would add the Lurie urban rooftop garden at Millennium Park in downtown Chicago.

Humans have been moving plants around the world for a long time. In *Good Plants, Bad Plants*, children learn the meaning of native vs. non-native plants. Tallamy defines native as "a plant that has been growing for thousands or millions of years in one particular place." Good plants are natives that support the most living things. Ninety-one native oak species in North America support over 950 kinds of caterpillars. Planting an oak from acorns like blue jays do is fun for children too. A plant from elsewhere is "introduced" and can become invasive. Asian Kudzu aka mile a minute grows a foot a day smothering native oak and cherry trees and goldenrods and asters. Kudzu supports one caterpillar, the silver-spotted skipper.

The chapter "Weeds Are Our Friends" profiles dozens of native weeds to plant in our yards. Search Native Plant Finder and Plants for Birds websites below.

The final chapter provides suggestions on how children can approach their principal and teachers about starting a native plant garden at school to let hope grow in the schoolyard too.

Native Plant Finder https://nativeplantfinder.nwf.org/
Plants for Birds https://audubon.org/plantsforbirds/

Sowing hope one seed at a time

Bolster Your Garden with Family Reading

The garden path leads to the public library. Whether the family is looking to start a garden, research organic methods, select plants to attract hummingbirds, or locate books to read together outdoors, the library is an adjunct to your garden.

Plow through the catalog of children's books related to your gardening efforts and interests. Then harvest a basket of books to take home to read in the garden.

Miss Rumphius by Barbara Cooney presents a role model to make a more beautiful world, a noble gesture for any age.

Grandparents often influence young gardeners through their actions more than their words as in *Grandpa's Garden Lunch* by Judith Caseley.

Eric Carle encourages close observation of one insect and its metamorphosis in *The Very Hungry Caterpillar.*

After picking fresh berries in your yard, read *Blueberries for Sal* by Robert McCloskey or *Strawberry Girl* by Lois Lenski.

Children are delighted when the seeds they sow turn into plants taller than they are. *Sunflower* by Miela Ford shares one girl's experience in planting a treat for herself and wildlife.

Have unwanted critters entered your garden? Add a scarecrow with ideas from *Scarecrow* by Cynthia Rylant or *Scarecrows* by Felder Rushing.

Eve Bunting reminds us in *Flower Garden* that beautiful gardens need not be in one's back yard. Reading round robin the classic *The Secret Garden* by Frances H. Burnett will have your family ordering bulbs from Brent and Becky's Bulbs.

Lois Ehlert has families growing meals together in *Growing Vegetable Soup* and *Eating the Alphabet.* A child and mother order bulbs and seeds each year in *Planting a Rainbow.* Follow the life cycle of a butterfly in *Waiting for Wings.* In *Leaf Man* children catch the falling leaves to create a cadre of leaf men to ride the autumn wind.

Understanding and appreciating the many beneficial and fascinating creatures living among our garden plants can be achieved through books such as *Fireflies* by Sylvia Johnson, *The Amazing Earthworm* by Lilo Hess, and *Ladybugs* by Gail Gibbons. In photo and text, this trilogy magnifies the functions of three otherwise secretive lives.

Bianca Lavies helps you build a compost pile along with her in *Compost Critters*. She captures the process of decomposition and the creatures responsible for recycling yard waste.

Whether books are used as bedtime reading or while out in the beds, your garden grows with amendments from the library as well as from the compost bin and garden center.

Chapter 2 - Horticulture and Human Culture

"We cared for our corn in those days as we would care for a child; for we Indian people loved our gardens, just as a mother loves her children."
Buffalo Bird Woman

Garden like a Native with the Three Sisters

Social science and natural science intersect in the garden. By replicating the ways societies have grown and prepared their indigenous food crops, children gain an understanding of gardening methods, the history and origin of foods, and an appreciation of cultural differences and contributions.

How might you and your children garden like a native at school or home? Enlist the three sisters, a Native American food management system trio to enliven your summer garden.

Throughout North America Native American diets relied upon three staple crops -- corn, beans and squash -- a trio that they called "the three sisters." As legend has it, corn was the tall elder sister with long yellow hair and a green shawl. Her younger sister, dressed in green, could only crawl and was always clinging to elder sister. The third sister wore yellow and had a habit of running off in every direction. The three sisters loved each other dearly and grew closely together so as to never be separated.

The legend describes two organic methods of gardening introduced by Native Americans -- interplanting and companion planting. Interplanting utilizes space efficiently by growing plants in close proximity to each other. Companion planting clusters plants in harmonious relationships for mutual support.

For Native Americans gardening was a way for people to become an integral part of the Cycles of Life. The garden and gardener are affected by the water cycle, nutrient cycle, life cycle, lunar cycle, night and day, seasonal cycles, and the cycle of giving and receiving.

Corn, beans, and squash need a site with six to eight hours of sunlight per day. Add a two-inch layer of compost or manure to the soil. In the center of the area build soil into a mound eighteen inches in diameter and six inches high. Sow three or four corn seeds atop the mound about six inches

Three Sisters Garden planted by fourth graders at Pontiac Elementary School

Fourth grader harvesting squash

apart. When corn seedlings are four inches high, sow four pole or runner bean seeds around the slope in the directions of north, south, east, and west. If beans are planted too early, they will overtake young corn and smother them.

Squash, both winter and summer varieties, may be planted at the same time beans are planted. Squash seeds may be planted in four mounds aligned with the compass directions built around the central corn/bean mound. Squash vines will spread across the ground.

Many native gardens were bordered with sunflowers, also an important native food. To avoid blocking sun from reaching the three sisters, plant the sunflower fence on the north border of the garden.

As the plants grow together one begins to see the benefits of companions. There is less loss of crops due to insect damage. The corn supports the beans and the squash controls weeds and holds moisture in the soil. Beans, being a legume, fix nitrogen in the soil. This is especially important because corn is a high consumer of nitrogen. The planting system packs a nutrient dense and varied diet in a compact space.

Harvest crops as they mature and re-create native recipes like succotash, sunflower seed balls, corn cakes, squash blossoms, roasted pumpkin and squash seeds, beans, or cornbread. Compost garden waste and return it to the earth as Native Americans would do.

A three sisters garden is just the opening act of what can be an inquiry into ethnic food crops and methods of growing them of your ancestry and those of students. The garden is a stage for the ongoing historical and scientific drama between people and plants.

Intersperse work in the garden with stories from *Buffalo Bird Woman's Garden* by Gilbert L. Wilson and *Native American Gardening* by Michael J. Caduto and Joseph Bruchac.

SOURCES

American Indian heirloom seeds often are available at health-food stores. To obtain seeds online, contact the following sources:

Native Seed SEARCH https://www.nativeseeds.org
Seed Savers Exchange https://www.seedsavers.org
Southern Exposure Seed Exchange https://southernexposure.com/

Trailblazing a Garden with Lewis and Clark

When President Jefferson commissioned Meriwether Lewis to lead the Corps of Discovery into uncharted territory west of the Mississippi, no one could have anticipated the wealth of scientific data awaiting discovery. Our nation's bicentennial commemoration (2004-2006) of the Lewis and Clark Expedition celebrated the

Growing up Gardening

importance of imagination, exploration and discovery.

The primary purpose of the expedition was to find a river route to the Pacific starting at the mouth of the Missouri River near St. Louis. But this was to be much more than a canoe trip. Among other priorities such as establishing ties with native tribes and charting the territory, Lewis and his co-leader William Clark were to observe, describe, and collect specimens of plants and minerals.

Jefferson, an avid gardener, envisioned the excursion as a way to find and experiment with new plants at his Monticello estate in Virginia and introduce new plants into the nursery trade. Thanks to Jefferson's foresight, many of the plants discovered grace our gardens today.

After visiting the "western garden" of Lewis and Clark, which still contains the specimens growing where the explorers first came upon them, some families are moved to design and plant their own historical garden honoring the expedition. Those who have not toured the route also can make history come off the page by gardening.

> **Resources available to help you trailblaze a garden at home are listed below:**
>
> **Books**
> *Lewis and Clark: Voyage of Discovery* by Stephen E. Ambrose
>
> *Lewis and Clark for Kids: Their Journey of Discovery with 21 Activities* by Janis Herbert
>
> *Plants of the Lewis and Clark Expedition* by H. Wayne Phillips
>
> *Plants on the Trail with Lewis and Clark* by Dorothy Hinshaw Patent
>
> *The Food Journal of Lewis and Clark* by Mary Gunderson
>
> *The Lewis and Clark Journals* edited by Gary E. Moulton
>
> **Expedition Web Sites**
> www.lcarchive.org
> www.lewis-clark.org
> www.lewisandclark.org
>
> **Seeds and Plants**
> https://nicholsgardennursery.com
> www.oldhousegardens.com
> www.seedsavers.org
> www.superseeds.com
> https://monticelloshop.org
> www.victoryseeds.com

What are some of the plants to include in a trailblazing garden? We'll focus on wildflowers and plants that can be harvested for food.

Many of the wildflowers found by Lewis and Clark are available in catalogs and nurseries today. The plains coneflower (*Echinacea augustifolia*), cousin to the purple coneflower, the blanketflower (*Gaillardia aristata*), and wild ginger (*Asarum canadense*) had medicinal uses by Indians and the Corps.

Blue flax (*Linum perenne lewisii*) is a dazzling bright sky-blue perennial whose seeds germinate in seven to ten days. Although each blossom lasts only a day, plants flower continuously from May to August. The Columbia tickseed (*Coreopsis tinctoria*) has yellow to orange rays with reddish brown base and brown disc flowers.

Elkhorns (*Clarkia pulchella*), named to honor William Clark, have pink to lavender flowers with lobed petals resembling antlers.

This sample wildflower collection is a butterfly paradise. All can be grown in South Carolina. Many grow or can be grown in USDA hardiness zones 1 through 8.

Lewis and Clark also learned about food in the wilderness. The food packed for the expedition was minimal, since the Corps would rely on hunting and gathering wild foods. Natives shared many wild edibles now grown in contemporary gardens. Sacagawea, the Shoshone teenage interpreter and only female joining the expedition, introduced the men to roots of the nutty-flavored sunchoke or Jerusalem artichoke (*Helianthus tuberosus*). The Shoshone mixed sunflower seeds and serviceberries with a relative of spinach called lamb's quarters (*Chenopodium album*) to make a bread.

The first winter the Corps camped among the Mandan, Hidatsa, and Arikara in what is now Bismarck, North Dakota. They survived on Arikara corn and beans and Mandan corn. When Jefferson received seeds of corn and beans from Lewis, he planted them at Monticello and reported on their fast growth cycle and appealing flavors. Today these seeds are available through Seed Savers Exchange.

Sacagawea, introduced the expedition to edible roots of the nutty-flavored sunchoke or Jerusalem artichoke, *Helianthus tuberosus*.

Gaillardia aka blanketflower

Poinsettia's South Carolina Roots

Mexico has contributed many of the colorful cultivated flowering plants in our gardens, including some of the easiest for children to grow successfully from seed. Among them are cosmos, four o'clock, marigold, morning glory, and zinnia.

One plant native to Mexico, the poinsettia, might have remained south of the border had it not attracted the attention of a South Carolinian.

The story of the flower's migration and its influence on two countries is a history lesson to share with children during Christmastide. Joel Poinsett, a Charlestonian and the first U.S. ambassador to Mexico (1825-1829), was an avid amateur botanist. While exploring Taxco, he discovered a plant with "painted leaves" classified as *Euphorbia pulcherrima*. He sent specimens back to South Carolina for propagation at his Greenville greenhouse and shared cuttings with plantsmen and botanical gardens throughout the United States. Bartram's Garden in Philadelphia was the first commercial nursery to grow the poinsettia outside of Mexico and introduced the plant to the public at the first Philadelphia Flower Show in 1829.

William Prescott, horticulturist and historian, coined the common name "poinsettia" to honor Poinsett's discovery.

The wild poinsettia found by Poinsett grows ten to twelve feet tall and barely resembles the ornamental cultivars of today. Thirty years of breeding and selection on the Ecke Ranch in California led to the development of the lush, compact potted plant sold at garden centers and grocery stores. The Ecke Ranch is responsible for seventy percent of U.S.-grown poinsettias.

In 2013 Congress declared December 12 as National Poinsettia Day, a day to enjoy the beauty of the festive holiday plant. The date marks the death of Joel Poinsett, who is buried in Sumter County.

National Poinsettia Day gives teachers and parents an opportunity to introduce history through a familiar plant. *Flor de la Noche Buena,* flower of the Holy Night, is one way Mexican children refer to the plant. In the thirteenth through the fifteenth centuries, Aztecs cultivated poinsettias to extract the white sap or latex to treat fevers and to produce a red dye from the leaves for cotton fabrics and cosmetics. Following the Spanish conquest of Mexico in 1521, Franciscan padres near Taxco began the tradition of using the flowers in Nativity processions.

Over the years a legend connecting the poinsettia and the Nativity was told from generation to generation. The legend speaks of a young child from a poor family who feels upset by not having anything to offer the baby Jesus. On the path to the Christmas Eve service the child picks some weeds and takes them into the church, placing them around the manger and praying. The weeds erupt into sparkling star-shaped blossoms, *flor de la noche buena.* Three children's books retell the beautiful legend and acquaint children with the culture through illustrations and words: *The Gift of the Poinsettia* by Pat Mora and Charles Ramirez Berg, *The Legend of the Poinsettia* by Tomie dePaola and *The Miracle of the First Poinsettia* by Joanne Oppenheim.

Around the World with Aromatic Herbs

My herb and spice cabinet conjures thoughts of faraway places and long ago events. The mere whiff of an herb can evoke a memorable meal: Rabbit stew on a rain-soaked day in Cognac, France (thyme, parsley, bay), my grandmother's Thanksgiving turkey dressing (sage), my mother's beef and kidney pie (cloves, bay, marjoram).

Herbs speak to our first, most primitive and direct sense, smell. A scent is an instant message and memory. The search for mysterious and magical scents from herbs and spices spawned the Age of Exploration. Early explorers found the world to be a highly scented map. Immigrants not only transplanted their families to new places but also brought their native herbs to grow and use in new lands.

Since odors register in long-term memory and scents stimulate learning and retention, why not use the potent power of herbs as a learning tool for advancing knowledge of history and world geography in contemporary classrooms!

Students can simulate the Age of Exploration by growing herbs, drying them, and researching their native habitat and present-day growing grounds. In the process, they reenact the migratory path of herbs now seasoning the globe. Their findings can be represented in herb-scented maps, aromatic reminders of Vasco da Gama, DeSoto, Columbus, and Magellan among other adventurers who for over two centuries of unprecedented exploration charted the map of the world we know.

> **References on the History of Herbs**
>
> *A Kid's Guide to How Herbs Grow* by Patricia Ayers
>
> *A Kid's Herb Book: For Children of All Ages* by Leslie Tierra
>
> *Herbs for Use and for Delight* edited by Daniel J. Foley
>
> *The Encyclopedia of Herbs* by Arthur O. Tucker and Thomas DeBaggio
>
> *This Noble Harvest* by Anne O. Dowden
>
> *Walking the World in Wonder: A Children's Herbal* by Ellen E. Hopman

Each herb is native to somewhere on Earth. However, the native habitat is not necessarily the county known for using the herb in its cuisine or where commercial quantities for worldwide distribution are grown today. For example, basil is native to India although best known for use in Italian cuisine. Today's major commercial supplies of basil are grown not in India or Italy but in Egypt's Nile River Valley. There are many excellent books on herbs that provide historical data for students to use and also direct them to the websites of commercial growers like McCormick, Spice Islands, and C.F. Sauer and the Herb Society of America.

Growing herbs from seed is easy indoors under florescent lights or along walls of windows. Some herbs like rosemary are easy to propagate from cuttings. When seedlings are two to three inches all, transplant to two-by-two-inch pots. As plants mature, students should snip stems and bundle them for drying. Hang bundles upside down in a sunless dry location with good air circulation. A teacher workroom or school supply room might suffice.

Cool hardy herbs for the fall outdoor garden include bay laurel, parsley, sage, rosemary, and thyme along with chervil, chives, garlic chives, oregano, salad burnet, and winter savory.

If growing herbs isn't an option, mapping the world in native herbs is still possible with an instant alternative – containers of dry herbs from the home pantry or grocery store shelf.

When the research on the

Herb Maps

native land of the herb is complete, it is time to share the data through an herbal map. The student draws or traces the native country of his herb on cardstock or drawing paper. He cuts out the map and prints the country and names of native herbs on the map. Then he spreads a thin layer of craft glue across the map and sprinkles dried herbs for that country atop the glue. Allow twenty-four hours for the map to dry before covering the entire surface with clear contact paper or laminating film. Punch a hole in the top of the map to attach a yarn loop or braid in the country's flag colors. Construct a trade route by hanging herb-scented maps throughout the classroom, school cafeteria, or media center before sending maps home to scent kitchens.

The exploration of herbs could prompt your students to establish an herb-and-spice trade zone with herb plants, cuttings, seed, dehydrated herbs, and recipes for swapping with peers, families, community members, and chefs.

Growing aromatic herbs with children brings history to life by opening a memorable route to learning about the distant past and contemporary seasonings.

Hands-On Hmong Farmers

On an educational tour of sustainable environments with the American Horticultural Society, I witnessed Hmong dedication to the land and food production at school and community gardens, urban farms, and farmer's markets in Madison, Wisconsin. For Hmong Americans farming is a lifeline to the land and connection to their culture in southeast Asia. Hmong culture doesn't celebrate birthdays. Instead Hmong say "I was born in the time of planting corn."

The Hmong are a southeastern Chinese ethnic minority from Laos, Burma, Thailand, and Vietnam. During the Vietnam War the U.S. CIA recruited and trained Hmong guerilla fighters in operation Secret War. Following defeat in the Vietnam War when communist leadership assumed control of Laos and North Vietnam, these allies were without a homeland. The U.S. relocated Hmong refugees to the states. The third largest Hmong population in the U.S. resides in Wisconsin.

Hmong gardening knowledge, tools, techniques, and plant varieties are used to recreate distinctly Hmong agricultural landscapes. In the culture each individual is a subsistence farmer growing food for and with their family in home and community gardens. Manual labor with hoes, shovels, and hand trowels is preferred to machinery. Farmers seed, thin, weed, water, and harvest by hand and practice chemical free farming. (Wisconsin has the second largest number of organic farms in the U.S.) Hmong farmers don't purchase synthetic fertilizer or patented seeds. They recycle the seed they brought from Asia as part of the annual gardening cycle. Seed Savers Exchange, Southern Exposure Seed Exchange, and Baker Creek offer Hmong seed.

Hmong children are assigned more farm tasks at an earlier age than North American children. Furthermore, Hmong children now garden at home and school. I visited Badger Rock Middle School's student-made food garden. A contiguous community garden on campus contains Hmong plots.

While aware of "Caucasian vegetables" like rhubarb and asparagus, Hmong grow staples of their indigenous Asian cuisine: arrowroot, asparagus beans, bitter melon, bok choy, bottle gourd, cabbage, Chinese broccoli, cilantro, corn, Daikon radish, Hmong cucumber, Hmong winter squash, lemon grass, mustard greens, pumpkin, rice, snow peas, taro, Thai basil, Thai eggplant, Thai peppers, and turnips. Menus are determined by which vegetables are in season and in their prime. Dishes are boiled, steamed, or stir-fried.

Hmong men engage in edible geography when it comes to a soil test. They taste soil for acidity (sour) or alkalinity (sweet). After soil preparation, they broadcast vegetable and herb seed as we might do with grass or wildflower seeds. By intercropping staples with other vegetables, herbs, and fruits, pest problems are reduced. Farmers build distinctive support systems and structures for vining crops using bamboo or tree limbs and fibers.

Hmong produce has revitalized farmer's markets in urban and suburban Wisconsin. The Dane County Farmer's Market on the Square in Madison surrounding the state capital, the largest producer-only market in the U.S., features Hmong produce each Saturday. Community GroundWorks, a nonprofit connecting people to nature and local food, values the traditional knowledge of Hmong farmers and provides community garden space at Troy Gardens. The Hmong American Farmers Association assists members reach additional markets including schools, hospitals and other large institutions.

Badger Rock Middle School students grow food on their urban farm campus.

While Hmong are as flexible as bamboo and tough as teak, hands-on Hmong are a resilient farming force from whom we can learn much.

Three Students Script a Teacher's Vision for Education

Charles was a late arrival to my fifth grade class of thirty-seven students in Washington Elementary School, Evanston District 65, a large integrated school district north of Chicago on the shore of Lake Michigan and home to Northwestern University. Charles was a tall, thin, olive-skinned African-American with curly hair and hazel eyes. He smiled a lot but rarely talked and always kept his hands in his pockets where he fiddled with something.

He did what was asked of him and followed classroom rules and procedures. But his failure to talk was a concern. So one day when we were away from the eyes of fellow students, I asked, "Charles, what's in your pockets? Can you show me?" He smiled and brought out handfuls of watermelon seeds. Then he told me his story. He had arrived from Mississippi where he had lived on a truck farm with his grandparents. They grew many crops and he helped with growing watermelons.

He missed Mississippi and needed somewhere to sow those seeds to connect to his family.

Evanston was an urban forest unlike the fields of rural Mississippi. However, my classroom was large like a field and we had walls of windows from counter to ceiling spanning half the room, perfect for growing vines. I asked Charles if he would teach his classmates and me how to grow watermelon since he had the seeds and I would get the soil and pots. Water was nearby in the classroom sink.

By teaching fellow students how to grow watermelon, he had to talk to them as well as show them how to grow watermelons. He became our classroom farmer. Although getting the fruit of their labor required the plants to be outdoors, we did have vines with flowers across the counters.

Seventy miles west in fertile farmland of rural DeKalb, Illinois, Chauncey Watson III entered my sixth grade self-contained class from the farm, which had been in the family since 1855. The farm grew corn as part of the Corn Belt Livestock Feeder Association. Chauncey was up before the sun working on the farm before coming to school and when he left school in the afternoon, he had chores until bedtime. Chauncey, a Caucasian of stocky build, curly brown hair and blue eyes, always wore denim overalls. He seemed trained to keep his eyes on the teacher and do everything just perfectly. He was attentive, cooperative, respectful, and a good student.

He shared his love for farm animals and for growing corn on acres of farmland for as far as the eyes can see. Chauncey was the epitome of agriculture in a town obsessed with corn. The first hybrid corn, DeKalb hybrid, was developed there.

Cherokee, a lean Native American lad with high-cheek bones and brown skin, attended the laboratory school at the University of North Carolina-Greensboro, where I was teaching. During a unit on Colonial America, third graders were replicating foods and folkways of colonists. They dipped bayberry-scented candles and brewed herbal Liberty teas using fresh mints and lemon balm. Colonists banned English teas.

Cherokee asked to introduce sassafras tea from the root bark of the sassafras tree, *Sassafras albidum*. The tea was popular in his home and with his people. He demonstrated how his mother and grandmother had taught him to make the tea and brought jugs of sassafras tea for classmates to sample.

The indigenous knowledge brought to classroom instruction by Charles, Chauncey, Cherokee, and each of our students is a pivotal point for successful instruction. Schools are either an integrating or an alien experience for students. Tapping the background knowledge of students makes practice enthralling and energizing for all involved. Plants are pervasive in human life and culture. The interaction between plants and people is reciprocal and dynamic.

SECTION SIX

COMMUNITY COLLABORATION

"Alone we can do so little; together we can do so much."
Helen Keller

SECTION SIX

COMMUNITY COLLABORATION

Chapter 1
Natural History Programs

"Come forth into the light of things. Let nature be your teacher."
William Wordsworth

Riverbanks Nature Preschool: Where Learning Comes Naturally

Young gardeners are sprouting and growing at Riverbanks Zoo and Botanical Garden right along with the plants. As research continues to tout the benefits of being in nature, Riverbanks has started a nature-based preschool to help get young children out in nature at an early age.

Amanda Segura, garden education manager, says the students participate in the preschool from September through May, five days a week. The children are indoors for only a short period at the start of each day to participate in a learning circle and discuss that week's theme. Then the kids head to the woods where there are two forest classrooms designed with youngsters in mind. Each outdoor space has climbing structures, mud kitchens, hammocks, reading areas, class circles, and lots of space to explore and play. Each week the theme and concepts change, but they are always working on developmentally appropriate skills such as social and emotional development, assessing risk, cognitive skills, and gross and fine motor skills. They learn all the same things that would be taught in a traditional preschool but with nature used as the catalyst. They count acorns, identify birds, and form letters from sticks, as well as dive deep into imaginative play. The children really thrive in the outdoor environment.

The classes are led by two instructors and have up to sixteen kids in each class, with two classes meeting each day. Riverbanks Nature Preschool is not confined to the forest classrooms but uses the whole campus as a learning opportunity. Each class works in the vegetable garden, planting, observing growth, and harvesting the produce for their snack. It teaches them the whole cycle of gardening, and helps them understand why they are composting. The kids go to the zoo to learn about animals, walk on the nature trail to explore wildlife tracks, and see how streams lead to the river. The experience really teaches children to be better observers of what is happening around them.

"Some of the benefits of the program are for children to be one on one with nature and to learn to do things which are applicable for the rest of their lives," Segura said. "The program fosters an appreciation of nature and conscientiousness about the earth." Visit www.riverbanks.org for more information.

Feast Your Family's Eyes on Nature's Wonders

Children are endowed with an affinity for the natural world. Even before they walk or talk, their eyes scan and locate objects of interest in the surroundings. Once bipedal they begin gathering natural souvenirs from pine cones to pebbles, feathers to fossils, and seed pods to shells.

Natural Curiosity, an exhibit at McKissick Museum on the University of South Carolina (USC) campus, explores man's penchant to collect, display, and organize nature. Since colonial times, the state has been a footpath for amateur and professional naturalists enamored with the rich biodiversity here. Faculty members and naturalists have contributed to the collections at USC.

Your family will find both familiar and far-out collections. Children will delight in the taxidermy specimens of bobcat, barn owl, gray fox, raccoon, and black bear. The full-length mounted eastern diamondback rattlesnake from Beaufort is the largest of its kind found. Two insect collections give children models for how to properly display and preserve specimens: Rudy Mancke's dragonfly collection and Richard B. Dominick's butterfly and moth collection. Naturalist's tools like hand lenses and the Peterson and Golden Nature field guides are displayed.

The variety of cabinets housing specimens may prompt you to seek new curio cabinets for your family's own fossils, shells, skulls, and rocks stashed away over the years in shoe boxes and paper sacks. Even plant parts pressed between blotting papers can yield a family's herbarium book. An extensive rock and mineral collection specifies tests to perform on your mineral specimens to determine their identity.

The exhibit will inspire you to imagine ways to use and display a family's ongoing collection. After cleaning and identifying objects, children can make display cards for each by hand printing or printing from a computer. Conduct "curiosity chats" so collectors can introduce the details of their finds to the whole family.

The exhibit prompts discussions on how to collect and preserve specimens without depleting the natural treasures. Naturalists kept journals and diaries; sketched and painted wildflowers and birds; and photographed wildlife. On a smaller scale, your family can start to develop a catalog of the flora and fauna in your back yard through field study rather than displacement by collecting.

At the back of the exhibit hall children can peer into a naturalist's office through a set design from the popular *Nature Scene* television series hosted by Rudy Mancke, naturalist in residence at USC. Clues to the naturalist's mind cover the desk.

Naturalist Rachel Carson observed that every child needs at least one adult companion who will share and encourage the child's inborn sense of wonder. After you take your children to the McKissick exhibit, explore the flora and fauna on the outdoor Horseshoe before returning home to revitalize your collection.

Recharge with a Walk at Belser Arboretum

For families with children, Sundays are a good day for togetherness and rejuvenation before the whirlwind school and work week begins. One of the most sensational spas for body, mind, and spirit is the W. Gordon Belser Arboretum in the Sherwood Forest neighborhood of Columbia. Weekdays are reserved for University of South Carolina classes, but the third Sunday of each month the arboretum is open to the public from one to four p.m.

Growing up Gardening

Looking skyward through bald cypress

Come prepared for a green experience like none other in Columbia. Leave electronic devices, food, toys, pets, and bicycles at home. Don your ecotour garb, including sunscreen, long slacks, hat, and walking shoes. A camera, hand lens, memo pad, pencil, and field guides to Eastern trees and wildflowers are useful.

The arboretum is a ten-acre preserve for natural communities of plants and animals. Start your self-guided tour at the Bloomwood Road entrance gate.

Once inside the gate you have stepped back to prehistoric time. The high ridge at the entranceway is evidence of the Atlantic Ocean shoreline millions of years ago.

FIND IDEAS FOR YOUR GARDEN

By following the main loop path, you circumnavigate the property and traverse ten biomes. Stay on the loop trail except to make side trips to botanical exhibits on spur paths. Take turns reading interpretive signage. Jot down ideas for your home garden from educational demonstrations throughout the property. One of the first side trips is Horseshoe Horticulture Grove, where a parade of sixty-eight native perennials is arranged along a rope fence according to sun and shade preferences. In the interior of the horseshoe grow twenty-five species of flowering small trees useful in home landscapes.

Back on the loop trail a seedling tree nursery sparks interest in propagating native trees from seed. Nearby is Chinquapin Glade, a stand of dwarf chestnut trees. "Companion trees" such as fringe tree, dogwood, redbud, red maple, and beautyberry are interplanted in the glade to maximize the beneficial interrelationships among plants and support biodiversity.

Resident Barred Owl

Seasonal wildflowers line the trail. Native azalea, sweet shrub, trillium, mayapple, hepatica, and wild ginger flower in April. Be on the lookout for the cranefly orchid.

In the Valley of Giant Poplars, hug a treasured tree. Count the summer rings on longleaf pine tree cookies to determine the age.

Taking a fast trip along the trail

WATERFALLS AND MICROCLIMATES

Opportunities to reflect come at several points. Longleaf pine stumps provide a place to pen poetry and prose. The Zen Garden is meant for meditation. Let a waterfall melt away tension.

The moist streambed around the waterfall is an ideal habitat for many wildflowers and ferns. The habitat serves as a relocation center for wildflowers rescued from construction sites.

Feel temperature changes along the trail. You are experiencing microclimates of this garden.

Belser is all about preserving natural communities. One eastern forest population of trees, the American chestnut, was threatened by a fungal blight in the late nineteenth century. Into the twenty-first century efforts to introduce blight resistant varieties of American chestnut continue with a promising Eagle Scout project at the arboretum. Just over the boardwalk is a native pawpaw patch. The delicious fruit can be grown in your home orchard. Flanking either side of Arboretum House, a museum and library, is "S and S Grove" of sparkleberry and sassafras, two picturesque native understory trees. The loop trail comes full circle along a high ridge of longleaf and loblolly pine overlooking an ancient streambed now the Bloomwood entranceway. Exit the Belser spa refreshed and ready for whatever the week may bring. To keep up to date on the arboretum, visit https://www.facebook.com/uofscarboretum/

The Plant Circus in Charlotte

In less than two hours from anywhere in South Carolina, you and your family can be under the Big Glass Circus Tent of wonderfully weird plants in McMillan Greenhouse at the botanical gardens at the University of North Carolina's Charlotte campus.

For over four decades ringmaster Larry Mellichamp had been researching, collecting, growing, propagating, teaching about, and sharing bizarre botanicals from as near as the Green Swamp Preserve in North Carolina to as far as Tasmania. The greenhouses contain a lifetime collection from tropical and temperate climates.

Mellichamp's flesh-eating carnivorous troupe includes pitcher plants, sundews, Venus flytrap, and butterwort. You can observe them in any one of four acts-- attracting, capturing, digesting, or absorbing prey.

Plant clowns entertain and make visitors laugh with their colorful costumes and charades. Pumpkins on a stick, *Solanum intergrifolium*, look like pumpkins doing acrobatics up and down the stem of a plant. It is really an ornamental eggplant with pumpkin-shaped orange fruit. Polka dot begonia, *Begonia maculata* var. *wightii*, has circular white dots on the upper green leaves and

White Bat Flower

burgundy dots on the undersurface of leaves reminiscent of clown costumes.

Every circus must have animal acts. The white bat plant, *Tacca integrifolia*, has clusters of black flowers from which two large white winglike bracts spread forth. Scores of thin white whiskerlike bracts trail two feet long from the black flowers. Black bat plants, *Tacca chantrieri*, have black wrinkled fruit that hangs down like roosting bats. Butterfly orchids, *Psychopsis papilio*, dance atop flexible stems like acrobats.

Two woodland ginger flowers resemble animals. Panda ginger flowers, *Asarum maximum*, are black and white with a furry texture like a Panda. The thick waxy flowers of wild ginger, *Asarum arifolium*, resemble piglets, hence the common name piggies ginger. The garden flower *Celosia cristata* or cockscomb displays its bright velvet crest like that of a rooster.

Tarantula Cactus

Spiders fascinate children. The tarantula cactus, *Cleistocactus winteri*, has long furry stems that bend and creep out of the pot but will never escape from its container. If you have had trouble keeping goldfish alive in a fishbowl, try a goldfish plant, *Nematanthus*, in a hanging basket. Floating throughout the waxy foliage are schools of orange goldfish flowers with puckered lips. Mellichamp notes that hummingbirds are attracted to the fishy flowers so you can expect two pets on one plant.

The succulent sideshow is really eccentric. These desert dwellers have a wide range of adaptations to hot and dry conditions. Old man cactus, *Cephalocereus senilis*, uses its spiny silk beard to cool itself from desert sun. Climbing onion, *Bowiea volubilis*, is a winter growing vine emerging from a bulb with stringlike forking stems rapidly growing upward and twisting around anything in a nine-foot tangled journey. Look out!

Lithops are finger magnets to children who must touch the mimicry succulents that blend in with their surroundings. They look like desert stones in size, shape, and color. Above ground each lithop has a pair of lip-like leaves that retain moisture; underground is a short stem and tiny taproot.

Mother of thousands, *Kalanchoe delagoensis*, is a leaf succulent flaunting its asexual prowess with vegetative propagation of baby plantlets in prodigious numbers along leaf margins. As plantlets fall off of their mother, they take root where they land to begin another population explosion.

The aerial acts in this circus are the air plants, the epiphytes. They appear to walk on air and absorb

Pumpkin on a Stick

moisture and nutrients as well as pollutants from the air. Spanish moss, *Tillandsia usneoides*, is a familiar Lowcountry epiphyte to South Carolina but there are numerous other epiphytic bromeliads and orchids under the circus tent.

A barbed wire posse of plants is circus security and comes equipped to thwart invasion. Flying dragon, *Poncirus trifoliata*, has long curved thorns. The prickles of blood red wingthorn rose, *Rosa omeiensis f. pteracantha*, dominate the stem. Devil's thorns, *Solanum pyracanthum*, produce potent spikes on stems, fruit and the midrib of leaves. Bed of nails, *Solanum quitoense*, has equally foreboding spines.

The late Dr. Mellichamp has been called the Plant Whisperer. During his tenure as director of the UNC-Charlotte Botanical Gardens, he and the former assistant director, Paula Gross, coauthored a book, *Bizarre Botanicals*, profiling seventy-eight weird plants for folks to grow at home. A greenhouse tour and the book can give children ideas for their upcoming science fair project.

The Outdoors Were In at the Conservation Station

Imagine a classroom with no roof, no walls, no carpet or tile on the floor, and no electricity! Was there a natural disaster? Quite the contrary. It's a natural wonder!

The Conservation Station was an open-air outdoor classroom sponsored by the Richland County Soil and Water Conservation District and Clemson University in the 1990s through 2011. The station grew out of a woodland setting at the Sandhill Research and Education Center and provided a laboratory for adults and children to investigate concepts and issues pertaining to natural resources affecting the quality of life and welfare of all citizens.

A trail system connected six instructional kiosks or classroom information stations for the study of six natural resources: soil, water, air quality, forests, wildlife, and geology. Each station complete with wooden desks and benches accommodated approximately thirty students. The large wooden kiosk at the front of each classroom had cabinets beneath stocked with lesson plans and teaching materials complying with state science standards.

At the Conservation Station students collected and interpreted data about the natural environment. The textbook was the natural world. In the forestry kiosk students interpreted the rainfall record from tree rings. At the soil kiosk students learned how to take a soil profile, then measure and read the layers. Lichens were used as air pollution detectors at the air quality kiosk. Minerals were tested and identified in geology. Plaster animal tracks were made to identify visitors to the wildlife station. Life forms in the pond water samples were observed, identified, and inventoried.

Designing and developing the Conservation Station's curriculum was a collaborative effort of numerous agencies including South Carolina's Departments of Health and Environmental Control; Natural Resources; Forestry Commission; Parks, Recreation, and Tourism; U.S. Department of Agriculture Natural Resources Conservation Service; and the S.C. Wildlife Federation. Mary Jane Henderson, education coordinator for the Richland Soil and Water Conservation District, spearheaded the structural and educational plan. Americorps and City Year volunteers and Department of Correction inmates constructed the kiosks. Colonial Life Insurance Company created the trail and bridge.

The Conservation Station served public and private K-12 schools as well as homeschool groups. Workshops trained teachers in use of the outdoor kiosks and curriculum prior to bringing classes to the Conservation Station.

Now picture a classroom with the sky and clouds as the ceiling and a star providing the lighting. Textured tree trunks make the framework on a soft earthen floor patterned in leaves. Wind conditions the air. Time is told in the shadows and evidence of wildlife appears everywhere.

Although the Conservation Station is no longer open, it serves as one model for establishing an outdoor classroom. During the pandemic when many school districts in the United States turned to online learning, the National COVID-19 Outdoor Learning Initiative emerged to revitalize use of outdoor classrooms across the country. Teams of interdisciplinary working groups created frameworks, strategies, and guidance on outdoor learning to support keeping schools open safely by using affordable on-campus or nearby park outdoor spaces as classrooms and to improve learning, mental and physical health, and happiness of students and teachers. An outdoor learning library is available online. https://www.greenschoolyards.org/introduction

Wildlife Conservation Station

Your Neighborhood Urban Forest

In the midst of summer one of the coolest retreats from the heat is an urban forest like Sesquicentennial State Park. Whether you choose a self-guided tour along one of the trails or sign up for a ranger-led nature walk, local residents and families can find clues to understanding their home property and neighborhood within the urban forest.

On a nature walk led by Interpretive Ranger Stacey Jensen, families explore the sand beneath their feet as being part of the Sandhills belt, South Carolina's seashore millions of years ago. Fast forward to today and view the diversity of wildlife inhabiting the ancient seabed.

Tall native switchgrass, *Panicum virgatum*, grows throughout the park sheltering wildlife and providing nesting for birds. The common name possibly came from being used to switch horses and naughty children. Today switchgrass is a biofuel candidate.

The native sassafras, *Sassafras albidum*, with aromatic leaves, stems, and root was a medicinal plant for Native Americans and colonists. Early root beer recipes used sassafras root. Since sassafras oil, safrole, was found to be a carcinogen, the Food and Drug Administration has banned its use in food and fragrances. The ban hasn't stopped whitetail deer from devouring leaves and twigs year-round or ripe fruit being eaten by squirrels, wild turkey and quail.

Muscadine grape vines, *Vitis rotundifolia*, climb twenty feet into the trees throughout the park. The southeastern native is easy to grow in the home garden with the proper support. Muscadine vines are tolerant of insect pests and diseases and do not require spraying. But you may have to contend with raccoons, squirrels, opossums, crows, bluejays, coyotes, and deer for your share of the harvest.

Like it or not, lichens are everywhere growing atop the forest floor, on tree trunks, and on rocks. Lichens are composite organisms composed of an algae and a fungus living in a symbiotic relationship for mutual survival. Lichens are often pioneer plants of an area, being the first life to inhabit otherwise barren land. Lichens may be small in size but their value is monumental. Since lichens have the ability to absorb air pollutants, scientists monitor air quality by analyzing lichens. They are often found in association with mosses.

The native prickly pear cactus, *Opuntia* spp., is another wild edible found growing in sandhill soil. Native Americans rubbed off the spines of the pads and fruit with rocks before preparing and eating. The purple pear-shaped fruit is eaten fresh or made into jams, syrup, candy, sorbet, and wine.

Children delight in the animate and mobile critters on the trail, passing among sweaty palms an earthworm found atop leaf litter and eyeballing the undulating walk of a fuzzy orange-and-black-striped caterpillar on a decaying log. They spot a brown skinned anole "camouflaged" on a twig and watch butterflies weave in and out of understory branches. They examine large fall webworm silken webs on persimmon trees, speculating on the moths to come. The bark of an old tree had been riddled with orderly rows of holes by the yellow-bellied sapsucker, a winter visitor to South Carolina.

Besides serendipitous findings along the route, Jensen has a backpack of surprises to show and tell eager eyes and ears. Evidence of white-tailed deer is everywhere at Sesqui. Jensen has a pelt to rub, antlers to hold, and scat to see. She informs that scat is often the best evidence for the larger animals in the park like coyotes, bobcats, foxes, and deer.

In addition to being an ecology lab for homeowners and natural history lesson for youth, an urban forest like Sesqui supplies part of the green infrastructure for healthy community development. Trees cool air temperature and save energy, filter the air and water, help control stormwater runoff, buffer noise, and link the ecosystem of the forest to the encroaching and surrounding built environment where you live.

Visit your neighborhood urban forest and see how cool it is! Sesquicentennial State Park has picnic shelters, RV and tent camping, fishing, boating, birding, hiking, biking, nature trails, and more. For park hours and seasonal programs visit https://southcarolinaparks.com/sesqui

Interpretive Ranger Stacey Jensen leads children on a nature walk.

A Schoolyard Herbarium

Pulling winter weeds in the school garden can be the start of a long-term floristic survey of the schoolyard. Floristic surveys document all the plant species found within a specified area. They are conducted by walking across campus many times during all growing seasons to identify plants and collect specimens. Collected specimens can then become part of the schoolyard herbarium, an indoor dried garden representing the plant diversity in the garden growing outdoors.

Pressing plant specimens in a plant press.

Start slowly by looking at one plant at a time. For example, students might find henbit, *Lamium amplexicaule*, a common winter annual weed growing on the school lawn. The square green to purple stems on this mint family plant hold kidney-shaped leaves with toothed margins. In early spring the two-lipped purple flowers bloom and attract a bevy of pollinators – honey bees, native bees, wasps, flies, and butterflies.

Linnaeus gave henbit its scientific name. Children should be introduced to Linnaeus because the great plant taxonomist is a key historical influence on the work students will be involved in when building a herbarium of schoolyard specimens. They will be able to view the online images of henbit and other plants from The Linnaean Herbarium at https://linnean-online.org/linnaean_herbarium.html

Whatever weed is the starting point, as students observe the plant on campus, they will record significant data in field notebooks--date of observation, location of plant in schoolyard, soil type, nearby plant associates, height of plant, flower color and scent, and identity of insects visiting plant. State wildflower and weed field guides will help identify the specimen. Students should take digital photographs of the plant, which also captures its habitat. Observations and photographs will become part of the documented history of each specimen.

On subsequent outings have students sketch the plant and tint the sketches with watercolor pencils. Sketching adds details that words may have failed to convey, and tinting adds another identity clue.

A field trip to the nearby established herbarium is a must for understanding how to establish a schoolyard herbarium. Residents in central South Carolina contact the A.C. Moore Herbarium on the University of South Carolina campus to schedule a guided tour. On the day of the trip dig up one specimen, from roots to flower, to contribute to the herbarium collection. Bring the data students collected on the specimen too. Students will be able to check the accuracy of their specimen's identity by comparing it to voucher specimens at the herbarium. Your specimen will also be used as an instructional model to show how botanists preserve, label, mount, and file plant specimens on a daily basis as part of their botanical research.

The herbarium curator, Dr. Herrick Brown, or his staff will use your plant to demonstrate the use of a plant press. The specimen is placed between layers of corrugated cardboard to allow airflow, blotting paper to absorb moisture, and newspaper to hold plant material before anchoring all between two rigid wooden lattice frames and tightening two straps around the entire plant press. Students can sketch the process in their notebooks before moving to the drying room. An oven the size of an upright refrigerator set at 110° F is the next step in the preservation process. The plant press sets upright in the oven for one week and is creating a two-dimensional specimen from the three-dimensional original.

Then the dry specimen is mounted with glue onto acid free cotton rag paper. A label with the field data collected by students is attached to the page prior to filing by taxonomic group and geographic region in airtight cabinets. Students can tour the "plant morgue" where their specimen becomes part of the historical botanical dried garden.

Back in the classroom your junior field botanists are now ready to construct plant presses, plan the location for the schoolyard herbarium archive, and continue the floristic survey and creation of a schoolyard herbarium for future explorations.

Healing Through Giving and Gardening

The Children's Center for Cancer and Blood Disorders at Prisma Health Children's Hospital recognizes the importance of supporting children and their families through the diagnostic and treatment phases of life-threatening illnesses and diseases. The Center provides patient support programs.

Lasting Impressions is one support group for teen patients ages thirteen through nineteen. Under the best of circumstances teenage years can be tumultuous with the many physical, emotional, and social changes of adolescent development. A diagnosis of cancer adds stress and feelings of fear, isolation, and frustration. Being the member of a group who listens to your journey of recovery and shares fun activities and service projects reduces stress and fosters positive attitudes. Dr. Julian Ruffin, Ph.D., coordinator of psychosocial programs at the Center through 2017, observed that teens thrive on peer support. Patients remain in the group six or seven years before graduating out. Cancer survivor graduates often return as volunteer adult chaperones.

In the spring of 2014 Lasting Impressions patients conducted a therapeutic horticulture service project for another group of children in crisis. They built a raised bed vegetable garden at the Nancy K. Perry Children's Shelter in Lexington County. The shelter is a residential setting for children placed there by public agencies.

The service scenario was simple. Two groups of youth experiencing pain would come together in a united effort for the common good of all. Ed Brogdon, owner of Back to Eden, a business empowering people to grow food year round for a healthier life, synchronized the service project. Twenty-eight teens were assigned to teams including safety, quality control, landscape preparation, calculations and measurements, sawing lumber, filling beds, pre-assembly, and assembly.

Two symmetrical raised bed vegetable gardens were built. One bed was shaped like a plus sign that stretched eighteen feet in each direction. A second bed, shaped like a couch, was twenty feet long with two eight-feet-long arms. Both beds would allow planting, weeding, and harvesting without stepping on the soil or into the beds. Beds were filled with a soil rich in composted horse manure.

When the garden beds were in place, teens stepped back and children's shelter residents eagerly took over filling the beds with future food. Children imitated Brogden as he modeled a planting procedure of squeezing pots to loosen transplants, using the hand as a digging tool, inserting plant roots downward, backfilling with soil, and washing hands in sand.

Children planted tomatoes anticipated to yield as many as two hundred fruits per plant along with red and yellow bell peppers, romaine, Bibb and buttercrunch lettuces, spinach, stevia, and strawberries. Brogdon and children surrounded the vegetables with marigold sentinels, a natural insect repellent plant.

Ed Brogdon (r) assists children plant the food garden.

Roscoe Moore, housefather at the shelter, managed the garden with the residents. He said at the time the children would love tending the garden and eating salad ingredients they had grown. But they would also share a portion of their bountiful harvests with others in need like at Sistercare, a non-profit for survivors of domestic violence, and Oliver Gospel Mission, a homeless shelter.

In five magical hours of collaboration, camaraderie, and caring, the patients, shelter residents, counselors, volunteers, and mentors experienced the power of healing through giving and gardening.

A Walk on the Wild Side

What better way would there have been to celebrate the end of classes and the beginning of summer vacation than a wilderness walk with the late naturalist Rudy Mancke? He was a teacher, a broadcaster, and curator, whose popular walks ended with his death in November 2023. Students in his Reinventing Natural History class, a seminar on the history of natural history at the University of South Carolina, joined Mancke in the field at the Congaree National Park, the largest old growth bottomland hardwood forest in the southeastern U.S.

Trees and water make possible an abundant habitat for all kinds of wildlife. Mancke noted, "The diversity of hardwoods here will blow your mind. Michaux and other Europeans were overcome with what was here. They must have felt like what we now feel when we go to places like Costa Rica for the first time."

Of the canopy of hardwoods, oak species are the most prevalent with water, laurel, overcup, swamp chestnut, Southern red, white, and black being visible along the trail. Wherever there are oaks, one finds oak galls, an abnormal growth of plant tissue usually caused by an insect. An insect like a wasp lays an egg in the plant leaf. The larva hatches and chews the leaf triggering the plant to produce a specific type of gall. Depending on the insect the gall may resemble large seeds, marbles, spiky sea urchins, fruit, or wooly masses. With his fingers Mancke dissected oak apple galls and wool sower galls revealing wasp larvae. The tannin in galls was used by Native Americans and early colonists. Some of America's early historic documents, the Declaration of Independence and Constitution, were penned with ink from oak galls.

Passing a wax myrtle shrub (*Myrica cerifera*) Mancke crushed the aromatic leaves for students to scent and recalled "Myrtle Beach is named for the shrub and bayberry candles are made with the waxy berries. Deer love to eat the plant so hunters crush up the leaves to attract the deer."

Many plants at the park triggered tastes and flavors of his childhood. Mancke's grandmother used wild plants in her cooking. The oblong leaf on the persimmon tree summoned her persimmon pudding and pie. Pokeweed salad and sassafras tea were springtime foods. As he pointed out new growth and heart shaped leaves on a greenbrier vine (*Smilax rotundifolia*), he recalled she ate the new growth raw or cooked the tips like asparagus. Where young paw paw trees lined the trail, he noted, "Every animal wants its banana-like fruit." The red mulberry (*Morus rubra*) provided sweet berries for grandmother's bakery. She used the elliptical red bay leaf (*Persea borbonia*) to flavor vegetable soup.

Nearly 175 species of bird have been sighted at the Congaree National Park. It is the summer nesting ground to many neotropical migrants overhead--a ruby-throated hummingbird, male and female summer tanagers, a prothonotary warbler and a white-eyed vireo. Year-round bird residents heard or observed were the turkey vulture, Northern cardinal, Carolina wren, red-shouldered hawk and red-bellied woodpecker.

The diversity of angiosperms at Congaree contributes to the varied population of moths and butterflies in the park. But unlike a home butterfly garden's emphasis on annuals and perennials, Congaree's trees are primary hosts. At the visitor's center a red admiral butterfly swirls above the moist soil. Zebra swallowtails use the paw paw as host plant. The magnificent tulip tree (*Liriodendron tulipifera*) is host to the eastern tiger swallowtail butterfly. The palamedes butterfly larvae feed on red bay leaves. Spicebush larva curl up in sassafras leaves. Dogwood and viburnum host the azure blue butterfly larva. The lovely luna moth lays her eggs upon persimmon, beech, sweet gum, cherry, alder, or hickory in the park. The tussock moth caterpillar prefers a diet of oak, elm, and willow leaves.

The woods display native plants attractive for the home landscape. The Virginia willow or sweetspire (*Itea virginica*) has slender arching branches with showy spires of white flowers in spring. The eight-foot shrub tolerates wet or dry conditions and full sun or partial shade. A picturesque petite tree of eight to ten feet tall, the sparkleberry (*Vaccinium arboreum*), has flaking red bark, crooked trunk, and twisted branches. Glistening foliage is offset with white bell-shaped flowers followed by purple berries relished by wildlife.

Mancke loved dragonflies and they clung to him as well. The diversity of habitat in South Carolina brings 110 species here. Adult dragonflies live throughout the summer or "until their wings wear out," according to Mancke. In monitoring their life span, he painted the wing tips with nail polish.

A naturalist reads directly from objects in the environment and indirectly from evidence. Mancke pointed out that bark scaled off of pines was evidence of pileated

Growing up Gardening

woodpeckers and the rows of holes around tree trunks were riveted in winter by yellow-bellied sapsuckers. Many fallen giants were evidence of Hurricane Hugo in 1989. A paw paw leaf with a semi-circular piece missing was the work of a native leaf cutter bee that uses the disc to make a nest cell. The nest is lined with nectar and pollen before the female bee lays an egg and seals the cell.

After a walk on the wild wide with Rudy Mancke, students felt an appreciation, enthusiasm, and anticipation to keep right on walking.

A big blue skimmer dragonfly clings to Rudy Mancke's nose.

Gateways to Gardening with Children

Chapter 2
Data Dialogs via Citizen Science

"Citizen science is a passport to the rights and responsibilities of engaging in validated systems of discovery." Caren Cooper

Winter is for the Birds in Your Back Yard and Schoolyard

Arousing curiosity about birds, their behavior, populations, anatomy, diet, song, territory, defenses, and habitat can start at winter holiday time and is as simple as one, two, three. There are a variety of bird events taking place throughout winter that bring birds to your windows or coax you and your children outdoors among the birds in the garden, field, and forest.

The Cornell Laboratory of Ornithology Project FeederWatch (PFW) is an annual winter census of birds visiting feeders at schools, homes, and businesses across North America from November 1 through April 30. The twenty-six week census counts birds at feeders mounted as close as the windows of your building to the outskirts of your property. You decide on the parameters of your count site and how much time you devote to counting throughout the twenty-six weeks of the census. The project supplies a poster of common feeder birds to expect, detailed instructions on how to count for an accurate scientific survey, and a website ornithology library. The data you collect is transmitted online to Lab scientists who make each count summary available to the public via an annual Winter Bird Highlights publication. PFW participants as data collectors submit counts to Lab ornithologists who analyze the data on bird population abundance, distribution, feeding preference, disease, behavior, habitat, and conservation research.

Participants will see unexpected avian visitors and migrants, as well as winter residents and native year-round residents. While watching feeder birds one could detect bird diseases, pecking order within and between species, or note predatory species coming to the feeder for birds, not seed or fruit.

Birding as a youngster encourages the development of lifelong habits of attention to wildlife and the natural surroundings. The Cornell Lab Ornithology K-12 Education provides resources and professional development across the country to assist in teaching science content and process skills that meet the New Generation Science Standards (NGSS) and inspires students. Contact Cornell Lab K-12 Education at https://www.birds.cornell.edu/k12

The National Audubon Society sponsors the Christmas Bird Count from December 14

The Great Backyard Bird Count

through January 5. The count originated to replace a long-standing Christmas Day tradition known as the "side hunt" when two groups (sides) of hunters competed to shoot the largest number of feathered and furred animals.

In 1900 ornithologist Frank Chapman wrote an article in *Bird-Lore* magazine, proposing changing the "side hunt" to a bird census over concern for dwindling bird populations. Today local Audubon chapters schedule count days and welcome novices to a circular flock of census takers. The count is taken in circular plots fifteen miles in diameter. Participant registration is required ahead of time. Joining a census group is a fabulous way for children and adults to learn species in their hometown. Additionally, participants can "shoot" birds with cameras.

The third segment of winter's bird watching marathon takes place each February around Valentine's Day. In 1998 the Cornell Lab of Ornithology, the National Audubon Society, and Birds Canada initiated the first online citizen science bird census to collect data on the distribution and abundance of birds in the winter landscape - the Great Backyard Bird Count (GBBC). The GBBC is a worldwide census where scientists, amateur birders, children and families participate in the free fun four-day count in mid-February. Although it is called the Great BACKYARD Bird Count, it can take place anywhere there are birds. National and state parks are popular places to join birds in the census, but also consider birding at botanical gardens, neighborhood parks, and, of course, your own back yard. Participants can spend as little as fifteen minutes or as long as they desire and report their sightings online at https://www.birdcount.org

The information gleaned from the census is used to look at the "big picture" about what is happening to bird populations over the long term and to answer questions like these:

How have weather and climate changes affected bird populations, numbers, and distribution?

What patterns appear in data of individual species and of bird populations in general?

How is the timing of bird migration changing over time?

How are bird diseases like West Nile virus and house finch eye disease affecting populations?

What are the differences in bird diversity in rural, urban, and suburban settings?

Winter Bird Watching Expeditions

https://www.audubon.org/community-science/great-backyard-bird-count
https://feederwatch.org/
https://www.birdcount.org/

The census data from GBBC becomes part of an Internet database available for exploration of migration patterns, year-to-year changes in abundance and distribution of birds, and trends that indicate how birds are faring under environmental pressures such as urbanization, climate change, and disease.

Put on a warm jacket, scarf, and gloves and grab your field guide and binoculars for a winter of bird watching.

Budburst – Citizen Science with Plants

Children are alert and adept at noticing subtle changes in their surroundings. Parents and teachers can tap into their perceptual acuity during the seasonal changes occurring in plants. Are trees leafing out earlier this spring? Will dogwoods blossom for Easter? Are daffodils blooming later? In February we notice leaf and flower buds swelling on bare branches of deciduous trees and shrubs, for example, red maple, alder, forsythia, and quince flower buds. In these species leaves will arrive later. But when?

In fall we may observe dogwood (*Cornus florida*), winterberry (*Ilex verticillata*), and photinia (*Photinia fraseri*) fruits being devoured by flocks of robins and cedar waxwings. Budding, flowering, leafing, and fruiting are changes or phenophases within the life cycle of plants. The study of the timing of plant phenophases is part of the science of phenology. The timing of phenophases is influenced by day length, by weather, and -- in the long term -- by climate.

To the close observer, child or adult, each plant can reveal a story of its life cycle phases. We can think of natural phenomena like trees and wildflowers as storytellers. Documenting the ongoing observational story of plants through sketching, photographing, and description is made possible through a citizen science program originally known as Project Budburst.

Since 2007 a national fieldwork network of plant observers in the United States has been monitoring plants through the seasons and recording and reporting observations to the program's ecological database for the science of phenology as it pertains to plants and the timing of their life cycle events. The timing of **when** plants leaf, flower, and fruit is the crux of the program. In 2017 Project Budburst was renamed simply Budburst and relocated to the Chicago Botanic Garden.

Anyone can join the free network. People from all ages, stages, and walks of life participate. Groups such as botanic gardens, botany classes, wildlife refuges, nature centers, museums, state forests, and national parks participate, as do day cares, public and private schools, and families. Participants make careful observations of species on their property or a selected property. To focus observation Budburst maintains a roster of plants by state in five categories--wildflowers and herbs, deciduous trees and shrubs, broadleaf evergreens, conifers, and grasses. Everyone in South Carolina is within arm's length or eyeshot of many of these plants, including dogwood, redbud, yellow jessamine, eastern red cedar, loblolly pine, southern magnolia, and live oak.

Reporting forms are downloaded from the Budburst website at https://budburst.org/. Forms request date of observation, common or scientific name, address or latitude and longitude of plant, and a brief checklist of phenophase observations for flowering, leafing, and fruiting.

The timing of when plants leaf, flower, and fruit is the crux of Project Budburst.

People have recorded phenological observations for centuries. The Japanese have logged the peak time for cherry blossom bloom for twelve hundred years. Swedish taxonomist Carl Linnaeus recorded the flowering time of plants in eighteen locations across Sweden in the 1700s. Britain's first phenologist, Robert Marsham, started recording his "Indications of Spring" journal in 1736 and his descendants continued until 1958. Henry David Thoreau's journals and Thomas Jefferson's *Garden Book* give detailed phenological data.

Gardeners, keen detectors of changes in their surroundings, often keep a journal on the first and last frost dates, first hummingbird arriving in spring, first leaf and flower buds to open, and rainfall readings.

While phenology offers evidence that climate change is happening now with significant effects on the life cycles of plants and animals, perhaps the practice of phenology offers a more important, close-to-home, immediate effect on children and their connection to the natural world.

Current research documents a major shift in the ways children interact with the natural environment. Direct sensory observation and immersion in nature-based activities have been replaced by a distancing from nature through indirect, more sedentary observation through electronic media. Budburst, however, brings nature back into the ecosystem of the family and school by prompting us to look closely at the cycles we share with other life forms on earth.

Data Dialogs with Natural Phenomena

Data flows and grows everywhere in the garden. Contribute yours to a citizen science project or brainstorm to plot investigations unique to your garden.

A butterfly garden at home or school provides flying data from spring to frost and can generate a flutter of questions. **Journey North**, headquartered at the University of Wisconsin Arboretum, is a citizen science program whereby individuals track the spring and fall migration of species including monarch butterflies, American robins, hummingbirds, and songbirds. Observers report sightings, which are recorded on tracking maps. For example, when monarch butterflies leave the Oyamel forests in central Mexico in spring and head north to Texas, observers track them. In fall observers report monarchs heading south to Mexico. Anyone can observe the tracking on maps at Journey North. https://journeynorth.org/

The North American Butterfly Association (NABA) sponsors several citizen participation programs for monitoring butterfly distribution, abundance, flight times and conservation.

Butterflies I've Seen is a personal checklist of butterflies observed by date, location, and species. Over time a butterfly checklist becomes a Life List, similar to the life list kept by birders of number of species observed in one's lifetime.

NABA has conducted the Butterfly Counts Program in North America since 1993. In spring, summer, and autumn a four-member count team compiles a list of butterflies observed within a fifteen-mile diameter count circle in a one-day period. The data provided allows scientists to monitor changes in butterfly populations and the effects of weather and habitat change on North American butterflies. To join a nearby count circle, refer to the map at https://naba.org/butterfly-counts/

Monarch Watch (MW), a research, education, and conservation program headquartered at the University of Kansas has been monitoring the fall migration of the eastern population of monarch butterflies since 1992 through a tagging program. Tagging a butterfly, like banding a bird, is an unforgettable experience for children and adults.

From August through November, eastern North America's landscapes are visited by monarch butterflies enroute to the Oyamel fir forests of central Mexico's Sierra Madre mountain range, their overwintering home. These daytime travelers are each year's fourth generation of monarchs and the longest living generation with a lifespan of nine months. Most adult butterflies live two to three weeks. The winged travelers, estimated to log fifty to a hundred miles per day, make rest stops for nectar to fuel their journey and may accumulate between two and three thousand frequent flyer miles one way. Their journey is fraught with many obstacles including high winds, rain, hurricanes, herbicide and pesticide use, drought, loss of habitat, predators, and vehicles.

Citizen scientists including school children, their families, and other volunteers conduct the catch, tag, and release protocol. Monarchs are caught in butterfly nets. Volunteers record the special tag number, tagging date, gender of butterfly, and geographic location before placing a small lightweight circular adhesive tag on the mitten-shaped discal cell on the underside of the hind wing.

After tagging, butterflies are released to continue their journey. In December tagging data are submitted to Monarch Watch and added to the database to be used in research. Tagged monarchs may be found on the ground along the migration route but most are found at overwintering sites. In Mexico local workers recover tagged butterflies and report tag numbers to Monarch Watch. By early spring recovered tag numbers are posted on the website.

By 2022 two million monarchs had been tagged and twenty thousand recoveries have been made at the overwintering sites. The tagging data present new information on the origins of monarchs that reach Mexico, the timing and pace of migration, differences among regions due to recolonization and weather, the effects of drought and habitat loss.

In 2005 Monarch Watch initiated **Monarch Waystations** to compensate for the loss of milkweeds and nectar plants. Monarch Waystations are patches of habitat providing the resources for monarchs to produce successive generations and sustain their migration. Schools, homes, businesses, parks, zoos, nature centers, and Department of Transportation roadsides are sites for monarch waystations. The basic guidelines for waystations appear on the Monarch

Tagging Monarchs during Fall Migration for Monarch Watch

Watch website https://www.monarchwatch.org/waystations/ Waystations are registered and mapped on the website. K-16 classes planting a monarch waystation may join the Monarch Waystation Network to facilitate ongoing use of the garden as a learning center, a place for inquiry, discovery, and self-instruction.

In spring 2014 pre-service and in-service teachers in my Life Science for Teachers course at the University of South Carolina installed a Monarch Waystation at the Sustainable Community Garden on campus. Students planted milkweed seed obtained from Ernst Conservation Seeds in Pennsylvania and plugs of *Aesclepias tuberosa* milkweed donated by Monarch Watch. For every host milkweed plant, we planted three nectar plants including cosmos, tithonia, ironweed, blanketflower, swamp sunflower, goldenrod, Joe-Pye weed, and two verbena - 'Homestead' and 'Bonariensis'. Plants were mass planted to give large splashes of red, yellow, orange and purple easily observed by the compound eyes of butterflies. Students included plants to stagger bloom from spring to summer to fall. All Monarch Waystations have the potential to be used as teaching gardens.

The Great Sunflower Project was created in 2008 by researcher and biology professor, Dr. Gretchen Lebuhn at San Francisco State University to better understand the reasons for and effects of declines in pollinator populations. Citizen observers identify, count, photograph, and track pollinators, honeybee and native bee populations in urban, suburban, and rural sunflower gardens across North America.

These fast growing, free-flowering lemon queen sunflowers have branching clusters of blooms four to six inches wide with lemon yellow pointed petals and chocolate center discs. They grow five to seven feet tall. When flowers bloom, observers count how many pollinators visit them and how often. The data is recorded on the project website.The data collected has helped create a nationwide online map of bee populations.

In a second program, **Pollinator Plants and Places**, volunteers identify important plants that support pollinators and the regions where they thrive. Participants make a pollinator count using plants in their yard or nearby green spaces.

The third program, **The Great Pollinator Habitat Challenge**, requires participants to evaluate pollinator habitat at their home, school, park, playground, or community center and draft and implement a plan to provide more pollen resources for bees and other pollinators. https://www.greatsunflower.org/

Kids leap for joy with **Frogwatch USA**, a toad and frog monitoring program organized by the Association of Zoos and Aquariums (AZA) designed to help protect and conserve amphibians. After volunteers are trained in the simple steps to frogwatching at their local AZA chapter including use of the online field guide to identify frogs and toads for their area, practicing a few frog calls and gathering their gear, observers are ready to hop to the bog during monitoring season from February through August. Frogwatch USA data include population, rare and invasive species, and changes in species diversity, range and seasonal timing. The findings are used to inform environmental protection and amphibian conservation strategies.

The Community Collaborative Rain, Hail and Snow Network aka CoCoRaHS invites anyone with a penchant for precipitation to join its grassroots observation network. By observing, recording, and reporting daily accumulations of rain, snow, and hail in rain gauges in their own back yards, volunteers help fill in "holes" in the official network of precipitation gauge data. The clear plastic rain gauges used by volunteers are four inches in diameter and hold 11.30 inches of precipitation. Reports are mapped on the CoCoRaHS website for anyone to view. www.cocorahs.org/

Who uses the recorded data? Over time, these local observations will serve as a record of local climate. Climatologists use the data to help put extreme precipitation events into historical context and to identify precipitation patterns.

Meteorologists, hydrologists, city utilities, insurance adjusters, engineers, builders, farmers, gardeners, mosquito control, and outdoor recreation venues are among the data users. CoCoRaHS offers education resources for K-12 teachers. Students are engaged in collecting, reporting and analyzing real scientific data while meeting state and national standards in science, math, and geography.

CoCoRaHS Regions in South Carolina
For Tracking Precipitation

Lure a Luminous Landscape

Pollinator gardens, butterfly gardens, and wildlife gardens are popular themes to direct conservation efforts for at-risk species and populations. Yet one summer insect that appears just after sunset, lighting up the night and capturing human hearts by magically flashing its luminous lanterns, has rarely received conservation attention.

Known by common names lightning bugs and candle flies, fireflies are not bugs or flies but beetles. As beetles, they undergo complete metamorphosis with four stages – egg, larvae, pupa, and adult. The complete life cycle can take several months or up to three years depending on the species. The majority of their life cycle is spent in the larval stage as a grublike creature eating its way through the dark underground. Adult fireflies live only three to four weeks.

The firefly family, *Lampyridae*, has 2200 species worldwide. The United States has 170 species. Mid-Atlantic and southeastern states have the greatest firefly diversity.

While fireflies are fascinating for their bioluminescence, anecdotal records from around the world report fewer individuals are observed each year. Realizing a need to study firefly populations more closely, several conservation, education and research organizations are collaborating to study firefly distributions, life histories, and extinction risks. Citizen scientists are recruited to assist with data collection.

Firefly Watch was an annual garden ritual of scientific research where a network of citizen scientists from across the country observed fireflies in their back yards to assist the Massachusetts Audubon Society and Tufts University biology professor emerita Sara Lewis and students in research to track and map the geographic distribution of firefly species and environmental factors affecting their abundance or decline. Participants spent at least 10 minutes once a week during firefly season observing fireflies on their property or a nearby field. All firefly sightings or lack thereof were considered valuable.

In 2024 the Firefly Watch program passed the torch to **Firefly Atlas**, a community science program launched in 2022 by the Xerces Society to better understand firefly species distribution, diversity, phenology, habitat associations and identify threats to their populations in North America. Register to participate in Firefly Atlas at https://www.fireflyatlas.org/get-involved/how-to-participate.

Firefly habitat requirements vary with species, but fireflies generally prefer moist places with wetlands, moss, and pond edges and warm places with tall grasses, native wildflowers, shrubs, and shade trees. Females lay eggs on the ground in leaf litter and brush piles.

Fireflies face some of the same challenges as pollinators including loss and degradation of habitat and pesticide use in lawns, gardens, and agricultural fields.

Neonicotinoid insecticides persist in soils where firefly larvae and their prey — snails, slugs, grubs, and earthworms -- live and contaminate their habitats. Aerial spraying of insecticides targeting mosquitoes is harmful too, especially if sprayed at dusk when fireflies become more active.

Additionally, fireflies need dark nights to use their built-in language of light to locate a mate. Light pollution from streetlights, signs, security and landscape lights makes it difficult for fireflies to detect luminous signals in the dark, thereby disrupting courtship and reproduction.

Doug Tallamy, entomologist and ecologist, notes that firefly habitats need four things--food, shelter, moisture, and protection from pesticides, foot traffic, and mowing. He recommends keeping part of your yard or garden wild, leaving shady spots with leaf litter and decaying wood, providing a clean water source, planting a variety of native grasses and flowers, and eliminating pesticide use.

Congaree National Park, an old growth bottomland forest in Hopkins, South Carolina, has a synchronous firefly species, *Photuris frontalis*. The common name is Snappy Single Sync firefly. Synchronous firefly males orchestrate their flashes to shine together in unison while searching for a mate.

In August of 2020 the International Union for Conservation of Nature (IUCN) issued a report assessing the species status of *Photuris frontalis* which states: "Despite potential threats from light pollution and trampling of larvae and ovipositing adult females at sites where people come to see the displays of this species, there is currently no evidence of decline. Due to its widespread distribution, relative abundance, and lack of evidence of decline, this species is listed as Least Concern."

Each year from mid-May to mid-June the park hosts a synchronous fireflies event. To protect firefly habitat and provide a safe and enjoyable experience for visitors, the park uses a lottery system and charges an event fee as well as informing visitors of prohibited items and viewing etiquette.

The meticulously choreographed light show of fireflies will inspire you to lure a luminous landscape to your back yard.

Grow Some Shade

Cities are often prepared for national weather emergencies like flooding, hurricanes, and tornadoes but not for rising temperatures. In his book *The New Shade Garden: Creating a Lush Oasis in the Age of Climate Change*, Ken Druse addresses issues gardeners are facing with rising temperatures. He observes that temperatures under shade trees can be ten to twenty degrees cooler than surrounding open areas. Have you compared the air temperature on your driveway, under the magnolia tree, and above your pool?

Columbia, South Carolina's 'famously hot' moniker is a matter of geography, the relationship between physical features of the earth and its atmosphere, and of human activity as it affects and is affected by these, including the distribution and density of populations and resources, land use, and industries.

Urban areas like Columbia experience higher temperatures than surrounding farms, forests, and rivers. The man-made built environment – buildings, roads, and other infrastructure - absorbs and emits heat more than natural landscapes like forests and bodies of water creating an "island of higher temperatures."

Climate change and heat islands interact. As temperatures steadily increase, the trend for intensifying heat islands occurs. Continued warming is expected to worsen heat island areas. As urban population density increases and natural features decrease, heat islands strengthen. According to the National Oceanic and Atmospheric Administration (NOAA) heat is the weather issue with the biggest public health impact.

In August 2022 University of South Carolina geography professor Kristin Dow and a crew of citizen scientists traversed Columbia on two consecutive days taking the temperature of the city using heat sensors mounted on car windows or bikes. Sensors record temperature, humidity, time, and GPS location in the morning, noon, and evening. The Heat Island Mapping Campaign program is part of a national initiative started in 2017 at NOAA. The data can be used to plan, place, and landscape bus stops, bike paths, pedestrian walkways, and shared spaces like parks and greenways.

Live oaks are long living evergreen shade trees.

One effective heat mitigation strategy is planting trees and vegetation to cool the environment. Trees and other vegetation can lower surface and air temperatures by providing shade and evapotranspiration.

Columbia Green, a nonprofit that improves and protects the natural beauty of greater Columbia by promoting sustainable plantings, preserving trees and green spaces, and educating the public about the environment, has launched a tree planting initiative to reduce heat island effects in the city. Grow Some Shade offers native canopy and understory deciduous trees for planting on residential land in the metropolitan area.

Over time Grow Some Shade plans to reduce Columbia's urban heat by planting one Green Square Mile of shade trees. Celebrate your state's Arbor Day with plans to Grow Some Shade on your property.

Chapter 3 – Carolina Children's Garden

"In a Child's Garden…Imagination Grows" Jane Taylor

Planting Future Generations of Gardeners

Since 1993 the American Horticultural Society (AHS) has cultivated imagination, innovation, and inspiration through its annual National Children and Youth Garden Symposium. The event has seeded an interest in children's gardening and provided a forum for people who share a vision for connecting children to gardening and nature to showcase successes and kindle creative collaborations.

The first symposium, entitled "Children, Plants and Gardens: Educational Opportunities," was held in Chevy Chase, Maryland, and at River Farm, headquarters of AHS, along the Potomac River in Alexandria, Virginia.

The three objectives of the symposium were "to ensure that K-8 educators obtain a vision and perspective of horticulture as essentially important to human wellbeing and survival, to inspire and enable educators to create or improve plant and gardening programs for children, and to have attendees return to their schools, community spaces, and back yards and fill them with the kinds of plants, gardens, and enriching landscapes that provide interest and challenge to children", according to Maureen Heffernan, AHS Education Coordinator.

The symposium attracted over 550 educators, horticulturists, and conservation and community leaders from across the country.

One of the most effective ways to document and dramatize the importance of gardening with children is by creating outdoor spaces for them to garden, play, pretend, learn, discover, imagine, and dream. Hence, AHS installed twelve children's theme gardens at River Farm for symposium participants to tour.

Four gardens were designed and planted by school groups in grades four through seven -- Butterfly Garden, Dinosaur Footprint Garden, Persian Carpet Garden, and Wildlife Discovery Pond. Eight gardens were designed and planted by professional landscapers in the Washington, DC area -- Imagination Garden, Little House on the Prairie Garden, Ditch Garden, Secret Grove Garden, Alphabet Garden, Child's Fantasy Garden, Sunflower House Garden, and the Colonial Wind, Weather, and Sundial Garden.

Persian Carpet Garden

Little House on the Prairie

Colonial Wind, Weather, and Sundial Garden

Each garden demonstrated simple ways to give children freedom to experience the sights, sounds, scents, textures, cycles, changes, and wonders of nature, and all were adaptable to home, school, or community sites.

The imaginative theme gardens captivated participants, as did the speakers and workshops, and provided the stimulus to start a children's gardening movement across the nation, which continues into the twenty-first century.

That first symposium inspired me to share the children's garden slides and experiences at River Farm with Stephen Verkade, horticulturist and director of Clemson University Sandhill Research and Education Center (REC), a six hundred-acre extension campus of farmland, forest, and lakes in Columbia, South Carolina. At the time the center focused on urban and environmental horticulture outreach and had initiated an Environmental Gardens Demonstration Program including a cottage garden, backyard wildlife habitat, home composting demonstration, square-foot garden, small tree arboretum, and xeriscape model.

I proposed adding a children's garden to put individuals and families in touch with nature and each other. Within a year Verkade traveled to River Farm to tour the children's gardens. When returning to Columbia, he established a children's garden birthing committee of himself and four others -- Rick Anderson, a landscape designer in Columbia whom I had met at the 1993 AHS symposium; Mary Anne Allen, county 4-H extension agent; Bootsie Manning, master gardener volunteer, and myself. As a committee our specific goals were three-fold:

- To provide an educational framework for the understanding of the relationships among plants, people, and ecosystems
- To create a landscape for imagination, discovery, and interest to grow
- To encourage extension, replication, or invention of gardens within the home and community.

We drafted a proposal document for the children's garden stating its purpose, goals, a brief background on the contemporary children's gardening movement, and a designer's sketch of the two-acre space. The proposal had to be approved by the board overseeing Sandhill REC and was also used as our first publicity to the public on plans for the garden. We sent copies to individuals, businesses, and organizations when soliciting designers for the theme gardens. With our letter of solicitation, we included a set of guidelines stating the parameters of the project:

- All designs, plant lists, sketches, and/or labor would be considered to be pro bono.
- The size of each garden would be approximately 150 to 400 square feet, contingent upon the garden committee's approval.
- Sponsors would be responsible for all plants/supplies needed for the initial completion of the garden plot. Basic garden tools would be made available to the sponsoring group(s) providing the maintenance.
- Volunteers would provide basic maintenance (watering, fertilizing, deadheading, weeding) of the gardens. Each garden had to submit a maintenance schedule.

Minimal pesticide use was highly encouraged.
- The sponsor and the garden committee would review each garden every two years. Evaluations would include effectiveness, sustainability, size, location, and maintenance.

Each sponsor was required to sign a pro bono agreement to select their garden site, draft a design plan, create a plant list, order plants and hardscape items, create an informative brochure on the garden to go inside a garden mailbox, and build and plant their garden. They would be responsible for maintenance and securing the funding for it.

The project was a collection of a dozen themed garden spaces:

Three Bears Homestead was sponsored by the South Carolina Department of Mental Health (SCDMH) and received a grant from the Carolinas Chapter of the American Horticultural Therapy Association. The garden was conceived, implemented, and maintained by SCDMH horticultural therapists Mary Blackburn, Pat Redmond, and Liz Fuller with the grounds crew from the Department of Mental Health. Patients and volunteers also assisted with the garden.

Pooh's Corner was sponsored by Woodley's Garden Center. Their horticulturist, Vivian Huggins, headed the design and implementation team with Cathy and Thomas Wendell, Claire Woodley, and students from a service learning project at Richland Northeast High School. When Huggins retired, Robin Chaves Klein oversaw the garden.

Andy and Carrie Graves, owners of The Happy Bookseller, sponsored and installed the **Reading Garden**.

The Carolina Butterfly Society sponsored the **Butterfly Garden**. Tommy Moody, a member and master gardener, designed and planted the garden.

Summit Parkway Middle School science teacher Dr. Arlene Marturano and her sixth-grade classes designed, planted, and sponsored the **Bird Garden**.

The **Growing Healthy Garden** was sponsored by the South Carolina Nutrition Council, a 501(c)(3) non-profit. Nutritionist Heather Mixon started the garden. When the Nutrition Council dissolved, Susan Kurta Wilkerson, nutritionist with Richland County assumed leadership.

Clemson's Landscapes for Learning director Brenda Vander Mey installed the **Carolina Fence™ Garden** as a teacher-training exercise at one of their Columbia conferences. Follow-up maintenance came from the South Carolina Wildlife Federation.

Mesozoic Memories, **Alphabet Garden**, **McGregor's Garden**, and **MacDonald's Historic Crops** were initiated by Stephen Verkade and maintained by community volunteers.

Hattie Monson, a master gardener who owned a garden installation business, installed the **Rain Garden**.

Those were the magical spaces that comprised Carolina Children's Garden.

Rick Anderson, landscape designer and owner of StonWurks in Columbia whom

I had met at the first AHS symposium, oversaw the master plan design for the entire garden and was on hand to address issues in each garden as they arose. He recruited The Greater Columbia Landscape Association to design and install the entranceway to the garden as a service project. And when a geologist at Ridgeway Gold Mine donated rocks for the garden, Anderson arranged for the appropriate trucks needed to haul tons of tailing pile rock from the mine to the garden.

Sharon Lovejoy, author and illustrator, designed and donated the logo for the garden. I had met Lovejoy at AHS conferences and introduced her to Dr. Verkade at the AHS symposium at Callaway Gardens in Georgia. Lovejoy visited Columbia to view the garden space before ground was broken. I set up a garden radio interview for her at Woodley's Garden Center. Summit Parkway Middle School hosted a book signing for *Sunflower Houses*, her first children's gardening book.

Additional labor for the installation of gardens came from the South Carolina Departments of Forestry and Corrections along with Clemson Sandhill REC grounds manager Joe Hudson and his crew. Sandhill REC carpenters built the cedar playhouse, Big Bird House, and amphitheater.

Eagle Scouts were recruited to build the bat house, benches for the amphitheater, and raised bed planters in MacDonald's Historic Crops.

Heyward Career and Technology Center High School students crafted picnic tables, wooden wheelbarrows, birdhouses, and wooden figures for Pooh's Corner and Mesozoic Memories that lasted for many years.

The Carolina Children's Garden (originally called the Midlands Children's Garden) held a ribbon cutting in October 1997. The American Gardener magazine featured an article on the new garden in the July/August 1999 edition.

In 2016 the AHS Children and Youth National Symposium was held in Columbia, and participants toured the Carolina Children's Garden. The American Gardener magazine featured an article in the September 2016 edition.

Two years later, when Clemson REC changed its focus to Agribusiness, the Carolina Children's Garden was closed and the land repurposed for trial crop research and hosting an incubator farm program for beginning farmers.

Spotlight on Youth Gardening Across the Nation

Each AHS National Children and Youth Symposium is held in a different state, where it features a children's garden, school gardens, and unique local youth gardening programs.

The Michigan 4-H Children's Garden at Michigan State University was designed for young visitors, not adults. Jane Taylor, founder of the garden, proclaimed its mission was "to promote an understanding of plants and the role they play in our environment and our daily lives; to nurture the wonder in a child's imagination and curiosity and provide a place for the enrichment and delight of children."

Denver Urban Gardens in partnership with Slow Food Denver has a garden-to-school salad bar program in Denver Public Schools. One-third of Denver community gardens are situated on public school campuses. Students harvest crops in September and October and sell the produce to their school cafeteria for meals. Local chefs demonstrate food preparation techniques.

The Chicago Public Schools' (CPS) Garden Team in the Office of Student Health and Wellness oversees Eat What You Grow, a school garden toolkit for teachers and school cafeteria staff. CPS recognizes that gardens have a myriad of wellness benefits including social-emotional learning, nutrition education, and stress reduction in outdoor growing spaces. Organizations like the Chicago Botanic Garden and University of Illinois Extension contribute consultation and teacher workshops.

In Columbus, Ohio, the state's former First Lady, Hope Taft, described how heritage gardens teach natural and cultural history. Between 1999 and 2007 she developed and shared with the public the Ohio Heritage Garden on the grounds of the Governor's Residence. Subsequent first ladies and a Friends of the Ohio Governor's Residence and Heritage Garden have continued the garden as a public amenity. In just one hour students can tour the state's five physiographic regions landscaped in indigenous plants.

The Luci and Ian Family Garden at the Lady Bird Johnson Wildflower Center in Austin, Texas, connects children and families to nature through interactive outdoor exhibits including a wildlife blind, grotto with natural cave and waterfall, a native shrub maze, giant bird nests made of grape vines, dinosaur creek, and an open-air shelter with lending library of children's nature, gardening, and plant books. The four-and-a-half-acre area of woodland and meadow is designed to get children moving and learning through outdoor play. The Stumpery is a cluster of upside down cedars and oak for hiding, climbing, and rearranging. The large green picnic and play space is covered in buffalo grass.

The Stumpery

Coyote Rodeo

The three-acre Ithaca Children's Garden (ICG) in New York has many theme garden rooms similar to children's gardens built over the last thirty years. But the singular distinctive feature setting this garden apart is the large space designated for unstructured play. The Hands-on-Nature Anarchy Zone is an adventure playground, a design concept popular in Europe after World War II. The ground of the Anarchy

Zone is dotted with randomly placed man-made and natural loose parts—tires, planks, pallets, ropes, straw bales, logs, limbs, culvert pipes, tarps, piles of leaves, fruits, pods among the trees, vines, shrubs, wildflowers, clay, sand, and stream bed.

The anarchy zone is full of loose parts to encourage free-range unstructured play.

The loose parts are pieces of the play puzzle. Since play is considered the work of children and a necessary part of their social, emotional, physical, and cognitive development, the Anarchy Zone encourages free-range unstructured play. Children initiate the play, whether solo, parallel, cooperative, dramatic, constructive, or whatever happens, making forts, slides, swings, and treehouses. They create nooks and tunnels to secret hideouts and run after imaginary and real animals. They sift in the sand, dig in the mud, make mud pies, and practice walking on a log to cross a creek. On International Mud Day, the garden invites families to take part in mud slides, mud pools, mud pies, and mud art.

Rusty Keeler, designer of the Anarchy Zone and author of *Natural Playscapes*, notes that children are the ultimate explorers discovering the planet they live on in the outdoors. Children need to test their own limits and parents and caregivers are expected to allow them to do so. He says, "You are where you play and what you play."

The Oregon Children's Garden, part of the Oregon Botanic Garden, is nestled in the fertile Willamette Valley of family farms and spruce and fir forests of the Pacific Northwest. The whimsical children's garden is designed for children to wonder why weird plants like toad lily, lamb's ears, and mouse tail have the shape they do; to pretend living in a jungle of tangled trees in the treehouse; to discover bones at the dinosaur dig among prehistoric Monkey Puzzle trees; to climb in and onto a Hobbit House, and greet a family of terra-cotta flowerpot people; to meet topiary animals; and travel on a G scale model Southern Pacific train along a track lined with dwarf conifers and

Monkey Puzzle Tree

miniature plants.

The children's garden at the Morton Arboretum west of Chicago is four acres of sensory exploration in theme zones. Adventure Woods includes Wonder Pond, surrounded by reeds and rushes where children splash and wade, searching for tadpoles, turtles, and toads. An elevated boardwalk in Adventure Woods takes visitors to the canopy of sixty-year-old conifers at Evergreen Lookout. Backyard Discovery Garden has beds of grandma's flowers with Bloom Zoom, musical flowers, and a Sprout Garden focused on pollination and seed dispersal. Children study roots, stems, leaves, flowers, seeds, and fruits through interactive exhibits, including larger-than-life models like a giant acorn for kids to crawl through. Every Which Way displays plants with contorted or twisting stems and roots. Children can stroll through the Kid's Tree Walk and Tree Finder Grove in the museum of trees, a green mansion in summer and a conflagration of color in fall.

In addition to getting fresh ideas from hosting states' gardens and programs, AHS symposiums are packed with inspiring presenters and general knowledge that participants can take home and apply.

No garden is successful without good soil. At one memorable symposium session, Gina Bundy, science teacher and inventor of WormWatcher®, informed participants on garden writer Jeff Lowenfels' work on the soil food web, in his *Teaming With Microbes* book. Participants took part in worm yoga to experience a way to interest children in the work of red wigglers.

Mary Appelhof introduced vermicomposting through workshops demonstrating how red wigglers, *Eisenia fetida*, quickly and efficiently process food waste and organic material into vermicompost, rich humus for houseplants and the garden. Her book, *Worms Eat My Garbage*, is responsible for thousands of worm bins in K-12 classrooms across the country.

At another symposium, Lolly Tai, professor of landscape design at Temple University and author of *Designing Outdoor Environments for Children* and *The Magic of Children's Gardens* detailed the design process used by playground equipment companies prior to placement into schoolyards and public gardens. Factors such as safety, accessibility, product life span, methods of production, and aesthetics influence equipment design but so does the play value of a piece. Play value must tap the cognitive, creative, social, emotional, physical, and sensory capacities of children.

Robin Moore, landscape architect and founder of Natural Learning Initiative at North Carolina State University, introduced Preventing Obesity by Design (POD). Working within the social service childcare system in North Carolina Moore's design team is modifying the outdoor learning environments of day care centers to increase children's physical activity and time spent outdoors while creating garden settings that introduce healthy diets with fruits, vegetables, and nuts in early childhood.

Wyoming's Wild West weather prompted school gardens there to experiment with hoop houses, also called "high tunnels." Solar heated and plastic covered, the dome-shaped structures shed snow and rain readily. They are strong enough to protect plants from wind, hail, and frost and easy enough for middle school students to build. Hoop houses greatly extend Wyoming's short 120-day growing season.

Using gardens for nutrition education has been a popular symposium theme.

Amanda Maria Edmonds, founder of Growing Hope in Ypsilanti, Michigan, described their intergenerational compact food gardens that revitalize urban neighborhoods and give growers the hope that comes from nurturing soil, seeds and self.

Founded in 1971, the Washington Youth Garden (WYG) at the United States National Arboretum provides life, environmental, and food science instruction to children and their families in District of Columbia schools. WYG offers gardening experiences for classes at the arboretum as well as technical support to school garden teams of parents, students, and volunteers. Participating schools sign a contract for a three-to-five-year school gardening internship program that permits the WYG to develop each school's capacity to independently launch, utilize, and sustain the garden as an integral part of the school curriculum.

All who work with youth gardening will find food for thought and a cornucopia of human and research resources at any annual AHS National Children and Youth Symposium.

Selecting Plants Helps Kids Grow to Love Their New Home

There's no better way to feel at home in new surroundings than planting a garden. Just as a new home's interior is made of rooms with specific purposes, the outdoor space can be thought of as having rooms too, garden rooms for the family. The solar and stellar lighting, fresh-air flow, natural temperature control, soft earthen flooring, and a surprising variety of wildlife make the home landscape a priceless investment.

The Carolina Children's Garden had twelve garden rooms, each with a theme to demonstrate how families can furnish outdoor living space.

From the **Bird Garden** redwood entrance arbor, a mulched path led to a variety of specialty rooms. A hummingbird nectary furnished in salvia, weigela, bee balm, and pineapple sage adjoined a woven wisteria nest bench for bird watching and picnicking. Beyond the bench was a birdseed plot of millet, corn, sunflower, and sorghum. A fruit bar of strawberries, grapes, blueberries and figs served frugivorous birds. A pine snag was a condominium to brown-headed nuthatches.

The Carolina Fence™ Garden, a wildlife habitat, displayed the natural and cultural history of South Carolina by incorporating native plants as food, shelter, and nesting material for wildlife around a horizontal split-rail fence. The state flower, the evergreen vine yellow jessamine, bloomed in spring across the fence accompanied by nesting boxes for the state bird, Carolina wren. Blue granite, the state rock, sparkled amid Indian grass, *Sorghastrum nutans*, the state grass.

The white-picket **Alphabet Fence** was a roll call parade of flowering annuals and perennials aligned in alphabetical order by common name from Ageratum to Zinnia. A laminated copy of local author JoAnn Stoker's children's book, *The ABC Book of Flowers for Young Gardeners,* was mounted on a platform for tots to read.

Growing Healthy was a kitchen garden showcasing fruits, vegetables, and culinary herbs that can be grown seasonally and plucked fresh from the plant at the peak of flavor and maximum nutrition. Arbors (grapes), teepees (beans), containers (basil) and raised beds (tomatoes) displayed the fresh food options.

The Reading Room provided a relaxing respite for reading beneath the mottled shade of tall pines or for closely viewing nature's bounty -- a pine cone, green anole, or heart-shaped redbud leaf.

A scarecrow stood guard over **Old MacDonald's Historic Crops**, a seasonal time line of historic crops important to the state's economy--soybeans, peanuts, peaches, watermelon and collards. A blueberry patch to titillate taste buds was donated by Hollis Organic Blueberries. An old-fashioned millstone served as a stepping-stone into a cedar farmhouse displaying photographs of crops.

Three Bears' Homestead peeked into the daily life of a family of friendly bears who dwelled in a log-framed house roofed in blue morning glories and sided by sunflowers. Bear's pawprint stepping stones led to the tree-stump table and chairs designed for the topiary trilogy's sit-down meals and for children to "try on for size." Mama Bear rang a dinner bell summoning Papa Bear from the fishing pond and Baby Bear from foraging for berries.

Pooh's Corner demonstrated animals' behavior and their habitats in Hundred Acre Woods. Child-sized versions of Pooh and his friends looked for giant carrots at Rabbit's Hole. Children played with Roo in the sand pit.

A **Butterfly Garden** encouraged observation and conservation of the life cycle of native Lepidoptera among their host and nectar plants. A stepping-stone path through the tallest flowers featured a ceramic monarch butterfly basking stone. "Real children" gravitated to the whimsical sculpture of a butterfly girl chasing flying flowers with her net.

Mesozoic Memories presented a landscape from dinosaur days when gymnosperms were the predominant plant and reptiles the predominant animal. Mosses, ferns, cycads, and conifers were the herbivorous diet of dinosaurs.

The Rain Garden offered a view of the flow of stormwater on the property, filtered stormwater runoff by using particular native plants that can tolerate wet feet for twenty-four hours but also are drought tolerant like swamp sunflower, bee balm, tall coneflower, and switch grass. The rain garden increased the amount of water that filtered into the ground, helped protect streams and lakes from pollutants carried in runoff, and provided habitat for bees, butterflies, and beneficial insects.

Swamp Sunflower, Helianus augustifolius

Mr. McGregor's Garden replicated Beatrix Potter's *The Tale of Peter Rabbit*, the main character being derived from the author's childhood pet. The adventures of the flopsy bunnies were relived under the watchful eye of Mr. McGregor.

Imaginative gardens designed for children are filled with ideas that families and schools can replicate on their own property. How might your child initiate a garden room of his own at home? Start small and with a theme. The theme of a child's personal garden should allow his imagination to grow along with the plants. Let the child select plant furnishings and accessories for his outdoor room.

Sunflower houses, bean tunnels and teepees, corn columns, flower mazes, and weeping mulberry trees make miniature rooms for hiding, drawing, playing, and reading.

Window boxes bring the out-of-doors into the bedroom. Baskets hanging at a child's height bring one face to face with blossoms, butterflies and hummingbirds.

The Autumn Garden ABCs

Young children first encounter the alphabet in a variety of ways – songs, rhymes, picture books, soup, cereal, blocks, magnetic letters, penmanship strips, flashcards, and, keyboards. The outdoors, especially gardens, is a favorite venue for kids and an alphabet free for all.

JoAnn Stoker, author, and Gerald Stoker, photographer, held a book signing at the garden in 2005.

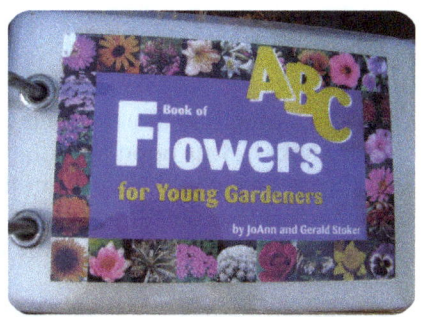

A laminated copy of their book was mounted on a platform at the Alphabet Fence Garden.

Parents can encourage alphabet play within the surroundings. Start with a bag of natural objects. Each item in the bag is to be matched with a visual letter of the alphabet. Children can collect and file objects with letters cut out or written on cardboard and spread out on the grass or sidewalk.

Alternately, each child might start with an empty bag and fill it with items beginning with each letter of the alphabet. Or line up twenty-six bags, each labeled with a letter of the alphabet and let children place objects in the bags for a designated period of time or until no more items can be found. Then children pick out and name items in front of family and friends.

The alphabet is useful as a classification system and can help a child organize his world in multiple ways. In autumn an alphabet game could focus on natural objects and events related to the season, A for apples, C for cicada, F for frost, H for harvest, P for pumpkin. By searching garden catalogs or garden centers with their parents, children can find pictures of blooming garden flowers which can be planted in an alphabet trail including A for asters, C for calendula, G for goldenrod, K for kale, M for marigold and P for pansies.

Parents can tag the surroundings with alphabet cards and children can name the object tagged, for example, T is tree, A is acorn, S is soil. To encourage word recognition, print the child's word on the card. A simple string dictionary made from the word cards can assist in alphbetizing and providing a pool of words for story writing. Punch a hole in each word card to thread a colorful yarn knotted at one end.

String dictionary

After reading aloud Lois Ehlert's *Eating the Alphabet*, plan an alphabet culinary experience by preparing and eating fresh garden soup, salad and salsas.

Children easily and eagerly learn the alphabet by growing their name in the garden with chia, cress, or radish seeds. Explore and enjoy the alphabet in your garden in autumn.

Peekaboo...Imagine Pooh and Friends Waiting for You!

Pooh's Corner, one of a dozen theme gardens for families at the Carolina Children's Garden, was popular with the sandbox set. Anyone thinking about a theme garden of their own could learn from the kinds of elements included in Pooh's Corner and the other gardens developed especially for children.

Children could explore the home terrain of Winnie the Pooh and his friends

Pooh

Eeyore

Rabbit

Piglet

Tigger

Kanga and Roo

Christopher Robin

Owl

under a shady pine canopy. From a comfortable bench Kanga watched (as any mother would) her offspring Roo model and move the sand in creative solo play or in social gestures with human play pals. Roo used twigs, stones, shells, and plastic toys along with his forepaws and hind feet to dig, sift, sculpt, pour, and draw in the soft, malleable material.

A variety of play props at Pooh's Corner enabled children to manipulate and transform the space imaginatively. Christopher Robin sat on his favorite rock eagerly awaiting the arrival of children of all ages. Children could hide inside Eeyore's House and peer into Rabbit's home, his Hole. They could cautiously reach into the trap for Heffalumps, look skyward to catch a glimpse of Owlet in his treetop dwelling, or track Tigger in search of food. Logs for balancing and jumping, stumps for drumming and tagging, and rocks for lookouts added adventure to the playground and encouraged gross motor development.

The plants in Pooh's Corner extended the range of play activity. They stimulated the senses and furnished the color, fragrance, and texture of an outdoor home. Plants in large tubs and shrubbery became foils in games of hide-and-seek. Beds of plants became the backdrop for dramatic play. Shrub enclosures became places for escape, relaxation, or conversation with friends and family. Animals were attracted to the garden plants, adding another dimension to the play environment for children.

Play is as basic an ingredient to a child's development as the sun is to a plant's development. The potential for inventive play abounded at the Carolina Children's Garden.

Venturing beyond Pooh's Corner, children could put the pieces of an alligator puzzle together in Papa Bear's fishing pond at Three Bears' Homestead. In the Dinosaur Garden, they competed in a Dinosaur Derby by riding a relic back to Mesozoic times. They followed the life cycle of gourds with Peter Rabbit in Mr. McGregor's garden. They could release a bouquet of scents by rubbing against the herbs in the Growing Healthy Garden.

A safe natural environment for children to grow through play was close to home. Winnie the Pooh and friends were always ready to play at the Carolina Children's Garden. They may be retired from the South Carolina space for now, but with imagination and effort, you can create your own version of a child-friendly play garden.

The World at Your Feet

Humans tend to seek exotic destinations and distant itineraries when the most marvelous discoveries can be just footsteps away in our local gardens and neighborhood parks. Carolina Children's Garden was one of those special finds that made people feel lucky to live in central South Carolina. Through its calendar of environmental education programs, the Carolina Children's Garden opened thousands of mostly local visitors' eyes to what was right there at their feet.

In fall the Little Leaves program encouraged young children's interest in collecting and identifying natural objects. On a nature walk, furtive feet found clues to the changing seasons.

No need to go on an African safari to learn basic bush skills with wildlife. The garden invited explorers to take part in a "poo walk" in October and find out about local wildlife from animal spoor. They just had to watch where they stepped. Those who did might have discovered the soil beneath our feet comes in a rainbow of colors. They could extract a soil profile to see the rainbow and other surprising soil characteristics.

In addition to scheduled public education programs, the garden provided a restful respite for self-guided tours, picnics, and imaginative play in the theme gardens. Visitors could breakfast with avian migrants, photograph monarch metamorphosis or lenticels on tree bark, sunbathe with skinks, mimic spring peepers, dance with the raindrops, and follow the call of the wild.

It might be easy to dwell on the absence of such a wonderful place with all the experiences it provided. It's better to focus for now on what families and children can do on their own without going far from home.

Did you know you can measure the pH of your own soil with a garden chemistry test and research on your own how pH affects soil and plants in a garden? Here are more things families can still learn and explore on their own in a home garden or other outdoor spaces without going far from home. You might try these ideas:

Observe how nature continually recycles in the garden before exploring ways to recycle with nature by creating something new in resources and recycling. When tree leaves fall to the ground, some decompose returning nutrients to the soil; some shelter insect larvae over the winter; others serve as mulch for bedding plants. Birds recycle grass, twigs, leaves, and string as nesting material.

Welcome winter with a celebration of the many ways children around the world commemorate the winter solstice. Find out the reason for the season by making a fruit model of the solar system. Find clues to what nature is up to on a mid-winter walk through the woods and around the ponds. Some public spaces may have naturalist-guided tours available.

Trek along the thickets, trails, and open fields in search of birds during the Great Backyard Bird Count. Each February experienced and novice birders team up in citizen science data collection to assist bird research and conservation.

Trees have a strong toehold in one place. During February Forestry practice identifying local trees, sight the layers of a forest landscape, learn how to interpret tree rings, and chant the life cycle of trees. Compare your height to a garden tree and give a bear hug to a tree.

Butterflies have their noses on their toes. Flutter your toes with the spring butterflies as you find evidence of their life cycle, observe butterfly behaviors, and compare butterflies and moths. Observe pollinators and predators entangled in the garden's food web. Butterfly gardening offers strategic planting tips to coax butterflies to the home or school garden.

Experience is the Best Teacher

Gardening has deep roots within the history of educational ideas. Comenius, Rousseau, Pestalozzi, Froebel, Dewey, and Montessori advocated the cultivation of gardens for a variety of instructional reasons. Workdays at the Bird Garden at the

Carolina Children's Garden found sixth graders practicing sound principles of both gardening and education.

The Bird Garden originated in the spring of 1997 when my class of thirty students from Summit Parkway Middle School's sixth grade formed committees to plan how food, water, shelter, and nesting material could be added to attract native and migrating species of birds for year round observation.

Each spring a new crop of sixth graders refurbished the garden using funds from service learning grants. It was for many years a favorite outdoor classroom for my sixth-graders and others and made memories for them and for me.

These are recollections from one of those workdays in the 1990's.

The underlying principle was from Comenius. He believed knowledge comes from studying things in the immediate surroundings – the sky, trees, flowers, and soil -- not by studying observations made by others and written in books. On this day, clearing away vines, students found a soft spongy brown object and came running to ask the teacher what it was.

The egg case was taken back to the classroom insect cage to await the emergence of hundreds of miniature praying mantids. These beneficial insects, often called "mantis," would then be returned to the garden for natural pest control. While working in the garden students described birds with the brown head, black cap, or red crest, finding that a field guide is only an adjunct confirmation to their own description of physical characteristics and behaviors.

Rousseau noted that children approach the garden wanting to touch everything. He encouraged use of the senses as the first guide to reason. Connie Chen, who planted redbud trees around the perimeter of the garden, said, "It was good to feel the dirt underneath my fingers. To plant trees we had to take big patches of grass out of the ground."

Krystal Rodgers felt the prickly stems of lantana against her skin while pruning last year's growth. Students learned a new meaning for M&M when loading and hauling wheelbarrows of manure and mulch. When students found grubs eating roots of plants, they reasoned that to destroy grubs with chemicals could also destroy beneficial insects or pass chemicals through the food chain when birds eat the grubs. They decided to squish the grubs instead.

Pestalozzi based all learning on sense perception and physical activity. He believed the child would experience intellectual power in surroundings real to him not from empty words, which have no background in his experience.
Jessie Buss planted a sunflower fence after clearing, turning and amending the soil. "I thought it was hard physical work but it gave me a feeling of self-satisfaction," she remarked.

Andrew Lail said, "Planting, pulling weeds, and turning the soil was really tough for me. When I got home, I took a nice long bath and went to bed."

Froebel said a garden was a place to build character and responsibility because one can see the consequences of actions in a very direct way.

William Hunter was surprised to see a weed patch become a flowerbed. "I had no clue how one adult, five boys, and one girl could pull all those weeds. However, working together we finished in no time. Then we mixed the soil, added fertilizer, and finally planted the hummingbird plants. We had made a big change. Flowers were everywhere. It was beautiful," he said.

Taylor Hopkins stated, "When we first got to the garden, we went right to work pulling up tons of weeds and digging up unneeded plants. We turned over the soil and replanted the hummingbird garden. A couple of weeks later my dad brought my sister and me back to the garden. It looked very good."

According to Dewey the activities of gardening engage children in the experimental method, in experiences that involve thinking and problem-solving. Before coming to the garden six student committees were formed to address specific garden problems.

One team had the task of designing and laying new pathways to keep foot traffic off planted areas. On site the team sprinkled white flour on the ground to mark off pathways. Then they dug up paths, raked the soil level, laid the stepping stones, tested the stride distance between stones, reset some stones, and mulched around them.

Mark Phillips was part of a team relocating bluebird houses to deter predators. The bird-fruit garden team added blueberry bushes and a fig tree to the strawberry patch, hoping to attract more frugivorous birds. They planted sorghum, corn, quinoa, and sunflowers for the seedeaters.

The birdhouse team planted a plot of birdhouse gourds for use in making purple martin and wren houses.

Montessori used the garden as a context for instruction and as food for school meals. A natural part of observing in the Montessori school garden was drawing. Since the bird garden needed an updated map, Dana Morris and Ashley Brunson volunteered for the task. Before drawing the map they had to consult with five other teams as they inventoried plants and hardscape items and measured the dimensions. Ashley said, "I was one of the architects. Dana got a bonus chore. Cleaning out the bird baths was nasty."

Bird house gourds grown in the Bird Garden

Being involved in so many aspects of a major undertaking like the Carolina Children's Garden gave the children a multitude of experiences most don't learn until later in life and a wealth of memories to last a lifetime.

The Children's Garden Was For the Birds

The children's garden always lured more than youngsters in winter. Garden educator Tim Nafziger observed an abundance of birds visiting the garden and surrounding woodlands during South Carolina's coldest months of the year. Wearing binoculars more often than not he kept a record of the passerines, waterfowl, and raptors on site.

One solitary bird is the loggerhead shrike, *Lanius ludovicianus,* also called the French mockingbird. The grey predatory songbirds with black masks perch alone on wires or fence posts scanning for prey. They hunt large insects, small rodents, reptiles, and small songbirds by pouncing on them from above and often impaling and storing them on barbed wire fences or thorny shrubs. Tim knew their perches.

A surprising view at the lake down from the children's garden was cormorants, usually seen at the coast. They are colony nesters and appear in flocks. As many as nine at one time were sighted while Tim was on watch. The lake supplied their diet of fish. In the water, the cormorant's dark plumage and snakelike head resemble an anhinga. Cormorants have a black downturned bill while the anhinga's yellow bill is sharply pointed and straight.

Flocks of robins and cedar waxwings took advantage of the "berried treasures" on shrubs and trees in the garden. Bluebirds frequently visited as well.

Tim held a class on Owl Pellet dissection indoors. Parents and children viewed slides of South Carolina owls as Tim described their habitat and habits. Then each student received a plate with a large barn owl pellet wrapped in foil.

"What's for dinner?" one might ask. Students unwrapped the foil to find a furry mass. Using fingers and forceps they separated fur from bones to find evidence – mandible, skull, femur, scapula, ribs, vertebrae, teeth, and more. Children made inferences about the diet of the owl and compared bones. Most

Family dissects owl pellet

pellets had two complete skeletons inside but one child found three skulls indicating a bird, a vole, and a mouse had been that owl's meal for the night. In addition children found rat and shrew on the menu.

Students began to put the bones together like pieces of a puzzle. They were given ziplock bags for their bones and instructions on how to create bone puzzles on black paper. Parents seemed as enthralled as the children.

Tim's Backyard Birds program introduced eager youngsters to the ingredients for building a backyard habitat for birds. Participants made bird feeders from juice bottles and took them home with a starter bag of birdseed.

Birds bring music, color, freedom of flight, and interest to our surroundings. They are sensitive indicators of the health of an ecosystem. What can we do to return their favors? For starters we can make our yards and neighborhoods bird friendly. The Bird Garden in the Carolina Children's Garden was designed, planned, and planted by sixth graders at Summit Parkway Middle School to develop a model habitat to include food, water, shelter, and nesting areas for birds.

The garden encouraged observation of bird behavior too. From a nest-shaped bench, visitors had an inconspicuous place to see birds using the garden as a nursery, airport, migration rest stop, spa, diner, oasis, and songfest site. In a brief visit one might glimpse a bluebird parent feeding its young, a house finch cracking sunflower seeds, a Carolina wren building a nest, and brown-headed nuthatches climbing in and out of woodpecker holes drilled in a dead pine condominium.

The entrance to the garden was a redwood arbor tangled with red cypress vine (*Ipomoea quamoclit*) by late summer. A cedar birdhouse mailbox held an informative brochure with map and plant list. Mulched pathways separated garden rooms. A hummingbird nectary of bee balm, columbine, globe thistle, hollyhock, lantana, phlox, pineapple sage, scabiosa, weigela, and zebrina surrounded an over-sized birdhouse that we called Big Bird's house for youngsters to peek out through rounded face holes painted as birds, butterflies, and flowers. The birdhouse was a favorite for taking photos of grandchildren.

Artisan Matt Kip wove the wisteria bird nest bench.

In summer the pink feathery blossoms of mimosa looked like tropical birds perched in the canopy. Mimosa pods are seed reserves for fall migrants. Other shrubs and trees selected to shelter and feed included eastern red cedar, hornbeam, wax myrtle, red buckeye, sparkleberry, winterberry, dogwood, and viburnum. In a plot thirty-three feet square were bountiful examples of plants to match the scale and budget of visitors' home property with the bonus of attracting birds.

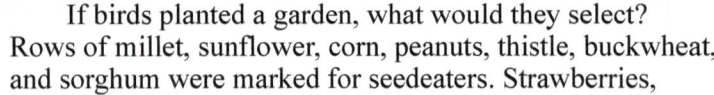

Big Bird's House

If birds planted a garden, what would they select? Rows of millet, sunflower, corn, peanuts, thistle, buckwheat, and sorghum were marked for seedeaters. Strawberries, blueberries, and figs were provided for frugivorous birds. The garden grew its own birdhouse gourds.

Details of hospitality to avian populations appeared throughout the garden. Water was provided in a standing concrete birdbath and a hanging terra-cotta one. A variety of bird nesting boxes and feeders were maintained within and around the periphery. Among them was a Duncraft Absolute II squirrel-resistant double- sided metal feeder filled with sunflower seeds and large enough to serve as many as twelve birds at once. The addition of a Peterson wedge-shaped bluebird nesting box quickly drew a nesting pair, then five blue eggs, and five bluebird fledglings.

The Duncraft Absolute II is a squirrel-resistant metal feeder.

It's no wonder that a favorite garden activity – along with counting birds, watching birds, feeding birds, and learning about birds – was to pack a picnic and dine al fresco with the birds at the children's garden.

Growing up Gardening

Mesozoic Memories: A Dinosaur Garden

Mesozoic Memories presented a landscape from dinosaur days when gymnosperms were the predominant plant and reptiles the predominant animal.

Imagine a world without flowers. Or, what would a bouquet have been from dinosaur days? The Dinosaur Garden gave visitors to Carolina Children's Garden some ideas of what a bouquet might have contained in those days. It presented a concentrated collection of the kinds of plants that once dominated Earth's landscape and introduced one chapter in the evolution of land plants. The theme garden contained non-flowering gymnosperms, the predecessors to angiosperms, the colorful flowering plants in our contemporary Cenozoic gardens.

The theme invited children to look through the eyes of dinosaurs to see their home landscape of two-hundred forty million years ago and to appreciate the relics from Tyrannosaurus' back yard in their own back yard – mosses, ferns, lichens, cycads like the Palmetto, palms, tree ferns, araucaria and pines, bald cypress, and gingko trees. The ferns of our shade gardens are contemporary miniatures from ancient tall fern forests.

Children could touch the fresh fast-food diet of herbivorous dinosaurs and imagine mouth-watering menus of moss mousse, conifer cone cakes, lichen burgers, cycad casserole, fern fritters, palm pudding, and gingko gruel. In their time dinosaur appetites consumed branches of trees and munched off tops of tender saplings. Dinosaurs were the first pruners in the garden.

Children could walk among large, colorful but ferocious dinosaurs and climb steps on a dinosaur's back, and slide down to be among stone alligators and tortoises.

As the Dinosaur Garden grew, a fossil-hunting bed, dinosaur nest, and fossilized footprints were planned to help retrieve Mesozoic memories.

Children were encouraged to bring their favorite dinosaur books to read among prehistoric plants and animals. Those usually included *Digging Up Dinosaurs* by Aliki, *Dinosaur Time* by Peggy Parris, *Dinosaur Garden* by Liza Donnelly, *Dinosaur Tree* by Douglas Henderson, *How do Dinosaurs Say Goodnight?* by Jane Yolen, *Dinosaurs* by Gail Gibbons, *Dinosaur Christmas* by Jerry Pallotta, and *Digging Up Dinosaurs*

or *Lily and Maia: A Dinosaur Adventure* by Jack Horner to read among prehistoric plants and animals. Older elementary and middle school students enjoy reading *Jack Horner, Dinosaur Hunter* by Sophia Gholz, the biography of the paleontologist who was Steven Spielberg's scientific advisor for *Jurassic Park*.

Trees: From Our Garden to Yours

Tree-planting season officially opens on Arbor Day, the first Friday in December in South Carolina. The Carolina Children's Garden took that occasion to recognize the attributes of the varied trees that were the backbone of the garden. The garden displayed candidates to consider for the home landscape.

In the Butterfly Garden the tulip poplar, *Liriodendron tulipifera*, a fast growing deciduous member of the Magnolia family, was featured. The tulip poplar presents a tulip-shaped yellow, green, and orange flower in April. Like its relative, the southern magnolia, the tree can achieve heights of over one hundred feet. The flower nectar feeds hummingbirds and the seeds are eaten by the evening grosbeak. Leaves of the tree host the eggs and larva of the Eastern tiger swallowtail, the state butterfly. In the same garden the Chaste tree, *Vitex agnus-castus,* also was showcased. The summer purple spikelike flowers

Tulip Poplar flowers

of *Vitex* become pungent berries by fall and attract bees, butterflies, and hummingbirds. The tree is easy to propagate from seed and grows rapidly to reach ten to twelve feet.

School board member Dottie Boatright assists sixth grade students from Summit Parkway Middle School plant an eastern red cedar, *Juniperus virginiana,* in the Bird Garden.

Baby Bear felt tall next to the dwarf Alberta spruce, *Picea glauca 'Conica',* at the entranceway to Three Bears Garden. The miniature slow-growing evergreen reaches ten to twelve feet in twenty-five to thirty years. In its early years the conifer is perfect for a child's potted Christmas tree to decorate indoors or outdoors. Most garden centers have a large selection in fall. After the holidays, the tiny tree can be planted in a permanent sunny location outdoors.

When the Carolina Children's Garden was developed, the Bird Garden site was selected because of a dead pine tree. The death of the pine opened a new world of life that made it a perfect teaching tool. The trunk riddled in holes by woodpeckers was a nesting spot for brown-headed nuthatches.

Hummingbirds fed on the nectar of the nearby mimosa and blossoms of two red buckeye trees. The lovely mimosa, *Albizia julibrissin,* is a small, supple tropical-looking tree with frondlike leaves and fragrant pink feathery flowers. The long, flat, brown pods reveal membership in the Legume family. In winter we hung suet and fruit from the limbs. Red buckeye trees, *Aesculus pavia*, have rich red panicles three to six inches long reaching toward the sky in April and May and one or two brown seeds in each capsule in fall.

Red buckeye tree flowers greet spring migrating ruby-throated hummingbirds.

And birds love the eastern red cedar, *Juniperus virginiana*, not only for its berries but also for its dense evergreen foliage, which protects them from weather and predators, conceals their nests, and harbors a feast of insects and spiders. Michael Dirr, professor emeritus of horticulture at the University of Georgia, described the red cedar as a "tough, irrepressible green soldier" thriving where few trees can survive. The aromatic conifer with a lifespan of three hundred years is often selected as the State House Christmas tree.

Plants in the Dinosaur Garden were gymnosperms, among the largest and oldest living plants on Earth. The ginkgo tree, *Ginkgo biloba*, is the only remaining species of Ginkgophyta on the planet. The slow-growing tree attains a height of forty feet in twenty years, transplants easily in any soil type, and is virtually pest free. The green fan-shaped leaves turn bright yellow in fall. We planted a male tree to avoid the foul-smelling fruit of the female.

The peach tree, *Prunus persica*, in the Old MacDonald's Garden was a reminder of one of the state's most important commercial crops. South Carolina is second only to California in production of fresh peaches. Individual homeowners can grow productive fruit trees in their own back yards.

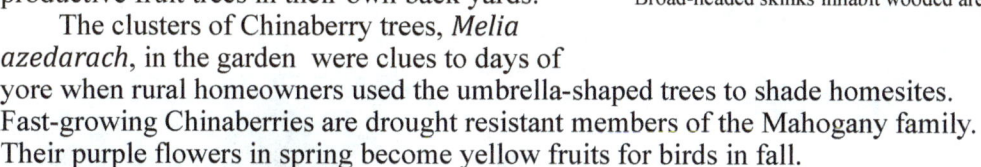

Broad-headed skinks inhabit wooded areas.

The clusters of Chinaberry trees, *Melia azedarach*, in the garden were clues to days of yore when rural homeowners used the umbrella-shaped trees to shade homesites. Fast-growing Chinaberries are drought resistant members of the Mahogany family. Their purple flowers in spring become yellow fruits for birds in fall.

Live Oak entranceway to the children's garden

Live oaks, *Quercus virginiana*, forming a natural arbor were selected as the shaded entranceway to the children's garden. Their location gave clues to the history of the site prior to acquisition by Clemson University. This magnificent long-lived tree asks only for sun and space to grow. In the children's garden broad-headed skinks used these trees as their gym.

On nature walks among the trees in the garden, children collected leaves, sprigs, twigs, berries, pods, cones, nuts, seeds, and feathers to make seasonal collages, pressed leaves, leaf prints, and nature bracelets.

Ralph Waldo Emerson wrote that in the woods we are all very young in comparison to the trees that surround us. Celebrate your youth on Arbor Day by planting a tree and visiting an arboretum.

Signs of Spring Hopped Out of the Children's Garden

Even though the ground hog might have seen his shadow and predicted six more weeks of winter, at the Carolina Children's Garden Peter Rabbit often saw early signs of spring. While he was hopping out of the wheelbarrow near Mr. McGregor's tool shed, a butterfly flew from the tiny lavender ajuga flowers to the hedgerow of Valentine red camellia sasanquas. Peter nibbled on the new leaves of hollyhocks sprouting along the white picket fence.

Peter Rabbit in Mr. McGregor's wheelbarrow

In the Bird Garden he watched bluebirds inspecting the bluebird boxes and noticed that birds were coming in pairs to the suet and seed feeders. The blueberry bushes had leaf buds unfolding.

When Peter met Baby Bear at the Three Bears Homestead, the young cub was rubbing the warm fuzzy leaves of lamb's ears on his nose. Peter remembered how his mother had made lamb's ear mittens for all of her Flopsy bunnies.

Under a heavy pine straw blanket along the Carolina Fence, verbena was peeking through the mulch after its winter nap. Peter smelled the leaves and remembered this was not the lemon verbena his mother had used for tea. At Frog Pond he sipped the water and wondered when frog eggs would appear in the pond.

Lamb's ear

In McDonald's Historic Crops Garden he gathered a bunch of parsley to nibble with the salad greens of wild onion and wild lettuce he found growing throughout the garden.

Until the soil got warm enough to sow seeds for the herb chamomile, he gathered tansy and thyme leaves from the Alphabet Fence, rosemary from the Growing Healthy Garden and bee balm

Carolina wren on rosemary

from the Butterfly Garden so his mother could brew a variety of soothing teas. He liked to bring long sprigs of rosemary's azure blossoms to his mother in their Sandhill home beneath the root of an eastern red cedar tree.

Growing up Gardening

Peter found the freshest, greenest grass in the Reading Garden and invited his siblings – Flopsy, Mopsy, and Cottontail--to the soft bed of greens. Nearby Pooh Bear was arranging a freshly cut crocus, hyacinth and daffodil birthday bouquet for Christopher Robin. He had gathered newly sprouted bamboo shoots from the Dinosaur Garden, Mesozoic Memories, for the salad course.

What signs of spring will you find in your home garden?

Daffodils along Mr. McGregor's fence

It's a Pleasure To Find Peter Rabbit

Unlike Mr. McGregor of Peter Rabbit fame, you can be happy to have cute creatures visit your garden. Having rabbits in the garden means it's thriving, plus rabbits perform a number of useful tasks such as eating weeds and gleaning crop leftovers after the season.

To visit Mr. McGregor's garden at the Carolina Children's Garden, you would start at the live oak entrance and walk up a slope to the grassy knoll, Hill Top. Our favorite children's garden from the past included a plot at the top of a grassy knoll where Mr. McGregor peered out of his tool shed searching for Peter Rabbit.

He found evidence of Peter the trespasser everywhere-- teeth marks in the cucumbers, footprints among the cabbages and potatoes, a blue jacket in the blackberries. Throughout the growing season, Mr. McGregor was on guard against predator rabbits. If he understood the habitat requirements and behavior of rabbits, he would delight in seeing rabbits on the farm. Cottontail rabbits like Peter need cover, food, water, and a place to raise their young. The woody cover of brambles, grape vines, honeysuckle, creeping juniper, forsythias, and wild roses provides protection for rabbits. Brush piles around the farm, which the Flopsy Bunnies call rubbish heaps, are also bunny cover. Even a recycled Christmas tree placed on its side along the garden fence can conceal rabbits. Tall grasses and weeds become nurseries for baby bunnies.

Expect to see rabbits in your garden.

In spring and summer, rabbit families share a wide variety of wild foods such as grasses, leaves, shoots, fruits, branch tips, buds, seeds, and bark. Rabbits pick such weeds as dock, clover, dandelion, chickweed, ragweed, poison ivy, wild blackberries, blueberries, and grapes.

In autumn they clean up fallen apples and corn and soybean debris left in fields after harvest. In winter when herbaceous plants are less abundant, a cottontail diet shifts to twigs and bark. The rabbits prune our cherry, dogwood, sumac, oak, and maple trees. Cedar and holly berries are desserts. Rabbits get most of their water from dew and succulent vegetation, but they will drink from natural stands of water.

If your farm or back yard supports a wide variety of plants for both cover and food, you should expect rabbits in the garden. Since humans like some of the same foods as rabbits, plant an extra row of lettuces, beans, peas, radishes, and sorrel for the rabbits in your neighborhood. Make sure to include a plot of chamomile to use in making a restorative cup of chamomile tea after a day in the garden.

Butterflies Flutter Amid Nectar-Rich Flowers

The butterfly section at the Carolina Children's Garden always was a carousel of colorful flowers, caterpillars, and butterflies by late summer. For over two decades the garden provided a place where children could find evidence of the life cycle of butterflies among the host and nectar plants. They could watch a tiger swallowtail lay eggs on tulip poplar leaves and see monarchs place their eggs on milkweed. A child could be enthralled by very hungry caterpillars and wait for wings to emerge from a chrysalis.

The Butterfly Garden also gave visitors a glimpse of key practices to entice butterflies to their own yard, including inspiration in creating their own butterfly botanical café:

- Locate the garden in a sunny area. Butterflies, their eggs, larvae and their menu plants require bright sun. Warm habitats allow eggs and larvae to develop more rapidly.

- Plant large splashes of nectar-producing flowers. Butterflies sip nectar through a straw-like proboscis but first find nectar through the taste receptors on their feet. Ageratum, azaleas, buddleia, chrysanthemums, goldenrod, lantana, purple coneflower, rudbeckia, verbena, and vitex are high-nectar-producing perennials and shrubs best planted in the fall. Annuals such as cleome, cosmos, marigold, pentas, salvia, vinca, and zinnia can be added in spring.

- Interplant host plants to support the eggs and larvae. Parsley, dill, fennel, and rue feed black swallowtail caterpillars. Milkweed feeds monarch caterpillars. *Cassia alata* aka *Senna alata* is a host plant for the cloudless sulfur butterfly. Plantains, gerardias, toadflax, snapdragons, beardtongue, spiderwort false loosestrifes, and wild petunia feed common buckeye caterpillars. White cabbage caterpillars feed on radish, mustard, and broccoli. The gulf fritillary feeds on passionvine.

- Include stones or rocks in the garden. Butterflies are cold-blooded and must bask on rocks and bare soil to collect the solar energy they need to warm their flight muscles to fly and remain airborne. They fly best when air temperatures are between 75 and 90 degrees Fahrenheit. The body of the butterfly is often

black, which helps in absorbing heat.
- Prepare a puddle pub. Male butterflies congregate to extract minerals and salts from moist soil. To make a puddling area, bury a bucket of wet sand or soil to ground level and then place sticks or rocks on top for butterflies to perch on while drinking. Periodically refill the bucket with water.
- Provide shelter and roosting sites. Where does a butterfly go at night or in the rain? Butterflies need safe shelter from wind, weather, and predators. Good protection is any tree with broad leaves; a hollow in a tree; a brush or woodpile; or the overhang on a shed or house.
- Use no pesticides in or near the butterflies' food supply. Pesticides disrupt the natural predator-prey relationships in the web of life.
- Become a butterfly watcher. Just as bird watchers learn how to identify birds, butterfly observers learn to recognize butterflies, their eggs, and larvae. Binoculars and a good butterfly field guide are essential.

Butterfly Girl Sculpture

Butterfly Garden Stepping Stone

Food Chains in the Garden

Gardens are man-made landscapes, and since most gardeners are continually adding trees, shrubs, vines, herbaceous edibles, and ornamentals, there can be great plant diversity leading to increased animal diversity. It's only natural and normal for the plant producers to bring the consumers.

I was reminded that food chains are everywhere in a garden when I happened upon an adult black rat snake eating a bunny breakfast in the Alphabet Garden at the Carolina Children's Garden. The bunny had been eating some of Mr. McGregor's Garden lettuces when the reptile slithered on the scene.

Black rat snake eating rabbit

The red-tailed hawks observed onsite fed on rabbits and snakes. In the Butterfly Garden eastern tiger swallowtails were drinking nectar from lantana while their larvae were chewing leaves of the tulip poplar, a host plant for the state butterfly. Carolina wrens nesting in the Carolina Fence Garden snatched swallowtail larvae. Nearby native pollen wasps were collecting nectar and pollen from the bottlebrush buckeye to feed to their young, and bumblebees were nectaring at the abelia.

Watching birds is a sure way to see food chains in action. Carolina wrens are voracious insect eaters throughout the garden but they also down small fruits like blueberries and grapes in the Growing Healthy Garden. Cardinals and house finches are attracted to the variety of seeds in all the gardens. The yellow-bellied sapsucker, a winter resident, traps insects in the sap wells he drills into the callery pear tree at the garden's entranceway. In early spring ruby-throated hummingbirds seek the sap wells for sustenance when they first arrive from Central America even before sipping nectar at native coral honeysuckle and other red tubular flowers.

Pines – loblolly, longleaf, and shortleaf - were the dominant tree in the garden, their cones and seeds ubiquitous. In daylight gray squirrels consumed pine seeds, acorns, hickory nuts, flower buds and blossoms, grapes, mushrooms, bird eggs, and baby birds. The night shift flying squirrels consumed a similar diet of acorns, seeds, berries, mushrooms, baby birds, caterpillars, and beetles. The arboreal broad-headed skinks in the live oak entranceway of the garden ate insects and even their own kind. Skinks became dinner for squirrels, hawks and snakes.

Humans were part of the food chain too, and that has not changed. Dragonflies capture mosquitoes before they bite us but they consume far more mosquito larvae than adult mosquitoes. While dragonflies dine by day, bats take on the mosquito menu at night.

Whether picnicking with your family at a children's garden or taking a closer look in your own back yard, play the game of Who Eats What? Write down the name of each predator and its prey on separate index cards. In the first food chain above lettuce, rabbit, snake fill three cards. With multiple observations over a season you will be able to diagram the complex web of feeding relationships involved in energy flow in a garden.

Hawk captured rabbit

Blueberries for Annika and You

One warm June day little Annika went with her mother to pick blueberries in the Growing Healthy Garden. She brought her small blue bucket and her mother brought a small blue bucket too. "We take our blueberries home to make muffins," said her mother. Little Annika picked three ripe blueberries and dropped them in her little blue bucket "kerplink, kerplank. kerplunk." She picked three more blueberries and ate them. Her mother walked slowly to the bushes and picked blueberries putting them in her pail. Little Annika followed behind picking blueberries and putting more in her mouth than in the pail.

On the other side of the blueberry bushes Mama, Papa, and Baby Bear were also picking blueberries for their breakfast pancakes to be eaten at their new oak stump table and chair set in Three Bears Homestead.

That scenario, which may sound similar to the children's book *Blueberries for Sal* by Robert McCloskey, is one of many I remember seeing and imagining in the Carolina Children's Garden during the years it was open. Hanna and her almost two-year-old daughter, Annika, came to the magical place every season of the year.

In summer after picking blueberries, Annika would head to the frog slide in the Dinosaur Garden and then on to Kanga and Roo's sandpit at Pooh's Corner. As a mother Hanna liked that the garden had sod and earth rather than hard gravel or tarmac like many parks, school grounds, and public gardens. Mother and daughter would listen to the wind chimes and search for the source of music coming from the tops of the pines. Being on a hill, the garden had a cooling breeze even on the hottest of days.

Blueberries are in season across South Carolina's Midlands from June 1 to August 15. At the Children's Garden blueberries grew in McDonald's Historic Crops Farm, Growing Healthy Garden, and the Bird Garden. The three gardens featured three benefits of blueberries – as a historic crop in the southeast, as a high source of antioxidants for human longevity, and as a food to share with wildlife.

Blueberries are one of the most productive and long-lasting edible landscape crops homeowners can grow. Once established, blueberry bushes can live twenty-five years. Rabbiteye and Southern Highbush varieties are best adapted to South Carolina climate and soils. Clemson Extension recommends a soil pH between 5.0 and 5.5. Fall and winter are the best planting times.

One goal of the children's garden was to demonstrate how families like Annika's can replicate favorite plants like blueberries in their home garden.

Annika and her mother

Annika picking blueberries

INDEX

A

ABC Book of Flowers for Young Gardeners, The (Stoker), 201
abelia, 220
acanthus-leaved thistle, 156
A.C. Moore Herbarium, 177–178
acorns
    as food for wildlife, 1, 5, 80, 220
    in handicrafts, 91, 114, 119, 126, 130, 139
Adamson, Nancy Lee, 17
ADHD (Attention Deficit Hyperactivity Disorder), 151
Africa, native plants, 95, 96, 101
African marigold, 156
African violets, 109, 112, 114
ageratum, 201, 218
air plants, 173–174
Aliki, 213
Allen, Mary Anne, 194
alley-orchids, 103
aloe, 9, 110
Alphabet Fence, 201, 216
Alphabet Garden, 193, 195, 219
alphabet play, 131, 205–206
alyssum, 64, 124, 132, 155
amaranth, 36, 72, 127, 132. *See also* globe amaranth
amaranthus, 124
amaryllis, 120–121
Amazing Earthworm, The (Hess), 158
American Academy of Pediatrics, 34, 91
American chestnut, 172
American Heritage Trees Project, 124
American Horticultural Society (AHS) National Children and Youth Gardening Symposium, 37, 193–194
American Horticultural Therapy Association, 195
American wisteria (*Wisteria frutescens*), 96
Anarchy Zone, 197–198
Anderson, Rick, 194, 195–196
angiosperms, 180, 213
anhinga, 211
animal consumption of fruits, 67
animals, dressing like, 143
animals, plants that resemble, 95–96, 173
annuals, 20, 23, 29, 84, 105, 124, 218
Appelhof, Mary, 199
arbor, 94, 96, 123, 129, 201, 212, 215
Arbor Day, 137, 192, 214, 216
"Ark" of animals classroom project, 36–37
Armitage, Alan, 102
arugula, 44, 57, 59, 64, 65, 150
Asian cuisine staples, 166
Asian greens, 65
Asian kudzu, 157
Atlanta Botanical Garden, 102

avocados, 75, 78, 116–117
azalea, 116, 129, 171, 218

B

baby's breath, 132
bachelor button, 55, 102, 124, 127, 132, 146
Backyard Birds program, 208, 211
Badger Rock Middle School, 165, 166
Bailey, Carolyn S., 138
Baker Creek, 89, 165
bald cypress, 171, 213
bales, planting in, 51
balloon flower (*Platycodon grandiflorus*), 23, 101, 103–104, 124, 156
balloon vine, 84, 97, 145
Barclay School, 81–82
bark in dyes, 143–144
bark in handicrafts, 138
barley, 9, 70, 72, 125, 132, 150
barley bales, 51
Bartholomew, Mel, 47–48, 51–52, 131
basil, 29, 93
    commercial supplies of, 164
    as a container plant, 201
    growing from cuttings, 150
    in a keyhole garden, 53
    in a pizza garden, 58
    as a salt alternative, 55, 70
    seed saving, 84
beans
    black beans, 72
    butter beans, 50, 89
    "Cherokee Trail of Tears" bean, 50
    climbing beans, 50
    garbanzo beans, 70, 71, 72
    growing, 49–50, 159
    hyacinth bean (*Lablab purpureus*), 50, 87, 92, 94, 96
    lima beans, 50
    in MyPlate plan, 72
    non-green varieties, 50
    scarlet runner bean (*Phaseolus coccineus*), 50, 87, 92, 94, 96
    in three sisters planting system, 55, 160
    as top plants for kids, 92
bean varieties
    "Calico Crowder", 50
    "Christmas", 50
    "Florida speckled", 50
    "Green Anellino", 50
    "Kentucky Blue", 50
    "Kentucky Wonder", 50
    "Kwintus", 50
    "Marvel of Venice", 50
    "Mountaineer", 50
    "Rattlesnake", 50

"Snow on the Mountain", 50
Trionfo violetto pole bean, 50
beardtongue (*Penstamon* spp.), 17, 20, 23
bear grease, 141
Beasley, Todd, 32
beds
    with a maze design, 129
    raised, 25, 31, 48, 178–179, 201
    square foot gardening, 43, 47–48, 51–52, 131–132
bee balm (*Monarda didyma*)
    in craft gardens, 150
    as drought tolerant, 204
    as a hummingbird plant, 4, 13, 23, 200, 212
    as a pollinator plant, 21, 22, 94, 204, 226
beeblossom (*Gaura lindheimer*), 20
beech, 24, 25, 180
bee-friendly garden, 20–21
bees
    bumblebees, 20, 220
    color vision, 21
    communication, 22
    creating an insectary for, 17–18
    declining populations, 17
    digger bee, 21
    European honeybees, 17–18, 22
    flower shapes and tongue length, 21
    gardens for, 22, 106
    leaf cutter bees, 181
    mason bee cavity nest, 22, 23
    mason bees, 22, 23
    native bees, 17, 18, 20, 21, 22, 23, 177, 181, 188
    pollination efficiency, 22
    solitary bees, 22, 23
    sweat bees, 21
    underground nesting, 21, 23
Bees and Blooms education initiative, 22–23
beets
    in bucket gardens, 55
    for cold frames, 44
    as a dye plant, 144
    fall planting, 57, 59, 64
    in MyPlate plan, 72
begonia, 124, 154, 172, 194
bells of Ireland, 92
Belser Arboretum, 25, 170–172
Bender, Steve, 102
Benjamin West and His Cat Grimalkin (Henry), 141
Berg, Charles Ramirez, 163
berries
    as dye plants, 143–144
    picking and eating, 93
    strawberries, 37, 62–63, 72, 93, 144, 200
    in wildlife diets, 1, 5, 148, 180, 200, 214, 215, 221
    See also blueberries
beta-carotene, 70
biennial, concept of, 103
Big Glass Circus Tent, 172
Billy's Goat Hill farm, 83
biodiversity, decline of, 157
Bio Dome Seed Starter, 85
bird fruit bar, 200
Bird Garden (Carolina Children's Garden), 195, 200, 208–212, 214
birdhouse gourd (*Lagenaria siceraria*), 6–7, 210
Bird-Lore, 184
birds
    cavity-nesting, 7
    census activities, 183–184
    in food chains, 220
    frugivorous, 37, 200, 210, 212
    munchie trees, 5, 79–80, 81
    natural feeder plants, 13
    nesting boxes, 13, 201–212
    seedeaters, 210, 212
    sightings in Congaree National Park, 180
birdseed plot, 200
birdsong, 30, 131
bird wreath feeder, 148
Bizarre Botanicals (Mellichamp and Gross), 174
black bat plant, (*Tacca chantrieri*), 172, 173
Blackburn, Mary, 195
black rat snake, 219
blanket flower
    Gaillardia aristata, 21, 22, 161, 162
    Gaillardia pulchella, 20
blazing star (*Liatris spicata*), 21
bleeding heart (*Dicentra spectabilis*), 123
bloom
    opening and closing times, 93, 155–156
    spring simulation for forcing, 115–116
    succession of, 20
blueberries
    Annika's berry picking experience, 220–221
    attracting wildlife with, 13, 217
    as bird food, 200, 210, 212, 220
    in Carolina Children's Garden, 202, 220–221
    as a dye plant, 144
    in MyPlate plan, 72
    pollinators of, 22
    varieties adapted to South Carolina, 221
Blueberries for Sal (McCloskey), 158, 221
bluebird, 210, 211, 212, 216
blue-eyed grass, 103, 124
blue flax (*Linum perenne lewisii*), 155, 161
blue flowers in floral fireworks, 124
blue granite, 201
Bonnie Plants, 41

Bonnie Plants 3rd Grade Cabbage Program, 32–34
books for family reading, 87, 158
Bottle Biology Project (University of Wisconsin-Madison), 48
bottlebrush buckeye, 219
boughs, 5, 80, 127
bouquet garden, 132
bouquets / bouquet flowers, 55, 124, 132
boxwood, 5, 94, 120, 129
braconid wasps, 35
Bradshaw, David, 50, 89
Brockman Elementary School, 27, 89–90
Brogdon, Ed, 178, 179
browallia, 124
Browder, Jamie, classroom of, 32
Brown, Herrick, 177
Brown, Karla, 23
Bruchac, Joseph, 160
brush piles, 11, 18, 190, 217
bucket gardening, 48–49, 51, 54–55, 68
buckwheat, 36, 71, 72, 132, 212
buddleia, 218
Buffalo Bird Woman's Garden (Wilson), 160
bulbs, 1, 7, 64, 98–99, 121, 158
Bundy, Gina, 199
Bunnies' Brew, 81–82
bunny's ears (*Opuntia microdasys*), 95
Bunting, Eve, 158
Burnett, Frances H., 98–99, 158
Burnham, Sarah, 89, 90
Burns, Alfred, 22
bur oak, 124
buttercup, 155
butterflies
  attracting, 25–26, 38, 94, 218–219
  eastern tiger swallowtail, 180, 214, 218, 219
  gulf fritillary, 25–26, 94, 218
  host plants, 13, 218
  monarch, 24, 37–38, 186, 218
  nectar plants, 20, 23, 38, 96
  red admiral, 180
  spicebush swallowtail, 25
  zebra swallowtail, 180
butterfly gardens, 24, 31, 100, 195, 203, 218–219
butterfly larvae, 25, 26, 38, 180, 218, 219
butterfly orchid (*Psychopsis papilio*), 173

C

cabbage
  as a bale plant, 51
  Bonnie Plants 3rd Grade Cabbage Program, 32–34
  as a cool-season plant, 57, 59, 64
  as health proactive, 70
  as a Hmong food staple, 166
  red cabbage, 144

Caduto, Michael J., 160
caladium, 95, 96, 124
calendula, 51, 64, 156
California poppy, 156
camellia, 129, 149, 216
Camp GLEA (Gardening and Literacy Education through the Arts), 52–54
canary creeper (*Tropaeolum peregrinum*), 97
candelabra, 124
canna, 23, 124
cantaloupe, 47, 62, 70, 72
Canterbury bells, 92
cape marigold, 156
cardinal, 79, 80, 180, 220
cardinal flower (*Lobelia cardinalis*), 4
Carle, Eric, 87, 158
carnation, 146, 156
carnivorous plants, 114, 172
Carolina Butterfly Society, 195
Carolina cherry laurel, 36
Carolina Children's Garden
  bird sightings, 211–212
  blueberry picking, 220–221
  creation of, 194–196
  education snake, 15
  environmental education programs, 207–208
  inspiration for, 193–194
  moveable landscape project, 100
  play potential, 94
  signs of spring, 216–217
  trees, 214–216
  See also Carolina Children's Garden themed gardens
Carolina Children's Garden themed gardens
  Alphabet Fence, 201, 216
  Bird Garden, 195, 200, 208–212, 214
  Butterfly Garden, 195, 203, 218–219
  Carolina Fence™ Garden, 195, 201
  Growing Healthy garden, 195, 201, 207, 216, 220, 221
  Mesozoic Memories, 195, 203, 213
  Old MacDonald's Historic Crops, 195, 202
  Pooh's Corner, 195, 203, 206–207
  Reading Room, 202
  sponsors, 195
  Three Bears' Homestead, 195, 202
Carolina wren, 7, 180, 201, 212, 216, 219, 220
carpeting, soft outdoor, 94
carrots
  in bucket gardens, 55
  for cold frames, 44
  fall planting, 57, 59, 64
  as health proactive, 70
  in MyPlate plan, 72
  in square-foot gardening, 132
Carson, Billy, 83–84

Carson, Rachel, 34, 157, 170
Caseley, Judith, 158
cassia, 218
catawba (catalpa), 36
catchfly, 156
caterpillar café, 23
caterpillars
    black swallowtail caterpillar, 23, 218
    cloudless sulphur caterpillar, 218
    ecological role, 24
    as food source, 24
    of gulf fritillary butterfly, 26
    host plants, 13, 23, 218
    monarch caterpillar, 23, 218
    oak species' support of, 157
    tussock moth caterpillar, 180
    white cabbage caterpillar, 218
caterpillar tents, 94
catmint (*Nepeta mussinii*), 9, 94, 156
catnip (*Nepeta cataria*), 9, 94, 125, 126, 156
cats, accessories and plant preferences, 8–9, 94, 125–126
cedar waxwing, 185, 211
celosia, 124, 127
cereal grains, 51, 132
chamomile
    as a dye plant, 144
    as insect repellent, 9, 125–126
    as soft outdoor carpeting, 94
    starting seeds, 150
    for tea, 94, 218
Chapman, Frank, 184
chard, 44, 51, 57, 59, 64, 65, 66
Charles (student), 166–167
Chaste tree (*Vitex agnus-castus*), 124, 214
Chen, Connie, 209
Cherokee (student), 167
Cherokee people, 105
cherry, 25, 94, 116, 180, 186, 218
chervil, 59, 64, 70, 94, 164
Chicago Public Schools (CPS) Garden Team, 197
chicory, 57, 65, 155
Children's Center for Cancer and Blood Disorders, 178
children's theme gardens at AHS symposium, 193–194
chinaberry (*Melia azedarach*), 215
Chinese greens, 52
chocolate cosmos, 101
chocolate mint, 9
Christmas cactus, 90
Christmas trees, reuse, 79–81
chrysanthemum, 109–110, 146, 218
cigar plant (*Cuphia ignea*), 4
citizen science programs
    Budburst, 185

Butterflies I've Seen, 186
Butterfly Counts Program, 186–187
Firefly Atlas, 190
Firefly Watch, 3, 190
Great Backyard Bird Count (GBBC), 184
Hummingbirds at Home, 4
Journey North, 4, 186
citrus fruit seeds, planting, 75
City Year volunteers, 62, 174–175
Clemson Sandhill Research and Education Center (REC), 17, 100, 174, 194, 196
cleome, 23, 124, 130, 154, 218
cleyera, 129
clock, floral, 154–156
clouds, 135
clover, 23, 91, 146, 217
clownish plants, 172–173
cockscomb (*Celosia cristata*), 173
cold frame, 43–44, 65
coleus, 124
collards, 51, 59, 62, 64, 65, 70, 202
Collins, Barbara, 28
Collins, Susan, classroom of, 28–29
Colonial Wind, Weather, and Sundial Garden, 193
color
    clothing in nature's colors, 142–143
    earth pigments, 141–142
    plant sources of dyes, 143–144
colorful flowers
    for floral fireworks, 124
    of Mexican origin, 162
    moveable butterfly garden, 100
color games, 130
Columbia Art Museum, 100
Columbia Green, 192
Columbia tickseed (*Coreopsis tinctoria*), 161
columbine, 20, 21, 23, 37, 212
Comenius on knowledge, 209
Community Collaborative Rain, Hail and Snow Network (CoCoRaHS), 188–189
companion planting, 159, 160
compost, making, 23, 37, 75, 83–84, 90
Compost Critters (Lavies), 158
Congaree National Park, 2, 13, 24, 179–181, 190
conservationists, 28, 157
Conservation Station, 174–175
containers
    bucket gardening, 48–49, 51, 54–55, 68
    cultivating mint relatives in, 9
    drainage, 54
    eggshells as, 149–150
    miniature, 59, 68–69, 76
    for moveable gardens, 68–69, 100–101
    for observing plant-insect relationships, 25–26
    for personal plots, 57

for starting seeds, 85–86, 149, 150
    terrariums, 114–115
convolvulus, 155
cool-season plants, 52, 57, 59, 64
Cooney, Barbara, 87, 158
Cooper, Chanda, 147
coral honeysuckle, 220
coreopsis, 17, 22, 23, 79, 84, 154, 161
cormorant, 211
corn
    as bird food, 79, 200, 210, 212
    colorful ears, 95
    corncob house, 139
    cracked, 18, 80
    growing, 59, 85, 159–160, 167
    on Lewis and Clark expedition, 162
    seedheads, 79
    in square foot gardening, 47
    in three sisters planting system, 55, 159–160
    vertical supports and, 94
Cornell Laboratory of Ornithology, 5, 184
    Project FeederWatch (PFW), 183
corn maze, 129, 130
corn poppy, 155
corn snake (aka red rat snake, garden snake), 14–15, 126–127
cosmos
    for floral fireworks, 124
    for a flower maze, 130
    as a nectar-producing annual, 13, 23, 188, 218
    seed saving, 84
Costello, Beth, 52, 53
cotton pods, 88
Cotty, Amelia, 100
creeping fig (*Ficus repens*), 97
creeping thyme, 130
crossvine (*Bignonia capreolata*), 4
crowder pea, 50
CSX Community Service Grants, 42
cucumber, 21, 29, 97
    as heat-loving, 59
    in MyPlate plan, 72
    in a private garden, 153
    starting from seed, 85
    as a trellis plant, 49, 94
cup and saucer vine (*Cobaea scandens*), 97
currant, 72, 153
cycads, 203, 213
cypress vine (*Ipomoea quamoclit*), 4, 84, 123, 212

D

daffodil, 64, 98, 149, 217
daisy, 21, 81, 91, 146, 156
dame's rocket, 156
dandelion, 143–144, 146, 156, 217
darkness, exploring, 13–14

daylily, 23, 39, 91, 156
delphinium, 124
Denver Urban Gardens, 196–197
Designing Outdoor Environments for Children (Tai), 199
devil's thorns (*Solanum pyracanthum*), 174
Dewey on he experimental method, 210
dianthus, 64, 84, 132
dietary guidelines, 59, 71–73
Digging Up Dinosaurs (Aliki), 213
dill
    as a companion plant, 153
    flavoring use, 55, 93
    as a host plant, 13, 23, 94, 218
    seed saving, 55, 70, 84–85
dinosaur garden. *See* Mesozoic Memories
Dinosaur Garden (Donnelly), 213
Dinosaurs (Gibbons), 213
Dinosaur Time (Parris), 213
Dinosaur Tree (Henderson), 213
Dirr, Michael, 215
doghouse rooftop garden, 46–47
dogrose, 155
dogs and gardens, 7–8, 46
dogwood (*Cornus florida*)
    berries and leaves, 5, 127, 131, 137
    fruiting phenophase, 185
    as a host plant, 180
    landscape uses, 171, 212
doll play
    doll-sized bouquet flowers, 132
    doll tea party, 94
    floral dolls, 91, 103
    Miss Hickory dolls and accessories, 138–139
donkey's ears (*Kalanchoe gastonis-bonnieri*), 96
Donnelly, Liza, 213
Dow, Kristin, 191
dragonflies, 180, 181, 220
dried plants, 9, 177, 178
Druse, Ken, 191
Dutchman's pipe (*Aristolochia macrophylla*), 96
dwarf Alberta spruce (*Picea glauca 'Conica'*), 214
dyes, plant sources of, 143–144, 163

E

ears, plants resembling, 95–96
eastern red cedar (*Juniperus virginiana*), 5, 185, 212, 214, 215, 216
Eating the Alphabet (Ehlert), 158, 206
Eat What You Grow toolkit, 197
Ecke Ranch (CA), 163
edamame, 72, 87, 92
Edmonds, Amanda Maria, 199
educational ideas in gardening, 208–210
eggshell crafts, 149–150

227

eggshell planters, 68–69, 150
eggshells as planters, 149–150
eggshells in garden crafts, 149
Ehlert, Lois, 32, 158, 206
elephant ears (*Colocasia antiquorum*), 95, 100
elkhorn (*Clarkia pulchella*), 162
Endangered Species Act, 157
English ivy (*Hedera helix*), 97
English plantain, 156
epiphytes, 173–174
eucalyptus, 5
European greens, 65
evening campion, 156
evening catchfly, 156
evening primrose, 14, 93, 105, 155, 156
evergreen shrubs, 129
exercise and gardening, 60–61
exotic love (*Ipomoea lobata*), 123
experiential education, 28–29, 81–82, 111–113, 208–210
experimental method in gardening, 39, 40, 111, 210
experiments with plants, 39–40, 48

F

fall garden herbs, 164
fall gardens for children, 50–52
fall planting, 64–66
fall seasonal activities
    collecting seed pods, 84–85, 87–89, 170
    flower colors in clothing, 143
    seed saving, 84–85, 89
    spider watching, 11–12
    squirrel watching, 1, 138
false indigo (*Baptisia australis*), 20
Farm to School programs, 73
Fellows, Rebecca Nevers, 147
ferns, 147, 172, 203, 213
fertilizer tea, 150
fig, 13, 67, 200, 210, 212
fig marigold, 156
finger puppets, 96, 130
firecracker vine (*Ipomoea lobata*), 97
Fireflies (Johnson), 158
firefly (aka lightening bug, candle fly), 2–3, 130, 189–191
Firefly Atlas, 190
firefly lantern, 14, 130
firefly larvae, 190
Firefly Watch, 3, 190–191
fireworks, floral, 124
Fisher, Erin, 28
Fitness the Dynamic Gardening Way (Restuccio), 61
floral chains and garlands, 146–147
floral clock, 154–156

flor de la noche buena, 122, 163
floristic survey, 177–178
flower chains, 91, 146
Flower Garden (Bunting), 158
Flower Grows, A (Robbins), 121
flowering plants
    bloom opening and closing times, 93, 155–156
    dependence on animal pollinators, 17, 18
    of Mexican origin, 162
flowering tobacco, 156
flower maze, 107, 130, 204
flowers, dried, 127, 147
flying squirrel, 14, 220
food chains, 219–220
Foodmap Container, 101
Ford, Miela, 87, 158
forget-me-not (*Myosotis sylvatica*), 49, 91, 123, 132
four o'clock, 93, 156
Fourth of July floral fireworks, 124
foxes, 2, 157, 176
Franklin D. Roosevelt Hickory, 124
French mockingbird, 211
French parsley, 64
fringed bleeding heart (*Dicentra formosa*), 123
fringed pinks, 156
Froebel on actions and consequences, 209
"Frog and Toad" series (Lobel), 10
Frogwatch USA, 188–189
From Seed to Plant (Gibbons), 87
From Seed to Pumpkin (Pfeffer), 87
fruits
    animal consumption of, 67, 176, 200
    fresh off the vine eating of, 97
    in MyPlate plan, 72
    planting citrus seeds, 75
Fruit Tree Planting Foundation, 41
Fukuoka, Masanobu, 44
Fuller, Liz, 195

G

games, nature, 129–134, 220
Garden Book (Jefferson), 186
gardening, history of educational ideas, 208–210
garden maintenance tasks, 58
garden spider (*Argiope aurantia*), 11–12
garter snake, 14
gas plant (*Dictamnus albus*), 124
gazania, 156
Geography of Childhood, The (Nabhan and Trimble), 151
George Washington tulip poplar, 124
Georgia-Pacific, 42
geranium, 124, 154
Gibbons, Gail, 87, 158, 213

gift-making, 119–120, 125–126
Gift of the Poinsettia, The (Mora and Berg), 163
ginkgo (*Ginkgo biloba*), 213, 215
Ginkgophyta, 215
Giovannone, Jason, classroom of, 32
glass jars, 76, 114
globe amaranth, 20, 127, 132, 145, 146
globe thistle, 212
goatsbeard, 155
Godden, Rumer, 148
Goff, Carla and Dylan, garden of, 19–20
goldenrod, 17, 105, 143, 188, 218
goldfish plant (*Nematanthus*), 173
gold star, 156
gourds, 6–7, 92, 207, 210
grains, 9, 69, 71, 72, 73, 79, 125, 132
grandparents, gardening with, 152–153, 154, 158, 167
Grandpa's Garden Lunch (Caseley), 158
grant funding, 40–42, 54
grapes (*Vitis* spp.)
  as food for birds, 5, 80, 200, 220
  as food for wildlife, 217, 220
  fresh off the vine eating of, 97
  as a healthy snack, 71
  muscadine grape (*Vitis rotundifolia*), 97, 176
  in a private garden, 153
  use of teepee structures, 49
  vines, 96
grapevine wreath, 147, 148
grass whistle, 92, 130
Great Backyard Bird Count (GBBC), 5, 184
Greater Columbia Landscape Association, 196
Great Sunflower Project, 188
greenbrier vine (*Smilax rotundifolia*), 180
Green Hour (NWF program), 152
greenhouse, mini-, 68, 85
greens
  European, Asian, and Southern, listed, 65
  harvesting leafy, 64, 66
  vitamin-rich, 59
Green Step School, 90
GreenWorks!, 41
grey squirrel, 2, 220
Gro More Good grants (Scott's Miracle-Gro), 41
Gross, Paula, 174
groundcovers, 7
grow buckets, 48–49, 51, 54–55
"Growing Healthy Across South Carolina" (Marturano), 70–71
Growing Healthy garden, 195, 201, 207, 216, 220, 221
Growing Vegetable Soup (Ehlert), 158
Grow Some Shade (Columbia, SC), 192
Guest, Seth, 53
gymnosperms, 203, 213, 215

H

hackberry (*Celtis occidentalis*), 25, 31, 36
hawks as predators, 2, 3, 219, 220
hawthorn, 36, 94, 116
healing through gardening, 178–179
health proactive theme gardens, 70–71, 195, 201
hearts-a-burstin (*Euonymus americanus*), 123, 127
heartsease (*Viola tricolor*), 123
Heat Island Mapping Campaign, 191
heat islands, 191–192
Heffernan, Maureen, 193
Helen Keller southern magnolia, 124
henbit (*Lamium amplexicaule*), 177
Henderson, Douglas, 213
Henry, Marguerite, 141
Henry David Thoreau red maple, 124
herbal world maps, 164–165
herbariums, 177–178
herbs, aromatic
  Age of Exploration and, 163–164
  bee-attracting, 21
  books on history of, 164
  in bucket gardens, 55
  for cold frames, 44
  cool-season, 64, 164
  growing from seed, 164
  native habitats, 164–165
  plants with kid appeal, 93, 94
  scent, 162–163
  as sensory play props, 92
  as top plants for kids, 92–93
Herb Society of America, 41
heritage gardens, 197
Hess, Lilo, 158
hibiscus, 23, 103, 143, 147
hickory, 124, 138
hickory horned devil, 25
hickory nuts, 91, 119, 126, 138, 148
High Line wild gardens, 157
Hmong American Farmers Association, 166
Hmong Americans, 165–166
holiday ornaments from natural materials, 119, 126–127
Hollis, Connor, 38
holly, 5, 94, 119, 120, 129, 148
holly and ivy wreath, 148
hollyhock (*Alcea rosea*), 102–103, 124, 212
Homegrown National Park, 157
hoop houses, 199
Hopkins, Taylor, 209, 210
hops (*Humulus lupulus*), 96
houseplants
  care, 109–113
  Plant 911, 110–111

plant hospital project, 111–113
propagation, 109–110
How do Dinosaurs Say Goodnight? (Yolen), 213
Hudson, Joe, 196
Hudson Valley School landscape painters, 100
Huggins, Vivian, 195
Human-Environment Research Lab (University of Illinois), 151
hummingbird feeder, 4
hummingbird habitat, creating, 3–4
Hunter, William, 209

I

Iceland poppy, 156
ice plant, 156
ikebana, 149
impatiens, 84, 124, 154
inchworms, 24
Indian corn, 79
Indian grass (*Sorghastrum nutans*), 201
Indian pink (*Spigelia marilandica*), 4
Indigenous knowledge in classroom instruction, 166–167
insectary, 17–18
insecticides, neonicotinoid, 190
insect pests, controlling, 35–36
insect repellent plants. See chamomile; marigold
insects, ecological services, 35
instant gardens, 50–52
International Paper (IP), 41, 62
International Union for Conservation of Nature (IUCN), 190
interplanting, 159
Interstellar Safari stargazing program, 13–14
ironweed, 188
Ithaca Children's Garden (ICG), 197

J

Japanese morning glory, 155
Japanese wisteria vine, 87
Jefferson, Thomas, 160–161, 162, 186
Jensen, Stacy, 175, 176
Jerusalem artichoke (aka sunchoke) (*Helianthus tuberosus*), 162
Jewel (tortoise), 30
jewel orchid (*Ludisia discolor*), 113–114
jimson weed, 156
Joe-Pye weed, 13, 23, 188
Johnson, Sylvia, 158

K

Kaiser Family Foundation research, 151
kale, 51, 57, 59, 64, 65, 70
kale, ornamental, 64
Kaleidoscope garden, 24
Katie's Cabbage (Stagliano), 33–34

Katie's Krops, 33–34
Keeler, Rusty, 198
keyhole garden, 52–54
Kids Gardening, 41
Kip, Matt, 212
kiss me over the garden gate (*Polygonium orientale*), 122
kitchen scraps, recycling, 75–76, 83
Klein, Robin Chaves, 195
Kniphofia spp., 20, 124
komatsuna, 57, 65
kudzu, 87, 157

L

lacecap hydrangea, 20
Lady Bird Johnson Wildflower Center, 45, 197
  Luci and Ian Family Garden, 197
Ladybugs (Gibbons), 158
Lail, Andrew, 209
lamb's ears (*Stachys abysantin*), 95, 100, 198, 216
lamb's quarters (*Chenopodium*), 162
Lampyridae, 2, 189
Landscapes Great and Small (exhibit) (Columbia Art Museum), 100
lantana (*Lantana camara*), 13, 20, 23, 26, 38, 209, 212, 218, 219
Last Child in the Woods, The (Louv), 151
Lasting Impressions cancer support group, 178–179
lavender (*Lavendula* spp.), 20, 127
Lavies, Bianca, 158
leaf hopscotch, 130–131
Leaf Man (Ehlert), 32, 158
learning activities, shared, 152–153
leaves
  colors in clothing, 142–143
  in gift making, 119, 120, 137–138
  in handicrafts, 137, 139–141
Lebuhn, Gretchen, 188
Legend of the Poinsettia, The (dePaola), 163
legumes, 49, 71
lei, 146–147
Lei for Tutu, A (Fellows), 147
lemon verbena, 94, 130, 150, 216. See also verbena
Lenski, Lois, 158
lentils, 70, 71, 72
Leopold, Aldo, 157
lettuces
  in bucket gardens, 55
  as food for wildlife, 218
  as health proactive, 70
  instructional planting of, 64
  in moveable gardens, 100
  in a raised bed therapeutic garden, 179

in a salad garden, 57, 65
shapes and colors, 66
Lewis, Sara, 190
Lewis and Clark Expedition, 160–162
lichens, 174, 176, 213
Linnaean Herbarium (website), 177
Linnaeus, Carl, 154–155, 177, 186
lion's ear (*Leonotis leonurus*), 96
literacy education, 52–54
lithops, 101–102, 150, 173
Little House on the Prairie Garden, 193
live oak (*Quercus virginiana*), 36, 185, 191, 215, 217, 220
lobelia, 4, 124, 132
loblolly pine, 36, 131, 140, 185, 220
loggerhead shrike (*Lanius ludovicianus*), 211
longleaf pine, 36, 138, 140, 171, 220 (could not find this tree on page 170)
loquat, 5
Lorrie Otto Seeds for Education Program, 41
Louv, Richard, 151
lovage (*Levisticum officinale*), 123
love-in-a-mist (*Nigella damascena*), 91, 122, 123, 127
love-in-a-puff (*Cardiospermum halicacabum*), 97, 122
Lovejoy, Sharon, 83, 102, 196
love-lies-bleeding (*Amaranthus caudatus*), 123
Lowenfels, Jeff, 199
Lurie urban rooftop garden, 157

M
mache, 44, 57, 65, 150
Magic of Children's Gardens, The (Tai), 199
Mancke, Jennifer, classroom of, 30–31
Mancke, Rudy, 170, 179–181
marigold
as a bale plant, 51
bloom opening time, 156
as a bucket plant, 55
for a flower maze, 130
as insect repellent, 179
as a nectar-producing annual, 23, 218
saving seeds, 84
Mark Twain cave bur oak, 124
Marsham, Robert, 186
Marturano, Arlene, 195, 239
"Growing Healthy Across South Carolina", 70–71
"MyPlate Inspires MyGarden", 71–74
mazes, 94, 129–130
McCloskey, Robert, 158, 221
McCoy, Barbara, garden of, 20–21
McGregor's Garden, 195, 204
McMillan Greenhouse, 172–174
measurement math, 53

Medicine Wheel Garden, 31–32
Mellichamp, Larry, 172, 173, 174
mesclun seed mixes, 51, 59, 65, 150
Mesozoic Memories, 195, 196, 203, 213
Metrolina Greenhouse, 90
Mexico, native plants, 116, 122, 162–163
Mexico in monarch migration, 186–187
Mey, Brenda Vander, 195
Mikolajcxyk, Jozefine, garden of, 153–154
mile a minute plant, 157
milkweed
Asclepias syriaca, 38, 88
Asclepias tuberosa, 38, 188
in habitat restoration, 37–38
as a host plant, 13
non-native vs. native, 38
planting, 188
seed saving, 84
symbiotic relationship with monarchs, 38
milkweed pods, 87–88, 91–92, 119, 127, 145
millet, 24, 72, 79, 95, 132, 200, 212
mimosa tree (*Albizia julibrissin*), 5, 87, 119, 148, 212, 214–215
mint plants
catmint, 9, 94, 156
as cool season herbs, 64
growing, 9
for herbal teas, 167
mint family, 177
mint medley garden, 55
mint relatives, 9
peppermint, 9, 94, 144
as a salt alternative, 70
starting seeds, 150
Miracle of the First Poinsettia, The (Oppenheim), 163
Miss Hickory (Bailey), 138
Miss Rumphius (Cooney), 87, 158
Mixon, Heather, 195
mizuna, 44, 57, 59, 64, 65, 66, 150
mockernut hickory, 131, 138
Monarch Story, The (Irmo Middle School students), 38
Monarch Watch (MW), 41, 187
Monarch Waystations program, 187–188
monarda, 4, 21, 100, 124, 130
mondo grass, 7, 94
monkey puzzle tree, 198
Monson, Hattie, 195
Montessori school garden, 210
Moody, Tommy, 195
moonflower, 14, 156
moonlight garden, 14
moonvine (*Ipomoea alba*), 97
Moore, Robin, 199
Moore, Roscoe, 179

Mora, Pat, 163
morning glory (*Ipomoea tricolor*)
    bloom opening times, 155–156
    for floral fireworks, 124
    Grandpa Ott's morning glory, 93
    trellising, 86, 92, 96, 123
Morris, Jim, 32
mosquitoes, 3, 10, 18, 220
mosquito larvae, 220
mosses, 176, 203, 213
moss rose, 156
mother of thousands (*Kalanchoe delagoensis*), 173
moths
    forested areas and larval stage, 24–25
    luna moth, 25, 180
    as pollinators, 17, 18
    rosy maple moth (*Dryocampa rubicunda*), 24
    tussock moth caterpillar, 180
mouse-ear chickweed (*Cerastium tomentosum*), 95
moveable gardens, 68–69, 100–101
Mr. McGregor's garden, 195, 204, 207, 217, 219
mullein, 156
Munsell soil color charts, 142
mustard
    as a cool-season plant, 52, 57, 62, 64
    food uses, 65, 66
    as health proactive, 70, 71
    as a host plant, 218
    planting in eggshells, 150
    planting in seashells, 69
mustard greens, 65, 70, 71, 166
MyGarden, 73
"MyPlate Inspires MyGarden" (Marturano), 71–74
MyPlate plan, 71–73

N

Nabhan, Gary, 151
Nafziger, Tim, 210–211
Nancy K. Perry Children's Shelter, 178
National Audubon Society Christmas Bird Count, 183–184
National COVID-19 Outdoor Learning Initiative, 175
National Farm to School Network, 41
National Garden Clubs, Inc., 41
National Poinsettia Day, 121, 163
National Pollinator Week, 19, 23
National Sunflower Association, 107
National Wildlife Federation (NWF), 22, 152
Native American Gardening (Caduto and Bruchac), 160
Native Americans

"Cherokee Trail of Tears" bean, 50
cycles of life gardening, 159–160
heirloom seeds, 160
Indigenous knowledge in classroom instruction, 167
Medicine Wheel Garden, 31–32
paint making, 141
recipes, 160
seed balls, 44
sunflower body paint, 106
three sisters planting system, 55, 159–160
use of persimmon fruit, 67
uses of native plants, 106, 176
native azalea, 171
native coral honeysuckle, 220
Native Plant Finder (website), 157
native plants
    adapted to sandy soil, 36
    at Belser Arboretum, 171, 172
    Carolina Fence™ Garden, 201
    Congaree National Park, 180
    defined, 157
    drought tolerant, 204
    in Heathwood Hall teaching gardens, 31–32
    for the home landscape, 180
    in a private garden, 19–20
    selecting, 45
    wildflowers native to South Carolina, 104–105
native sassafras (*Sassafras albidum*), 175–176
Native Seed SEARCH, 160
native species pollinator garden, 22
native switch grass (*Panicum virgatum*), 175, 204
natural classroom teaching and learning, 30–31
Natural Curiosity (exhibit), McKissick Museum, 170
Natural Playscapes (Keeler), 198
nature
    displaying, 169–170
    feeling a part of, 157
    restoring interest in, 151–152
"nature deficit disorder", 151
nature games, 129–134, 220
Nature's Best Hope (Young Reader's Edition) (Tallamy), 156–157
Nature Scene television series, 170
nectar café, 23
nectary, hummingbird, 200, 212
nepetalactone, 9
New Shade Garden: Creating a Lush Oasis in the Age of Climate Change, The (Druse), 191
newspaper, uses, 78–79
nicotiana, 14, 124, 132
night blooming cereus, 156
night blooming stock, 156

night phlox, 14, 156
nocturnal creatures, 2, 14
North Carolina Strawberry Grower's Association, 63
nutrition guidelines. *See* MyPlate plan
nut shell handicrafts, 137, 138

O

oak galls, 144, 179–180
oak species, 157, 179
oats, 9, 35, 51, 70, 72, 132
Obama, Michelle, 72–73
okra pods, 88
Old House Gardens, 64
Old MacDonald's Historic Crops, 195, 202
onions, 57, 58, 64, 70, 72, 144
Oppenheim, Joanne, 163
Oregon Children's Garden, 198–199
organic gardening
    biointensive method, 153, 154
    Hmong gardening, 165–166
    introduced by Native Americans, 159–160
    in a school garden, 34–36
outdoor classrooms, 31–32, 36–37, 81–82, 174–175, 209
Outdoor Learning Garden (Gadsden, Elementary School), 61–62
owl pellet dissection, 211

P

pak choi, 57, 59, 65
parasites, 2, 17, 35
Park Seed Bio Dome Seed Starter, 85
Parris, Peggy, 213
parsley
    as a cool-season plant, 44, 64, 164
    in health proactive gardens, 59, 70
    as a host plant, 13, 23, 94, 218
    as a seasoning ingredient, 55, 58, 150, 163
Pasco, Victoria, classroom of, 36–37
passion vine / passionflower (*Passiflora incarnata*), 25–26, 156, 218
pathways, creating, 210
paw paw, 180, 181
peach (*Prunus persica*), 202, 215
peanuts, 5, 71, 72, 79, 81, 87, 202, 212
peas, 49, 50, 55, 70, 71, 97, 100, 218
pentas, 23, 29, 100, 218
pepper pods, 88
periwinkle, 7, 11, 94
persimmon (*Diospyros virginiana*), 25, 66–68, 137, 176, 180
persimmon recipes, 67
Pestalozzi on sense perception and physical activity, 209
pesticides
    and declining bee populations, 17
    disruption of predator-prey relationships, 219
    eliminating to allow beneficial insects, 3, 8, 12, 190
    harmful effects on children, 34
    harmful effects on pollinators, 17, 23–24
    nepetalactone testing, 9
    preferred practices over use of, 21
pest trap crops, 36
Peter Rabbit (fictional character), 55, 216–217
petunia, 93, 124, 154
Pfeffer, Wendy, 87
phenological observations, 185–186
Phillips, Mark, 210
Philosophia Botanica (Linnaeus), 155
phlox, 14, 23, 94, 212
photinia (*Photinia fraseri*), 185
picket fences, 52
pillow pack gardening, 51
pine
    in Carolina Children's Garden, 220
    dead, 214
    needles, 44, 98, 127, 138, 140
    straw, 99, 119, 127, 137, 140
pine cones
    as bird feeders, 79, 148
    in handicrafts, 119–120, 141, 148
pine snag, 200
pizza pan garden, 58–59
plains coneflower (*Echinacea augustifolia*), 161
Plant 911, 110–111
plant circus, 172–174
plant hospital, 111–113
Planting a Rainbow (Ehlert), 158
plant press, 177–178
Plants for Birds (website), 157
play
    about, 91–92
    alphabet play, 131, 205–206
    equipment design, 199
    rooms, hideaways, and enclosures, 92, 94–95
    top ten plants for kids, 92–94
    unstructured, 91, 152, 197–198
    See also doll play
pocket survey, 152
pods, dried, 127
pods, milkweed, 87–88, 91–92, 119
Poinsett, Joel, 122, 162
poinsettia (*Euphorbia pulcherrima*)
    books for children, 163
    choosing and preserving, 121–122
    history, 162–163
    keeping as a houseplant, 89–90
    legend of, 163
pokeweed, 104, 143, 180
Polish plant names, 154

polka dot begonia (*Begonia maculata* var. *wightii*), 172–173
pollen wasps, 219
pollination, human assistance with, 6
pollination as an ecosystem process, 18
Pollinator Plants and Places program, 188
pollinator plot, plants for, 20
pollinator resources, 19
pollinators
    Bees and Blooms education initiative, 22–23
    conservation campaigns, 19
    declining populations, 18–19, 22
    ecological services, 18
    windshield phenomenon, 18
pollinators, predators, and parasites (three P's), 35
pollinator seed mixes, 17–18
Pooh's Corner, 195, 196, 203, 206–207
popcorn, 5, 55, 71, 72, 79, 81, 92
poppy pods, 88
popsicle sticks, 76
potatoes, 99–100
Prescott, William, 163
preserving plants, 145
Preventing Obesity by Design (POD), 199
prickly pear aka "beaver tail" (*Opuntia compressa*), 95, 176
primrose, flower structure, 97
primrose party, 14, 155
Prisma Health Children's Hospital, 178
propagation, 109–110
protein in MyPlate plan, 72
pumpkin on a stick (*Solanum intergrifolium*), 172, 173
pumpkins, 70, 72, 76–77, 166
pumpkin seeds, 77, 85, 97, 160
purple chaste tree, 124, 214
purple coneflower (*Echinacea purpuannualsrea*), 13, 20, 161, 218
purple love grass (*Eragrostis spectabilis*), 123
purple salvia, 20
pussy ears (*Kalanchoe tomentosa*), 96
puzzle garden, 131–132

Q
quinoa, 71, 132, 210

R
rabbit ears (*Ruttya frutivos*), 96
rabbit manure, 62, 81–82
rabbits, 217–218
radicchio, 64, 65, 66
radishes
    as aioli, 31
    as cool-season plants, 52, 55, 64
    as fast-growing, 57

sowing seeds, 100
    in square foot gardening, 47
    as a top plant for kids, 92
Rain Garden, 31, 195, 204
rain gauge, 134, 135, 189
Reading Garden, 195, 217
Reading Room, 94, 202
red bay leaf (*Persea borbonia*), 180
red buckeye (*Aesculus pavia*), 4, 212, 215
redbud (*Cercis canadensis*), 20, 116, 171, 185
red clay, 45
red flowers in floral fireworks, 124
red globe amaranth (*Gomphrena haageana* 'Strawberry Fields'), 20
red hot poker (*Kniphofia uvaria*), 20, 124
red maple (*Acer rubrum*), 24, 124, 171, 185
Redmond, Pat, 195
red mulberry (*Morus rubra*), 180
red mustard, 65, 66
red rocket crepe myrtle, 124
red-shouldered hawk, 180
red-tailed hawk, 219
red wriggler worm (*Eisenia fetida*), 37, 83–84, 199
reindeer lichen, 127
Restuccio, Jeffrey P., 61
rice, 9, 70, 71, 125, 132, 166
Riverbanks Botanical Garden, 102
Riverbanks Nature Preschool, 169
river birch, 25, 137, 138
Robbins, Ken, 87, 121
robin, 30, 185, 186, 211
rock pink, 156
rodents, 1–2, 14, 18, 76
Rodgers, Krystal, 209
roofs, green, 46–47
rooftop garden, 157
Roots and Shoots, 41
root vegetables, 44, 57, 64
rose hips, 88, 127
rosemary (*Rosmarinus officinalis*), 29, 216
    as a cool-season herb, 64
    as a groundcover, 7
    as a landscape filler, 100
    as a pollinator plant, 20, 21
    propagation, 164
    as a salt-alternative, 70
    sensory aspects, 94
    in wreath-making, 120
rosemary rinse, 9, 126
Roundstone Native Seed, 17–18
Rousseau on senses, 209
royal walnut moth larvae, 25
ruby-throated hummingbird, 3, 4, 180, 215, 220
rudbeckia, 79, 84, 218
Ruffin, Julian, 178

Rushing, Felder, 158
rye, 9, 35, 51, 72, 125, 132, 206
Rylant, Cynthia, 158

S
safflower, 20
sage, 20, 21, 70, 94, 150, 163, 164
   pineapple sage (*Salvia elegans*), 4, 200, 212
   Salvia coccinea 'Jewel Red', 20
   Salvia microphylla 'Hot Lips', 20
   scarlet sage (*Salvia splendens*), 4, 13
salad gardens, 57, 59, 65–66, 69
salad greens, 43, 44, 47, 51, 55, 57, 65, 150
salad necklaces, 69
salsify, 155
salvia
   as attractive to butterflies, 218
   as attractive to hummingbirds, 4, 20, 23, 37, 200
   for floral fireworks, 124
   seed saving, 84
Sandhill REC carpenters, 196
Sandhill Research and Education Center (REC), 13, 17, 100, 174, 194
sandwort, 156
sassafras (*Sassafras albidum*), 36, 167, 172, 175–176
sassafras leaves, 25, 91, 131, 180
sassafras tea, 167, 180
Savannah River Ecology Lab, 15
scabiosa, 37, 84, 212
Scarecrow (Rylant), 158
Scarecrows (Rushing), 158
scarlet pimpernel, 156
scavenger hunts, 130–131, 183
schizopetalon Milky Way, 156
school gardens
   Brockman Elementary School, 27
   combining nutrition and fitness, 61–62
   Eat What You Grow toolkit, 197
   funding, 27–28, 40–42, 61–62
   Heyward Career and Technology Center, 28–29
   Lawn, Garden and Gifts Enterprise course, 28–29
   monarch habitat restoration, Irmo Middle School, 37–38
   Montessori school garden, 210
   organic gardening, 34–36, 47
   parent participation, 27–28, 40
   pond, 37
   produce garden, Pinewood Prep, 33–34
   Sandhills School, 29–31
   Satchel Ford Elementary School, 28
   school garden survey, 40
   S.E.ED (School Environmental Education), 31, 32
   special-needs students' participation in, 28–29
   teaching gardens, Heathwood Hall Episcopal School, 31–32
   wildlife garden, Catawba Trail Elementary, 36–37
school lunches, 59–60, 106
schoolyard herbarium, 177–178
Schoolyard Strawberry Project, 63
scientific method, 39–40
Scrabble® Gardening, 132–134
seashell planters, 69
seashells as planters, 66, 67
seasonality, 73
Secret Garden, The (Burnett), 98–99, 158
seed balls, 44–45
seed libraries, 88
seedlings, hardening off, 87
seed packet cards in Scrabble® Gardening, 133
seeds
   books for children, 87
   broadcast sowing, 18
   heirloom, 50, 89, 154, 160
   pollinator mix, 17
   saving, 84–85, 88–89
   sowing, 18, 86
   starting, 85–87, 149
   wildflower mixes, commercial, 105
Seeds (Robbins), 87
Seed Savers Exchange, 89, 160, 162, 165
seed tapes, 93
Segura, Amanda, 169
sensitive briar (*Mimosa microphylla*), 92
sensitive plant (*Mimosa pudica*), 92
sensory plants, 92, 101
Sesquicentennial State Park, 13, 25, 175–176
shade trees, 191–192
Shealy, Joyce, 27
Silent Spring (Carson), 34
skinks, 208, 215, 220
Slither, Ms. (education snake), 14–15, 126–127
Slow Food Denver, 196
smilax, 36
snail vine (*Vigna caracalla*), 97
snakes, 14–15. *See also* Slither, Ms.
snapdragon, 21, 23, 64, 91, 93, 124, 130, 132
snappy single sync firefly (*Photuris frontalis*), 190–191
soapwort, 84, 88
soil
   amending urban, 23
   bare, 7
   for bucket gardening, 54
   colors, 141–142
   potting mix, 86
   sandy, 36, 37

for square foot gardens, 47
soil thermometer, 134
South Carolina Department of Agriculture, 40
South Carolina Department of Mental Health (SCDMH), 195
South Carolina Department of Natural Resources, 15
South Carolina Departments of Forestry and Corrections, 196
South Carolina Native Plant Society, 45
South Carolina Nutrition Council, 195
South Carolina Seed Foundation, 50
South Carolina Wildlife Federation, 24, 195
Southern Exposure Seed Exchange, 50, 89, 160, 165
southern greens, 64, 65
southern magnolia (*Magnolia grandiflora*), 124, 139–140, 185, 214
space program inspired gardening, 59–60
space-wheel amulets, 60
Spanish moss (*Tillandsia usneoides*), 174
sparkleberry (*Vaccinium arboreum*), 36, 172, 180, 212
spelling and vocabulary game, 132–134
spider frame, 12
spider watching, 11–12, 173
spiderwort, 23, 104, 155
spinach
　in bale gardens, 51
　in bucket gardens, 55
　in cold frames, 44
　as a dye plant, 144
　in MyPlate plan, 72
　in salad gardens, 44, 51, 57, 59, 64, 65, 66, 70, 179
Spiraea japonica 'Anthony Waterer', 20
spring, signs of, 216–217
spring simulation for forcing blooms, 115–116
square foot gardening, 47–48
squash in three sisters planting system, 55, 159, 160
squirrel-resistant bird feeder, 212
squirrels, 1–2
stabilimentum, 11
Stagliano, Katie, 32–34
stargazing, 13–14, 151
Star of Bethlehem, 156
State Farm, 42
St. Bernard's lily, 156
Stoker, JoAnn, 201, 205
stones, living, 101–102
Story of the Holly and the Ivy, The (Godden), 148
Story of the Sunflower, The (coloring book), 107
straw bale gardening, 51
Strawberry Girl (Lenski), 158
strawflower, 127, 145, 156

string dictionary, 205
Suber, Linda, 23–24
Suber, Von, 23
succulents, 77, 101–102, 173
Sudoku puzzle garden, 132
sugarberry (*Celtis laevigata*), 25
Sumayah, intergenerational gardening experience, 152–153
sundial plants, 93, 154–156
Sunflower (Ford), 87, 158
sunflower (*Helianthus annuus*)
　about, 106–107
　fence, 71, 106, 160, 209
　Great Sunflower Project, 188
　growing, 106–107
　as play props, 92, 93, 130
　in a pollinator garden, 20, 21
　seedheads, 79, 148
　in square foot gardening, 47
Sunflower House Garden, 193
Sunflower Houses (Lovejoy), 83, 156, 196
sunflower seeds
　as bird food, 5, 24, 79, 80, 212
　in recipes, 160, 162
　saving, 84
　starting indoors, 85
supports for plants
　picket fence, 52
　teepee structures, 6, 49–50, 92, 94, 96, 201

swamp sunflower (*Helianus augustifolius*), 188, 204
sweet Annie, 130
sweet gum (*Liquidambar*), 3, 5, 25, 137, 140, 143, 180
sweet gum balls, 5, 91, 127, 148
sweet gum leaves, 91, 127
sweet pea, 52, 94, 156
sweet potatoes, sprouting, 75–76
sweetspire (*Itea virginica*), 180
Swiss chard, 64
　'Bright Lights', 57, 66
switch grass (*Panicum virgatum*), 175, 204
sycamore bark, 143
sycamore leaves, 130–131, 137, 140, 143
synchronous firefly, 190–191

T

Taft, Hope, 197
Tai, Lolly, 199
Tale of Peter Rabbit, The (Potter), 204
Tallamy, Doug, 157–158, 190
tall coneflower, 204
tall goldenrod (*Solidago altissima*), 105
tannin, 66, 180
tansy, 127, 216

tarantula cactus (*Cleistocactus winteri*), 173
tatsoi, 57, 59, 65
Taylor, Jane, 196
Teaming With Microbes (Lowenfels), 199
Team Migration Nation (TMN), 37, 38
temperatures, rising, 191–192
temperatures, South Carolina, 191–192
tendergreen, 44, 57, 65, 66, 150
terrariums, 114–115
Texas Red Yucca (*Hesperaloe parvifolia*), 20
Thai basil, 166
thistle, 148, 212
Thomas, Sudie, 17
Thoreau, Henry David, 186
thorny plants, 174
Three Bears' Homestead, 195, 202, 216, 221
three sisters legend, 159
three sisters planting system, 55, 159–160
thyme, 21
    as a cool-season herb, 64, 164
    in a floral clock, 155
    planting in eggshells, 150
    as a salt-alternative, 55, 70
    sensory aspects, 94, 130, 163
tickseed (*Coreopsis* spp.), 20, 161
tie-dye, 143, 144
Tiny Seed, The (Carle), 87
tithonia, 79, 84, 100, 130, 146, 188
toads, 10–11
tomatoes
    cherry tomatoes, 55, 58, 60, 100
    in a keyhole garden, 53
    in moveable gardens, 100
    in MyPlate plan, 72
    in a pizza garden, 58
    in a private garden, 20, 153
    ripening, 78
    seed starting, 149
torenia, 91, 93, 124, 154
Tractor Supply Company, 42
travel kabobs, 60
trees
    companion planting, 171
    greet a tree game, 131
    for the home landscape, 214–216
    as host plants, 180
    as larvae hosts, 24–25
    materials for gifts and decorations, 137–138
    named after historical figures, 124
    W. Gordon Belser Arboretum, 25, 170–172
Trimble, Steve, 151
tropism, 98
trumpet creeper (*Campsis radicans*), 4, 13, 92
trumpet honeysuckle (*Lonicera sempervirens*), 4
tubular flowers
    multi-colored, 97, 123
    of nectar plants, 3, 20, 21, 37, 220
    as play props, 92
    resemblance to ears, 96
tulip poplar (*Liriodendron tulipifera*), 25, 124, 180, 214, 218, 219
turnips, 57, 59, 64, 65, 166
Tyler, Jamie, classroom of, 29

U

umbrella milkwort, 155
University of South Carolina (USC)
    A.C. Moore Herbarium, 177–178
    Green Quad, 46, 53
    Horseshoe Horticulture Grove, 25, 171
    McKissick Museum, 25, 170
    Sustainable Carolina Garden, 53, 188
urban forest, 175–176
USDA MyPlate Plan, 59, 71–73
USDA Natural Resources Conservation Service, 17

V

Valentine's Day, 122–123
vegetables
    cool-season, 52, 57, 59, 64
    encouraging consumption of, 59
    fresh off the vine eating of, 97
    heat-loving, 59
    Hmong American staples, 166
    in MyPlate plan, 59, 72
    for planting in bales, 51
    in square foot gardening, 47–48
verbena
    for floral fireworks, 124
    as groundcover, 7
    lemon verbena, 94, 130, 150, 216
    as a nectar plant, 13, 38, 94, 188, 218
    as a plant spiller, 101
    in a private garden, 154
Verkade, Stephen, 194, 195, 196
vermicomposting, 31, 83–84, 199
Very Hungry Caterpillar, The (Carle), 158
vesper lily, 156
viburnum, 180, 212
vinca, 218
vines
    anatomy, 97
    cooling effect, 96–97
    perennial, 4, 25–26, 87
    as play props, 96–98
    thigmatropism, 98
Virginia creeper (*Parthenocissus quinquefolia*), 11, 97
Virginia willow, 180
vitex, 23, 214, 218

W

Waiting for Wings (Ehlert), 158
WalMart, 42
wasp larvae, 179–180
wasps, 12, 18, 23, 35, 177, 219
watermelon, 22, 62, 72, 166–167, 202
Watson, Chauncey (student), 167
Watson, Lori, 22
wax myrtle (*Myrica cerifera*), 5, 13, 120, 180, 212
weather detectives, 134–135
weather observation network, 189
weather-related activities, 189
weeping cherry, 94
weigela, 4, 38, 94, 200, 212
Wendell, Cathy and Thomas, 195
W. Gordon Belser Arboretum, 25, 170–172
wheat, 9, 35, 51, 125, 132, 150
White, David, 62
white bat plant (*Tacca integrifolia*), 172, 173
white flowers in floral fireworks, 124
white-tailed deer, 176
Who Eats What? game, 220
Whole Foods Foundation Garden Grant, 42
wild daisy, 156
wildflowers
    honoring the Lewis and Clark expedition, 161–162
    with medicinal uses, 161
    native to South Carolina, 104–105
    use by Native Americans, 105
wildflower seed mixes, 105
wild ginger (*Asarum canadense*), 11, 161, 171
    panda ginger (*Asarum maximum*), 173
    piggies ginger (*Asarum arifolium*), 173
wildlife, attracting, 13
wildlife garden, 36–37
wildlife watching, 12–14
Wildlife Watch program, 13
Wild Ones, 41
Wilkerson, Susan Kurta, 195
Williams, Andrea, 61, 62
willowleaf butterbean, 89
Wilson, Gilbert L., 160
Wind in the Willows (Graham), 10
windsock, 134–135
wingthorn rose (*Rosa omeiensis* f. *pteracantha*), 174
winterberry (*Ilex verticillata*), 185, 212
winter bird watching, 183–184
winter gardening, 43–44, 57
winter greens, 57
Wisconsin Hmong population, 165–166
wisteria, 5, 96, 119, 200
wisteria nest bench, 200, 212
Woldt, Becky, classroom of, 30

Woodley, Claire, 195
Woodley's Garden Center, 195
worm castings, 83–84
Worms Eat My Garbage (Appelhof), 199
wreath making, 119–120, 147–148

X

Xerces Society for Invertebrate Conservation, 17, 19, 190

Y

yarrow (*Achillea millefolium*), 17, 20, 37, 127, 144
yellow-bellied sapsucker, 36, 176, 181, 220
yellow butterfly vine (*Stigmaphyllon ciliatum*), 97
yellow gentian, 156
yellow jessamine, 185, 201
Yolen, Jane, 213
youth gardening, nationwide
    Eat What You Grow toolkit (Chicago Public Schools), 197
    garden-to-school salad bar program (Denver Public Schools), 196
    Growing Hope (Ypsilanti, MI), 199–200
    Ithaca Children's Garden (ICG) Anarchy Zone (Ithaca, NY), 197–198
    Luci and Ian Family Garden (Austin, TX), 197
    Michigan 4-H Children's Garden, 196
    Morton Arboretum children's garden (west of Chicago), 199
    Ohio Heritage Garden, 197
    Oregon Children's Garden, 198–199
    Washington Youth Garden (WYG) (District of Columbia), 200

Z

zebrina, 212
zinnia
    for bouquet flowers, 55, 132
    as a dye plant, 144
    as easy to grow, 93
    for floral fireworks, 124
    for flower chains, 146
    as a nectar producing annual, 23, 94, 100, 218
    seed saving, 84
zucchini, 58, 70, 72

MEET ARLENE MARTURANO

Photo courtesy of
Jay Browne Photography©

Arlene Marturano grew up gardening with her family in northern Illinois. She credits her undergraduate training in outdoor education at Northern Illinois University with uniting her enjoyment of teaching and of gardening. In her career as a classroom teacher and teacher educator, she uses gardening as an organizing thread for instruction and a universal language for initiating a dialogue with nature.

She authored and field tested Reading the Environment, an environmental reading program using natural phenomena as teachers – trees, butterflies, frogs, wildflowers, and streams – to introduce reluctant readers to printed reading sources.

As Christa McAuliffe Fellow for South Carolina, she established Growing Healthy Through Gardening programs in K-8 schools across the state. A public demonstration Growing Healthy Garden for families was installed at the Carolina Children's Garden in Columbia with assistance from the SC Nutrition Council.

For a decade she was a GrowLab consultant for the National Gardening Association's KidsGardening program. Currently she directs the South Carolina Garden-based Learning Network, a research, teaching, and resource network and consulting firm.

She is a frequent speaker at conferences and youth gardening events. Her writing appears in numerous education journals, book chapters, and newspaper columns. In 2024 she received the Silver Laurel Media Award from Garden Communicators International for "Spring Fervor" in her Columbia Star garden column.

For her work in outdoor and environmental education, she was honored as the 2025 Lifetime Achievement Environmental Educator by the Environmental Education Association of South Carolina (EEASC).

PRAISE FOR GROWING UP GARDENING

"A Classroom Without Walls," one of the topics in Arlene's newest book, *Growing Up Gardening: Gateways to Gardening*" is a near matchless description of her life's journey collaborating with Educators and with Parents.

And I can assure that readers of this book—like myself—will genuinely appreciate just how much passion of herself that Arlene poured into this "must read" A-Z educational publication on the practice of gardening with children in mind!

Ed Brogdon
Director of Horticulture at Holy Angels in
Belmont, North Carolina
Owner of Back to Eden, LLC

Wonderfully written with so many great gardening ideas and resources.

A powerful inspirational gardening book that will draw anyone to the joys of gardening.

Liz Fuller, Horticulture therapist
Director of Horticulture/Horticulture Therapy
South Carolina Department of Mental Health

Growing Up Gardening: Gateways to Gardening with Children, is a well researched, meticulously organized, remarkably comprehensive, yet practical book for anyone who has a sincere desire to engage children in the splendor of nature.

Praises to Arlene Marturano! The best book I have read on the topic of Gardening with Children.

Donna Banas-Early Childhood Educator
Founder/Advisor- Children's Garden Project of Elwood in Illinois

🌱 Whether you're an adult wanting to connect the next generation to nature or an educator responsible for guiding students in learning, this book is filled with inspiration, practical tips, and beautiful writing! All plants and animals (including humans) are welcomed into a reciprocal relationship with the earth through gardening and Dr. Marturano provides a path to move into this type of relationship.

Susan Licher
Learning Coordinator
Cornell Lab of Ornithology | K-12 Education Team

🌱 Arlene's comprehensive knowledge, personal experiences, and detailed gateways to gardening make this book an invaluable resource for gardeners of all levels and all ages. Her love of nature, learning, and teaching is contagious and plants a seed within us to keep growing!

Pat Redmond, Horticulture Therapist
South Carolina Department of Mental Health

🌱 Some books are hothouse productions, forced to bloom for an occasion, then lie dormant on a shelf. Dr. Arlene Marturano's *Growing Up Gardening: Gateways to Gardening with Children* is more perennial, likely to be opened and used again and again. It grew from roots deep in the author's own childhood and is enhanced by her remembrance of fireflies in a Mason jar, hollyhocks along a fence, garden toys, and garden games. A teacher, she also remembers by name individual children and how they were delighted by class garden projects or spaces like the Carolina Children's Garden that Dr. Marturano inspired and helped develop.

Growing the book itself has taken some seasons, in which I was blessed to be involved, sowing commas and the like, and occasionally helping train a few spreading words. And here we are. Dr. Marturano has produced a bounty of ideas for garden learning experiences that children will carry into adulthood as she did.

Growing Up Gardening is a guide for families to flourish through gardening together or participating in public service. It's a sourcebook for home schooling and an overall inspiration for healthy, environmentally sound living. Not a read-through/put-down kind of a book, this one is a collection of life lessons presented as fun discoveries and activities children will enjoy, remember, and share.

Margaret N. O'Shea
Profession
Writers' Consultant

www.ingramcontent.com/pod-product-compliance
Lightning Source LLC
Chambersburg PA
CBHW060454030426
42337CB00015B/1586